OXBOW INSIGHTS

CW01023956

A GEOGRAPHY
OF OFFERINGS

*Deposits of Valuables in the Landscapes
of Ancient Europe*

Richard Bradley

OXBOW | books
Oxford & Philadelphia

Published in the United Kingdom in 2017 by

OXBOW BOOKS
The Old Music Hall, 106–108 Cowley Road, Oxford OX4 1JE

and in the United States by

OXBOW BOOKS
1950 Lawrence Road, Havertown, PA 19083

Paperback Edition: ISBN 978-1-78570-477-2
Digital Edition: ISBN 978-1-78570-478-9 (epub)

A CIP record for this book is available from the British Library

Library of Congress Control Number: 2016958733

Printed in Malta by Gutenberg Press

For a complete list of Oxbow titles, please contact:

United Kingdom	United States of America
Oxbow Books	Oxbow Books
Telephone (01865) 241249	Telephone (800) 791-9354
Fax (01865) 794449	Fax (610) 853-9146
Email: oxbow@oxbowbooks.com	Email: queries@casemateacademic.com
www.oxbowbooks.com	www.casemateacademic.com/oxbow

Oxbow Books is part of the Casemate group

Cover images: Animated water. Detail of the cataract at Allt Coire Phadairlidh, Scotland, whose name connects it with a water sprite (Photograph: Richard Bradley). Artefact photographs courtesy of National Museums Scotland.

'My roots go down through veins of lead and silver, through damp, marshy places that exhale odours, to a knot made of oak roots bound together in the centre. Sealed and blind, with earth stopping my ears, I have yet heard rumours of wars.'

Virginia Woolf, *The Waves*

Contents

List of Figures and Tables

Figures

Table

Preface and Acknowledgments

Be warned. This is an extended essay and not a work of synthesis. It considers some of the problems of the prehistoric and early historical periods, but it makes no claim to have solved them. Instead its aim is to explore a theme which extends over a longer period of time than is usual in archaeology. It also draws on a wider range of evidence. Its composition has led me into new areas, although my expertise is all too obviously limited to the pre-Roman period. It is because studies of later phases are so absorbing that I have ventured outside my comfort zone. Even a cursory examination of these sources shows that they are investigating similar questions to prehistorians who work in Western Europe.

It makes a specific case, but anyone who has studied law (as I did long ago) knows that every argument invites a counter-argument. Even the most precise observations can be interpreted in more than one way. More cautious statements abound in the professional literature and consider some of the same material, but, true to the spirit of this series, this is a work of advocacy and needs to be recognised as such. Readers may disagree with what it says, but I hope that it does not misrepresent the information on which my arguments depend.

I have emphasised its distinctive character and the character of the series in which it appears, but I should make it clear that, although I am one of its editors, I had no hand in choosing the referee for this proposal and have benefitted from his or her anonymous advice like any other author. Thanks are due to Hella Eckardt who read the first draft and more than once encouraged me to keep going. I must also thank Clare and Julie at Oxbow for supporting this proposal and Katherine for coping with a partner who became obsessed with the distant past. Courtney Nimura edited the text with her characteristic flair and attention to detail – I cannot thank her enough. As so often, Aaron Watson prepared wonderfully lucid figures, and on this occasion he did so at very short notice.

Much of the book was written as an academic visitor to the Institute of Archaeology in Oxford, where I have felt very much at home since my retirement from university teaching. The invitation came from Chris Gosden and this book is dedicated to him with my thanks for his support and enthusiasm.

1 October 2016

CHAPTER ONE

Beginning Again

Where does a project begin, and how can it be said to conclude? The research described here had several false starts and at least as many false endings. So far they have spanned roughly thirty years.

So much depends on the language archaeologists use. Some time ago I offered an analysis of 'prehistoric hoards and votive deposits' (Bradley 1998[1990]), but all these terms give problems. The category of 'hoard' was considered as if its modern usage reflected some reality in the ancient world. In fact it applied to different phenomena at different times in the past. The idea of a 'votive deposit' fared little better, for in most cases it was treated as a residual category made up of collections of objects whose composition resisted a practical interpretation. Even the adjective 'prehistoric' was confusing. Over large parts of Europe it was synonymous with the pre-Roman period, but beyond the Imperial frontier it had another connotation, so that in Northern Europe it extended until the end of the Viking Age. Those problems are still with us today. Not only are similar phenomena studied by scholars working in separate traditions, there can be institutional barriers to communication between them. The period studied in *The Passage of Arms* was too short (Bradley 1998[1990]). Roman practices were quoted as a source of influence on indigenous communities, but nothing was said about developments in the 1st millennium AD when the archaeological record poses the same problems as it does during earlier phases.

I tried to compensate for some of these shortcomings in later publications, but always in discussing a more general theme. Thus one of the chapters in *An Archaeology of Natural Places* considered deposits of artefacts and animal bones in terms of where they were found. In the case of hoards it even proposed an amendment to the conventional view (Bradley 2000, chapter 4). Was it possible that certain kinds of places required particular kinds of offering, so that the *relationship* between the types of artefacts deposited and the character of the site should be the object of study? Topography and typology needed to be brought together.

Another amendment to my earlier account was to emphasise the life histories of individual objects and the ways in which they were treated before they entered the archaeological record. *The Past in Prehistoric Societies* did not say enough about the biographies of artefacts and the ways of studying them, for its main concern was with monumental architecture (Bradley 2002). *Ritual and Domestic Life in Prehistoric Europe* took an equally cautious approach, although it ventured a little further by considering the roles of incomplete objects in the Bronze Age (Bradley 2005). In particular, it argued that certain parts of broken artefacts were deposited at the expense of others (Bradley 2005, chapter 5). The idea was not taken any further as the aim of that study was to show that many of the practical activities undertaken in ancient Europe were characterised by rituals. Metalworking was only one of them.

Perhaps it is time to begin again, but on a broader chronological and geographical scale. The book has two main aims. The first is to move this kind of archaeology away from the minute study of ancient objects to a more ambitious analysis of ancient places and landscapes. It aims to break down the conventional division of labour between those who study artefacts in the museum or laboratory, and archaeologists who investigate landscapes on the ground. The second is to recognise that the problems considered in successive editions of *The Passage of Arms* were not restricted to the period between the Neolithic and the Iron Age. Mesolithic finds have a place in this discussion, but, more important, so do those of the 1st millennium AD. Every phase has its own literature, and archaeologists who study individual phases are confronted with similar problems although they may not be aware of it. As a result the same debates are repeated within separate groups of scholars. That is worrying enough, but it is still more troubling that they arrive at different conclusions from one another. What is needed is a review that brings these discussions together and extends across the entire sequence. If it lacks the fine detail that specialists have mastered, it suggests an approach that should apply to much of their material. Archaeologists often complain that they lack sufficient information to offer persuasive interpretations of the past. Sometimes this is true, but here is a case in which they have too much material at their disposal and not enough ideas with which to address it.

There are two ways of investigating such a complex subject. The first would be a comprehensive study of all the available material, spread over different countries and written by a team of researchers. At the moment this seems to be the preferred model for academic research, but it is an approach which is most appropriate in the sciences. The alternative is a single-author study which makes no attempt at completeness and places more emphasis on the ideas that have directed research in this field. It would not be conceived as a synthesis, but as one contribution to a discussion that is likely to continue. For that reason it could be comparatively brief. That is the approach that I have taken here. Rather than offer a comprehensive survey of evidence that has expanded beyond anyone's control, this is an extended essay about the strengths and weaknesses of current thinking. It also considers the possibility of approaches that can be followed in the future.

The discussion is divided into ten chapters which are mainly concerned with the archaeology of Western and Northern Europe between about 5000 BC and AD 1000 (Fig. 1). Chapter 2, 'A chapter of accidents' considers the main strands in the interpretation of specialised deposits and the difficulties of interpreting them in anecdotal terms. In particular, it compares the work of archaeologists studying this evidence on either side of the Roman frontier. There is much to learn from the 'long Iron Age' of Scandinavia, and the discussion compares the ideas that have been employed in Western Europe with thinking in Northern Europe where scholars can draw on literary sources for knowledge of pre-Christian beliefs.

That discussion continues in Chapter 3, 'Faultlines in contemporary research', which considers the institutional division between

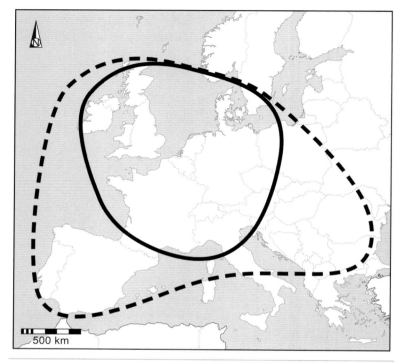

Figure 1. Map showing the extent of the study area. The main regions considered are within the continuous line. The dashed line encloses areas providing additional examples.

pre-Roman, Roman and early medieval archaeology. It compares the interpretations of specialised deposits between different researchers and different regions of Europe and asks how far the contrasts between them result from practices followed in the past and how far they reflect traditions of modern scholarship. In particular, it argues that work in this field has been influenced by one particular conception of the role of early coins and by the adoption of Christianity during the 1st millennium AD. It advocates a new approach to hoards and related collections based on the histories of individual artefacts and the places where they were deposited. It ends by suggesting that their distinctive character provides vital information on the concerns of people in the past. In taking this approach, field archaeologists can build on what has been achieved by traditional research.

Chapter 4 is called 'Proportional representation' and considers the range of specialised deposits and the way in which certain categories of material can dominate the discussion. The obvious example is metalwork. There are regions in which less attention has been paid to stone artefacts such as axeheads, or to wooden objects, food remains and pottery. Is it because the character of these collections changed, or does it reflect the division of labour between different groups of specialists in the present? It comments on the relationships between two different strands in prehistoric archaeology: sacrificial deposits characterised by large quantities of animal and human bones; and other collections which are dominated by finds of stone or metal artefacts. For some time they ran in parallel or overlapped, and this account traces their histories from the Mesolithic period to the Viking Age.

Chapter 5, 'The hoard as a still life', begins with a comparison between hoard finds, mainly those of the Bronze Age, and the collections of valuables depicted in 17th century Dutch paintings. These pictures had two key elements. They portrayed exotic and costly objects collected during the expansion of trading networks to Asia and featured new materials such as porcelain and lacquer. At the same time they assembled these striking objects into formal compositions that offered a medium for conspicuous consumption. The chapter argues that ancient hoards had some of the same properties; this interpretation is suggested by prehistoric rock art. The discussion also draws on the archaeology of the 1st millennium AD to suggest that the artefacts recorded as hoards and single finds may be all that survive of public displays of special objects taken out of circulation as their use lives came to an end.

Chapter 6, 'The nature of things', explores the character of the material found in these collections. It considers some of their properties that have been overlooked in the past: properties that extend well beyond their mechanical performance. In particular it investigates the distinctive character of worked stone and metalwork, drawing on new analyses of important artefacts. Ethnographic sources shed even more light on their original significance. Then Chapter 7 takes the discussion further by asking how different elements were treated as they entered the archaeological record. Why were certain features selected at the expense of others, and how did that choice determine the condition in which they are found today? For example, some stone artefacts were re-sharpened before they were discarded, but others were destroyed. The same applies to later finds of weapons. This account also draws attention to the anomalous position of the smith in ancient society and the peculiar practice of depositing incomplete objects.

Chapter 8, 'Vanishing points', discusses the reasons why deposition took place. Drawing on literary texts, it reviews current interpretations, from conspicuous consumption to sacrifice. It also considers the dangers posed by objects with special attributes or associations and the risk that their powers would be dissipated if they were treated as private wealth. That could have been one reason why they were removed from circulation. Finally, it emphasises the importance of gift-giving and suggests, as others have done, that this practice extended to dealings between people and the supernatural.

Chapter 9, 'A guide to strange places', considers the topographical setting of special deposits. Although there are notable exceptions, it contends that most scholars have treated the subject too casually. In particular, they have attempted to define specialised offerings according to practical considerations. Where material was buried and could be recovered, it might have been hidden in the ground. No doubt there were times when that did happen, but where it really was inaccessible – in a rock fissure, for example, a river or a lake – a different interpretation was required. The problem is that this approach said little about the character of the places where these artefacts were discarded. Water was not just a medium from which they would be difficult to retrieve; it had distinctive properties of its own. The same applies to dry land, for the character of the findspots is equally idiosyncratic. This chapter compares the evidence from Northern and Southern Europe and tries to identify those elements.

Finally Chapter 10, 'Thresholds and transitions', brings these observations together and proposes some new ways of studying the ancient landscape. It explores the importance of animism and the character of ancient cosmologies. The basic conclusion is simple. Hoards and related deposits have been studied for over a hundred years and analyses of their contents are rapidly approaching exhaustion. At a time when they have achieved many of their original aims, it is worth asking whether their results can be deployed in a different way. It suggests that this can be achieved by developing a 'geography of offerings'. In that case some of the most traditional studies can play a new role in a more ambitious approach to the past.

Why is a change of emphasis needed now? Over the last 20 years the development of metal detectors has transformed the character of archaeology. In some parts of Europe it is subject to few limitations; in others, it is more or less illegal. There are cases in which their use makes a direct contribution to fieldwork. This is especially true in Northern Europe, but provisions for recording the finds made on unprotected sites differ from one country to another. Even where progress has been made, as it has with the Portable Antiquities Scheme in England and Wales, metal detecting has serious consequences for the character of research. Although there have been worthwhile studies that use this source of information (Naylor & Bland 2011), it can easily encourage a new antiquarianism, concerned with the minute analysis of ancient artefacts at the expense of their wider significance.

In short it is essential to put this material to better use. There are many ways of achieving it, but here the premise is straightforward. It is to treat the deposition of distinctive artefacts and their associations as evidence of the cognitive geographies of people who left little else behind. That is why this material is still important and why it provides the point of departure for this book.

CHAPTER TWO

A Chapter of Accidents

This account begins with four notable discoveries, separated from one another by time and space. They share the common feature that these finds were first interpreted in practical terms and have since been reassessed.

The Broadward hoard

Discovery and initial interpretation

In 1867 a large deposit of metalwork was discovered near the border between England and Wales. The Broadward hoard dates from the end of the Bronze Age and is associated with radiocarbon dates between 980 and 820 BC (Bradley *et al.* 2015). It is composed almost entirely of weapons. Not all this material survives, yet even today the finds in the British Museum account for about 50 spearheads, five ferrules, two swords, a chisel and a chape. Many of the artefacts were broken and were in a single deposit interpreted as the stock of a smith.

The artefacts were found in digging a well on the edge of a poorly drained fen beside a tributary of the River Clun (Fig. 2). The hoard was located at the junction between the wetland and an area of dry ground:

> '[It was] at the extreme edge of the swampy ground, where it rises abruptly to a higher level. [The findspot was] on the very edge of [a] former morass ... Spear-heads and fragments of various patterns lay in a confused heap ... Many were taken from the earth cemented together with the gravel into large lumps, the points laying in all directions' (Rock & Barnwell 1872, 344).

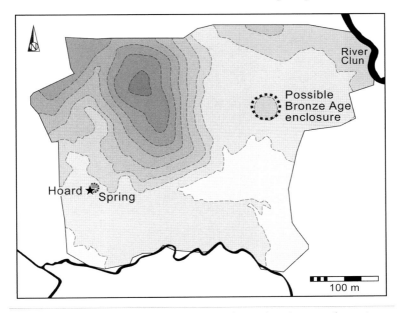

Figure 2. Outline plan of the Broadward complex showing the spring where the Late Bronze Age hoard was found and the position of a circular enclosure apparently of similar date. The two locations cannot be seen from one another and are separated by an area of higher ground. Information from Bradley et al. *(2015).*

One account records that these artefacts were associated with 'large teeth … chiefly of a small equine species' (Barnwell 1873, 80). Another report went further and offered an explanation for the finds: 'Whole skulls of ox and horse … were taken up with the spears and other bones of the animals, as if beasts of burden and their freight had been swamped in the bog' (Rock & Barnwell 1872, 343).

The Mästermyr hoard

Discovery and initial interpretation

A similar interpretation was suggested for a hoard from Gotland where, in 1936, a wooden chest was discovered at Mästermyr. It dated from the late 10th century AD and was associated with entire or fragmentary cauldrons, anvils, tongs, and a variety of tools (Arwidsson & Berg 1983). Other kinds of object were represented by single examples and were for preparing food, wood working and iron production. There were also whetstones and a piece of unworked brass. Again these items were interpreted as the property of a smith. More puzzling was the presence of three bells.

If that was difficult to explain, there seemed no problem in deciding how the deposit had formed. It was discovered on the edge of a bog, and pollen analysis suggested that the local environment had been similar when the artefacts arrived there. According to the definitive account of this find:

> 'It is generally accepted that the chest – which was presumably too heavy to carry – and the objects found near it were lost while crossing an ancient waterway, that it fell from a capsized boat or perhaps from some vehicle travelling on the ice' (Arwidsson & Berg 1983, 6).

This idea is remarkably like an interpretation of the Broadward hoard. The coincidence is striking and typifies the anecdotal explanations that became so common in archaeology. These finds are especially revealing since both have been reassessed during recent years. Not only do they suggest new ways of studying these collections, they illustrate entirely different methods of analysis.

Reassessments

The findspots at Broadward and Mästermyr have been excavated, but with contrasting results. At Mästermyr no trace was found of the original position of the hoard, which had never been recorded in much detail, although agricultural work did reveal an axehead (Arwidsson & Berg 1983, 6). At Broadward, where the surviving documentation was more precise, new fieldwork located the position of a pit cut by a 19th century well. It was exactly where the findspot was marked on the earliest map of the area and had been dug into the edge of an active spring (Bradley *et al.* 2015). It included a bone gouge which provided a radiocarbon date in the Middle to Late Bronze Age. Although that is a little earlier than the metalwork from the site, it is almost certain that the weapons came from the part of the pit removed in 1867. Analysis of samples from a nearby palaeochannel showed that the area had been a wetland throughout the postglacial period. Nearby there was a circular earthwork enclosure most probably of the same date (Fig. 2).

The results of this work dispose of the idea that the deposit of Late Bronze Age artefacts was the result of an accident. It had been buried beside a natural spring where water inexplicably issued from the ground. Is there more to say about this striking collection? In the definitive account of the Broadward hoard Colin Burgess and his co-authors suggested that it could have been a votive offering (Burgess *et al.* 1972). They based their argument on three features: the presence of large barbed spearheads which might have been too unwieldy for use in combat; the association between the metalwork and finds of animal bones; and the idea that the hoard was beside a prehistoric round barrow. Ironically, they reached the right conclusion, but for the wrong reasons. Barbed spearheads of the kind discovered at Broadward show signs of combat damage – they were not made solely for use in rituals (Mörtz 2010). None of the animal bones discovered in the new excavation dated from the same period as the hoard. Although their distribution focused on the spring, they were deposited there during other phases, from the Early Bronze Age to the post-medieval period (Bradley *et al.* 2015). Lastly, the new study showed that the findspot suggested in 1972 was not where the hoard was found, and in any case two of the features described as burial mounds in the early sources were a glacial hillock and a medieval motte.

Examination of the surviving material by Tobias Mörtz (2010) has raised a new possibility. His study has established that certain of the artefacts from comparable hoards show combat damage as well as the treatment they received when they were buried. He argues that these collections record the sacrifice of weapons after a battle. He interprets them as offerings of war booty similar to examples in northern France and south Scandinavia where their chronology extends from the pre-Roman Iron Age to the Migration Period. Other studies of Late Bronze Age weapons, including those from the Thames, have identified the same kinds of damage.

If the new analysis of the Broadward hoard drew upon excavation, pollen analysis and the surviving finds, those from Mästermyr have been reinterpreted by a different method. Pagan beliefs in Scandinavia were documented in oral literature that was only written down during the Christian era in the 13th and 14th centuries AD, but they described events that may have happened between the 9th and 11th centuries (Andrén 2014, chapter 1). These texts share enough features with archaeological evidence to be deployed as a source of evidence on the character of Old Norse religion. The Gotland hoard is one of a small group of finds which contain similar collections of artefacts. They are defined by the presence of a wooden chest associated with tools. Nine examples are documented, all of them dating between 950 and the early 11th century AD. Although their contents suggest a link with metalworking, other common elements include keys and bells. Like the collection from Mästermyr, they were associated with water, and most of them were on the shores of lakes.

These collections have been studied by Julie Lund (2006). She argues that in the oral sources both keys and bells were connected with the role of the smith and played an important part in ritual. Indeed, the bells resemble those buried with priests. Still more important, in such accounts smiths were associated with the supernatural and with a process of transformation that could extend to human bodies. It took place on the banks of lakes or rivers. The hoards did not come from the places where metal was worked. Rather, ['their] locations … mark the *idea* of where the smith and the smithy belonged in the cognitive landscape' (Lund 2006, 338).

Again the explanation proposed when the hoard was discovered fails to take account of its wider context. As a result the 'generally accepted' view of Mästermyr can no longer be accepted.

Bridges and troubled waters

Anecdotal explanations of this kind have enjoyed a wider currency. They apply to even larger bodies of finds and to the archaeology of other periods. Consider the exceptional collection of artefacts from the edge of a lake at La Tène in Switzerland, or the unusual quantity of Roman objects recovered from the River Rhine near Mainz. Although these finds vary in their composition and chronology, both have been explained as the result of catastrophic accidents.

Iron Age deposits at La Tène

Discovery and initial interpretation (Fig. 3)
At La Tène it was thought that the loss of so many artefacts was caused by a sudden rise in the level of Lac Neuchâtel which flooded an important settlement and caused two bridges to collapse. Many weapons and other artefacts were lost to the rising water, including so many pieces decorated in a distinctive manner that they have given their name to a phase of the European Iron Age and even to a widely distributed style of prehistoric art. As well as these elaborate pieces there were everyday tools, items of agricultural equipment, human bodies and animal bones. The investigators claimed that the inundation of the principal site at La Tène was not an isolated event, for similar deposits were found elsewhere together with the remains of structures of the same kind (Ramsmeyer 2009). So striking were the artefacts recovered in the 19th and early 20th centuries that their presence was taken for granted. Thus a monograph on the swords and their scabbards which was intended as the first part of a comprehensive catalogue of the finds devotes just over two pages to this question (De Navarro 1972, 17–19).

Roman artefacts from the Rhine

Discovery and initial interpretation
A similar approach has been taken to the Roman artefacts from the Rhine between Mannheim and Bingen. In this case the argument is even more circumstantial (Künzl 1993). It depends on several

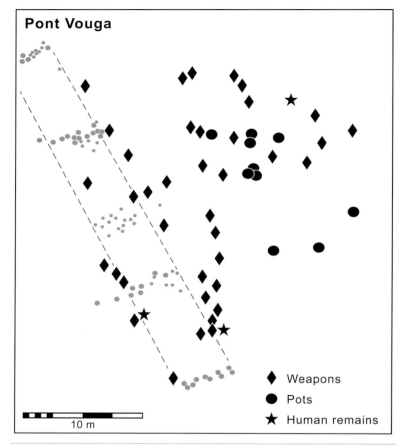

Figure 3. The remains of a wooden bridge at La Tène, Switzerland, showing the distribution of pottery, weapons and human remains in the water. Information from Vouga (1923).

observations. The material in question consists of elaborate items, principally metal vessels and weapons. Some of them have parallels in inland regions a considerable distance away, and were deposited along a restricted length of the river. There was a major concentration of metal vessels at Neupotz, and finds of swords came from the site of a bridge at Mainz. For the author of the definitive account they had been acquired during raids on prosperous villas and were being taken across the frontier into the barbarian world. In this case disaster happened when vessels overloaded with loot sank together with their cargoes. Indeed this account goes further. It enumerates the contents of entirely hypothetical villas from which the treasure had been taken. Even if the raiders used boats to escape with their spoils, it is hard to see how so many separate accidents could have occurred, for the finds extend for almost 100 km along the Rhine. Despite all these difficulties, this was the example chosen by Kenneth Painter (2015) to question the idea that the distinctive objects in European rivers had been placed there intentionally. On the other hand, Anthony Snodgrass (2006) has used the same example to compare the approaches taken by specialists on the Roman period and those favoured by prehistorians.

Reassessments

Neither interpretation of these finds is convincing, but it has taken archaeological studies of a traditional kind to expose their shortcomings. There may have been more than one episode when artefacts entered the water at La Tène. Their distributions, where they are known, suggest that some of them had been thrown from bridges (Vouga 1923). Far from being the victims of accidental drowning, several people whose remains were recovered had been pinned down in the water by pieces of timber; it is not clear whether this happened before or after they had died. According to Patrice Meniel (2009) the animal bones from the site contain an unusually high proportion of horses and dogs: species whose remains figure prominently at dryland sanctuaries, some of which were replaced by Roman temples. He has argued that in France they were employed as sacrifices, whilst pigs, cattle and sheep were consumed at feasts on some of these sites. The bodies of horses are also found in pits in the centre of the country dating from the 2nd and 1st centuries BC; as many as twenty of them could be buried together with the remains of adult men (Foucras

2013). Another link with the sacred sites of the same period is the treatment of human corpses whose heads had been removed after death (Jud 2007; Jud & Alt 2009). A new generation of research is under way at La Tène and its preliminary results add weight to the argument that the finds for which the site is famous were deposited there intentionally.

A different approach has been taken to the Roman artefacts from the Rhine. There are technical arguments which suggest that not all of them entered the water simultaneously (Kappesser 2012). There is the problem that these collections feature a small number of Iron Age weapons and that certain sections of the river include a sequence of prehistoric objects whose chronology extends back into the Neolithic period. Detailed analysis of the positions of the original findspots even suggests that swords were dropped from a bridge in the way that happened at La Tène. Weapons and metal vessels are unusually well represented among the material in the Rhine, and it seems much more than a coincidence that similar assemblages are associated with other rivers in Europe as well as with hoards of the same date on dry land. In short, more systematic study undermines the colourful story that originally accounted for these finds.

Literary sources

In each case an essentially anecdotal interpretation can be questioned on the basis of archaeological evidence, but again a fresh perspective is provided by literary sources. Roman texts are closer in date to the deposits considered here, but further insights can be gained from accounts of Anglo-Saxon and Old Norse beliefs.

Classical sources

The Classical texts have been assembled with a commentary by Bruno Boulestin and his colleagues in an account of European river finds (Boulestin *et al.* 2012) and by Thomas Grane (2003) in a study of sources referring to the Germans. Thus they refer to practices beyond the Roman Empire as well as those within its frontiers. These accounts have serious limitations. Although some scholars have considered the use of rivers, bogs and lakes for sacrificial offerings, the sources do not say much about this practice.

According to Grane, Tacitus records that before a battle the protagonists might dedicate the enemy and their possessions to the gods in the event of a victory. He describes this as 'a vow which consigns, horses, men [and] everything on the defeated side to destruction'. There are descriptions of similar practices in Gaul, where Osorius reports that 'clothing was torn apart and thrown away, gold and silver were thrown in the river [and] the men's armour was cut to pieces … There was neither booty for the victors, not mercy for the vanquished' (Grane 2003, 146).

Otherwise little more is said about the equipment of defeated enemies. Some were put on display, and others were burnt as sacrifices to the gods. Those taken from the losing side could also be destroyed. Prisoners and their horses might be killed before their remains were deposited in water. There is evidence that trophies were displayed at several locations: in the open air where no one was allowed to touch them; at temples; inside the houses of victorious warriors; and also in constructions formed of severed heads. There is literary evidence to suggest that the same elements were deposited in water, and archaeology provides compelling evidence that this happened. Analysis of some of the metalwork and human skulls raises the possibility that they were first displayed in sanctuaries before they were consigned to rivers and lakes (Jud & Alt 2009). That argument applies to the finds from La Tène. It might also apply to the Roman finds from the Rhine which bear a striking resemblance to the contents of hoards on dry land. Had they been transferred from one specialised context to another as their histories came to an end?

Tacitus also says that bogs were places of execution where social outcasts were killed. In another context he describes how the slaves who attended the goddess of fertility, Nerthus, were put to death to protect the secret location of the island on which she lived. All that is clear is that water and watery environments enjoyed a special significance among indigenous communities.

There is no doubt that they retained their sacred character within the Roman world, but they were rarely associated with deposits that can be described as treasures. Perhaps the best known example is the sanctuary that developed at Fontes Sequanae, the source of the Seine. Although it featured a series of monumental buildings, the site is famous for its votive offerings (Detys 1994). Classical writers record others associated with rivers, but metalwork rarely features. Most accounts focus on the golden treasure in a sacred lake at Toulouse, but this could be the exception that proves the rule, for it was deposited there *by the local population* after a raid on Delphi (Boulestin *et al.* 2012, 410–16). Its contents, which included a number of ingots, were recovered and sold during the Roman period. In that case there was an obvious contrast between indigenous and Roman attitudes to the same material.

Early medieval sources

It is not certain when the Anglo-Saxon poem *Beowulf* was written down, nor is it obvious how far it referred to events in the past. The definitive text is a mixture of pagan mythology and Christian doctrine and may have codified an oral epic whose contents accrued over time. A further complication is that it is set not in England but in Scandinavia (Bjork & Niles 1997).

Water features in two ways. The first is the account of a funeral in which the dead person is set adrift in an empty boat, accompanied by funeral offerings. This seems to be related to beliefs that were already present in Bronze Age archaeology where burials in the form of ships have been identified on both sides of the North Sea. It may also be related to the drawings of boats associated with mortuary monuments in Scandinavia. They depict vessels which were not provided with paddles and lack any means of locomotion. The evidence of Arctic ethnography suggests that they show the journey to the Otherworld and that the sea was associated with the dead (Zvelebil & Jordan 1999).

A second reference to the significance of water can be found in *Beowulf*. This is the fen from which Grendel and his mother emerged to attack the living. It was a dangerous place, associated with evil and destruction, and it was where the hero travelled in order to kill them. Beneath the water was 'treasure in abundance'. Among them there was a sword, 'an ancient heirloom from the days of giants … so huge and heavy that only Beowulf could wield it in battle'. Its blade melted in the monster's blood, but, once the fight was over, he removed its hilt, which was made of gold, and presented it to his lord. In Seamus Heaney's translation it is described in these terms. It was a 'relic of old times … engraved all over … There were rune-markings correctly incised … recording for whom the sword had been made and ornamented with its scroll-worked hilt' (*Beowulf*, lines 1688–1698). In the poem water is associated with violence and death, but also with valuable relics.

Norse references to the significance of water are much more helpful. Lakes were associated with important rituals at sites like Mästermyr and some of them have names which refer to those of pagan gods such as Odin, Tyr or Frey. Others emphasise the dangerous character of these locations. Rivers, springs and estuaries were just as special. Again their names provide a clue to their original importance. These observations are supported by archaeological evidence. Julie Lund (2010), who has studied the earliest literary sources, suggests that in many cases bodies of water separated the living from the dead. In Old Norse sources distinct 'groups of beings – men, gods and giants – lived on different sides of a river' (Lund 2010, 52).

In contrast to the Classical source, there are references to rivers that 'flowed with swords and seaxes' (Lund 2010, 52). They could extend around sanctuaries or the homes of the gods, and the water might even connect this world and *Hel* – the Nordic river Slidr extended between the land of the living and that of the dead. Bridges were important because they also linked those domains. That could be one reason why their construction was commemorated by runestones. It is also why rituals were needed where people crossed the water. A similar argument applies to the siting of Bronze Age and Iron Age burials on offshore islands along the coast of Scandinavia. Many of them were too small to sustain a resident population, suggesting that the dead would have been taken there by boat (Bradley & Nimura 2013, 21–22).

It is generally assumed that deposits of archaeological material in rivers and lakes were taken out of circulation in perpetuity. They would have been difficult or impossible to recover. A particularly telling example is Eberhard Sauer's (2005, 91) study of the 4500 Roman coins deposited in a thermal spring at Bourbonne-les-Bains in France where 'needless to say the 66°C hot water made recovery impossible'.

Although interpretations of this practice are by no means uniform, most researchers would agree that it contrasts with the treatment of similar material on land.

Ritual and non-ritual, religious and secular deposits

This contrast has given rise to an extensive literature, but again what appears to be a simple idea conceals a number of difficulties. The first is that specialists on separate periods have made similar observations but have explained them in very different ways. A second is that detailed analysis of the findspots of dryland hoards has shown that the distinction between terrestrial deposits and those associated with water is not as obvious as those authorities claim. North European sources relating to Anglo-Saxon and Viking collections introduce another complication.

One common element among the metalwork supposedly associated with dry ground is that it includes both whole and fragmentary artefacts, often belonging to the same types. It also features the kinds of material found in watery environments (Bradley 1985). This is especially true of personal ornaments which are common during three main parts of the sequence in south Scandinavia: the Late Bronze Age, the Migration Period and the Viking Age. To a smaller extent finds from the British Isles illustrate the same diversity, but here there are more hoards with broken metalwork in the Late Bronze Age than there are in other phases.

Two influential studies have examined the distinction between wetland and dryland deposits in Northern Europe.

The Late Bronze Age

In 1982 Janet Levy explored this distinction in a study of Bronze Age hoards in Denmark. On analogy with ethnographic examples, she divided them into two groups: ritual hoards and non-ritual hoards (Levy 1982).

Levy identified *ritual hoards* according to three criteria. They occupied specialised locations: in her study area, they were mainly bogs, springs and wells. They contained a restricted range of material, with a high proportion of weapons and ornaments, occasional food remains and what she called 'ceremonial objects'. Lastly, most of those artefacts were complete and might have been placed in the ground in a formal pattern. The important point is that they would have been difficult to recover.

By contrast, *non-ritual hoards* were generally buried in dry ground and the positions of a few examples were indicated by a stone. They contained a wider variety of objects, with a high proportion of tools. The ornaments could assume simpler forms than those in ritual hoards, and the same applied to any weapons. Certain kinds of objects were represented by several examples; that was especially true of axeheads. Among these collections there were freshly made objects, damaged or broken artefacts and metalworking residues. In this case they could have been retrieved. Levy's argument was so persuasive that it influenced the first edition of *The Passage of Arms* (Bradley 1998[1990], chapter 1).

The Migration Period

Because of the time frame chosen for that book it overlooked the fact that a similar scheme was proposed in Lotte Hedeager's (1992) study of hoarding in the Migration Period. The two groups of material were separated by an interval of about 1000 years. Again Hedeager emphasised the importance of distinguishing between finds from wet environments and those discovered on dry land, and to some extent her interpretation depended on practical considerations. How easy would it have been to recover these artefacts after their initial deposition – if it was possible at all?

Her analysis placed more weight on another criterion. How were the contents of hoards organised in the ground? Like Levy, she needed to explain the presence of complete personal ornaments – in this case arm-rings, neck-rings and the medallions known as bracteates – as well as fragments, some of them belonging to the same kinds of artefacts. Instead of a distinction between ritual and non-ritual hoards, she preferred a different terminology and identified what she called *religious* or *secular* deposits. Religious hoards were characterised by sets of objects which had been deposited with some formality – they were not meant to be recovered. Their contents were comparable to those of graves in other phases.

Secular hoards, on the other hand, consisted of more varied collections of valuables. They were concealed at times of crisis and were meant to be retrieved. This group included broken fragments which may have been assembled to make up a set weight of metal. Some could have been meant for recycling and might be stored in containers to make them easier to recover. Hedeager (1992) concluded that the hoards of the Migration Period served three different purposes. There were 'official' or religious deposits. Rather like grave goods, a second group may have been personal property for use in the afterlife: a feature documented by the Law of Odin. The third kind of hoard consisted of temporary stores of material that had been concealed with the aim of recovering them. They might be associated with smiths. The parallel with Levy's analysis is striking, although Hedeager's tables show less of a contrast between 'wet' and 'dry' deposits. The same point is made by Johan Nicolay (2014, chapter 11) who suggests that, while metalwork was buried beside streams, the importance of coastal locations has been underestimated. Here cliffs and promontories were particularly important.

The Viking Age

For a long time it was supposed that the practices described so far lapsed during the later 1st millennium AD, as deposits of treasure became increasingly associated with new power centres in Scandinavia. Hedeager (2011, chapter 7) has questioned this view. She makes the point that an association between hoards, other valuables and water is also present in the Viking Age, and can sometimes be recognised in the same locations as earlier finds. It seems as if those places retained their power whether or not artefacts were deposited there continuously. The same problem has been identified across large parts of North-West Europe between the end of the Bronze Age and the later years of the pre-Roman Iron Age. During that interval river finds and hoards were scarce.

Other researchers favour a practical interpretation for the collections of Viking metalwork (Graham-Campbell & Williams 2007). To a large extent this is because they include complete and damaged silver coins, but they also contain personal ornaments and a quantity of hacksilver. The arm- and neck-rings had been worn on the body and yet they contained set weights of imported metal. They could also be reduced to fragments and mixed with other broken pieces. Authorities like Birgitta Härdh (1996) see this as the first stage in the development of a monetary economy. There seems to be a further division between the contents of silver hoards and the iron weapons found in rivers.

The ubiquity of water

It is not clear that the distinction between wet and dry contexts is as useful as commonly supposed. That is due to the virtual ubiquity of water. There are two reasons for questioning the orthodox scheme. The first is that so many studies depend on this contrast *in the modern landscape*. The second is that until recently the findspots of these hoards had been studied on a piecemeal basis when what was required was a large enough sample from one region to identify any general trends.

The question to ask is whether the distinction between wetland and dryland deposits applies to the ancient landscape. There have been some important studies of hoard sites in Europe, but only occasionally can these discoveries be related directly to their original settings. Of course this can be worked out on a site-by-site basis, as it was at

Broadward and Mästermyr, but what is needed is to relate individual finds to developments in the natural environment. Were some objects deposited in bogs or pools which subsequently dried out? And were areas of dry ground containing metal finds later invaded by water?

Studies of changing sea and lake levels are especially important here. This applies to two recent projects. One is Martyn Waller's (1994) reconstruction of the changing environment of the English Fenland. The other is by Martin Rundqvist (2015) and considers an area of Sweden focussing on Lake Mälaren. Waller's work was based on a study of stratigraphic sequences supported by radiocarbon dates. Rundqvist based his research on models of isostatic uplift which traced the postglacial shoreline as the land rose and open water withdrew. Both regions contain concentrations of Bronze Age artefacts. Those in the English Fenland include large numbers of intact and broken weapons. The Swedish case study places a special emphasis on finds of axeheads, which occur both singly and in hoards; there were smaller numbers of weapons and ornaments. Each area had already featured in wider discussions of artefact deposition. The concentration of rapiers in the Fenland has attracted attention since Bridget Trump wrote about them in 1968. More recently, the metal finds associated with Lake Mälaren and its surroundings have been investigated by Christina Fredengren (2011).

The English Fenland

In 2010 David Yates and the writer combined Waller's reconstruction of the changing environment of the Fens with the distribution of Bronze Age metalwork which had expanded considerably since the research of Trump (1968). It soon became clear that a simple distinction between terrestrial and wetland finds was no longer adequate (Yates & Bradley 2010a). Nor was the conventional contrast between single finds of weapons in wet locations and discoveries of hoards on dry land. Although weapons were generally associated with water, there was an important difference between the single finds from rivers, and hoards containing similar material associated with bogs or shallow bays. Sometimes they included ornaments. Weapons also feature among the fragments in terrestrial hoards near to the water. In some senses the key site is the Isleham hoard – the largest collection of prehistoric metalwork ever found in Britain (Malim *et al.* 2010). It was buried in a pit cut into a ditch terminal, but a recent investigation has shown that it was also located beside a palaeochannel which was gradually drying out. Although there may have been a settlement, a wooden building and fields in the vicinity, this is a case in which such a hoard was closely connected with water. There was no simple distinction between collections of this kind and the single finds from bogs and rivers.

Lake Mälaren and its hinterland (Fig. 4)

Rundqvist's (2015) study identified some obvious patterns among the metalwork in his study area. During the Early Bronze Age axes and spears were associated with inlets of the sea, but swords and daggers concentrated in bogs where these other types did not occur. The pattern changed during the Late Bronze Age. In contrast to the situation in Denmark, axes were deposited in wet environments and were uncommon on land, whilst it was the discoveries from dry ground that included a series of personal ornaments.

Of the finds of Bronze Age metalwork in his study area 33% are described as in (or by) a lake and another 26% showed the same connection with marine inlets; 16% were in (or beside) a stream and a further 8% came from bogs. Not every site could be diagnosed, but only 13% of the findspots in Rundqvist's (2015) sample were unambiguously associated with dry ground. His hesitation over the precise contents of other discoveries is entirely understandable, for they were located very close to the water's edge. It made little difference whether or not they were submerged. The significant point is that the meeting of land and water seems to have been significant, while entirely terrestrial locations account for few of the finds. It is obvious that the resulting patterns were too subtle to be explained by the chances of retrieving these objects.

South-east England

The same conclusion finds support from a second project in lowland England (Yates & Bradley 2010b). Like Rundqvist's (2015) research, it

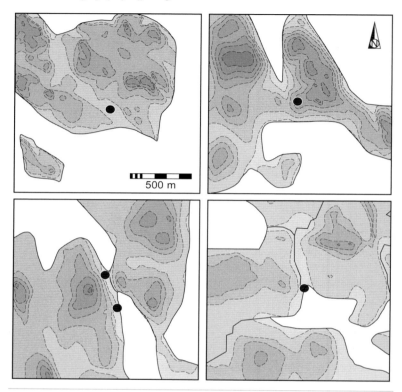

Figure 4. The locations of Bronze Age metalwork finds in middle Sweden, in relation to coastal inlets, lakes and rivers (unshaded). Contours at 5 m intervals. Information from Rundqvist (2015).

was not based on map analysis or a Geographical Information System but on the understanding of the findspots that can only be obtained by seeing them on the ground. One hundred well-provenanced hoards were studied in south-east England. The work was conducted by David Yates, David Dunkin and the writer, but, in contrast to the Fenland, this was an area in which hoards of tools and broken metalwork were common and finds of weapons were comparatively rare. Some collections did include ornaments, but there were few river finds. As a result the two studies are complementary and produce different results. Almost all the material dates from the Middle and Late Bronze Ages.

In principle this was a study of dryland hoards, but the results of the work revealed some unexpected patterns. They were similar to the outcome of work in the Fens – again the clearest association was with water. These finds did not come from wet locations. Rather, they were located beside or overlooking significant expanses of water in a similar way to the findspots documented by Rundqvist. Particular features were emphasised at the expense of others. Hoards were found beside springs, recalling the evidence from Broadward. They could be buried on small areas of higher land beside confluences, and were more closely associated with tributaries than the principal watercourses; this is another feature found at Broadward. Close to the Channel coast they emphasised the sections of streams and rivers with fresh water rather than their lower reaches where salt water extends upstream at high tide. Although many of the hoards may have been deposited in, or along the edges of, the settled landscape, they were not found everywhere. This is important as the area that was studied contains a series of upland farms that have been excavated on a large scale. Here there are fewer finds of Bronze Age metalwork, although ornament sets are occasionally discovered. By contrast, the distribution of hoards focused on lowland areas which were associated with flowing water. Again the distinction between wetland finds and those from dry land seems to be too doctrinaire. The same conclusion arises from the study of another 230 sites between the High Weald and the Fens – a region in which weapons are more often represented in hoards. I must thank David Dunkin and David Yates for details of this work.

Hidden in plain sight

The study of hoards in south-east England benefitted from cooperation with the metal detectorists who discovered them. The composition of these assemblages has been recorded by the Portable Antiquities

Scheme, with the result that more is known about the kinds of material represented. Discussion with the people who found it suggests another perspective. Why is it that certain people locate more hoards than their colleagues? It soon became clear that they had developed a clear understanding of how the metalwork was distributed. Long before any archaeologists had arrived at similar conclusions, they had worked out that areas like the springline were prime targets for investigation. In one sense this was reassuring, for it suggested that the results of fieldwork could be supported by another method, but it had serious consequences for time-honoured interpretations of these finds.

The traditional scheme was enunciated most clearly in the work of Gordon Childe (1958, chapter 10), whose approach extended to large parts of Continental Europe. Dryland hoards, especially those containing unfinished artefacts or scrap metal, had been stored by the smith with the intention of recovering them later. Alternatively, they were collections of valuables hidden during times of crisis. How effective would these procedures have been if metalwork was deposited according to widely shared conventions? That would hardly preserve it from interference. If the aim was concealment, surely the locations of this material should have been less predictable; that was obviously not the case. If these deposits can be recovered with no difficulty 3000 years later, the conventional model must be wrong.

Again the epic poem *Beowulf* sheds light on some of these issues (Bradley 2009a). Two collections of metalwork feature in this account. The first consists of the artefacts, mostly weapons, consumed with the hero's body on the pyre. Some were gifts from the living, but others were heirlooms he had inherited from important people in the past. The second consists of a hoard of metal objects deposited inside a megalithic tomb, perhaps an ancient passage grave. The collection was made up of vessels and ornaments which are specifically described as antiquities. People knew that they had been deposited there, as these treasures had not been concealed. They were guarded by a dragon. The poem shows how disaster followed when the hoard was disturbed and one of its contents was stolen. The violence that followed led to the hero's death. So great was the danger posed by the ancient treasure that it was buried with Beowulf's body, but, unlike the weapons displayed at his funeral, it was not consumed on the pyre. Instead it remained intact but inaccessible. There was no longer any risk that it would be appropriated as a source of private wealth.

In such cases it seems likely that the positions of metalwork deposits were known but respected. It is impossible to say whether they remained entirely undisturbed, for some must have been encountered by chance, but so many have been discovered over the last 200 years that it should apply to most examples. Again it is worth comparing this evidence with what is known of Viking silver hoards in Scandinavia, for here again literary evidence and folklore shed some light on this question. Torun Zachrisson (1998) has already studied the places where they were found, following a similar methodology to the Bronze Age cases mentioned earlier. Her research in middle Sweden suggests that those hoards are associated with estate boundaries, settlements, runestones, rivers, lakes and the entrances of farmyards. It is clear that the locations of buried material were sufficiently predictable to be identified, but they were left undisturbed. In a literal sense they were hidden in plain sight.

The god Odin knew the positions of all the gold and silver buried in the earth, but their positions were protected and could be recognised because they were indicated by firelight; in *Egil's Saga* a will-o'-the-wisp plays the same role. They were also commemorated by distinctive place names. People performed incantations when hoards were deposited in the ground, and it was believed that the locations of these collections were protected by special spells. They were guarded by mythical animals.

Drawing on these sources, Zachrisson explains that:

'Treasures could be perceived distinctly in the landscape, but at the same time they were impossible to reach for anyone but their true owners. If someone wanted to obtain a treasure by force, he either had to have knowledge of the enchantment that bound it, or he had to cross symbolic boundaries in silence. *If a person succeeded in obtaining a treasure, he or she usually sustained a misfortune*' (Zachrisson 1998, 220–21; my emphasis).

That is exactly what happened in *Beowulf* when the dragon's treasure was disturbed.

It suggests that in some cases it is not necessary to maintain the distinction between ritual and non-ritual hoards or to imagine that those buried in the ground were accessible to anyone who could find them and remove their contents. In the situation described by Zachrisson the significant element was not the discovery of where the treasure had been buried, for that was known. Nor was the feasibility of digging it up again. Even a deposit that was hidden or stored was protected by powerful beliefs. It remained intact due to such prohibitions and not to the ingenuity of people in choosing where to hide their valuables. It would be quite wrong to imagine that what may have been the custom in the Viking Age is directly relevant to earlier periods, but this account has identified enough anomalies to question some of the assumptions that prehistorians have taken for granted. The challenge is to devise other ways of thinking about this material, and that is pursued in the following chapters.

CHAPTER THREE

Faultlines in Contemporary Research

Chronological faultlines

By now, if not before, a critical reader might ask whether it is acceptable to make so many comparisons between the hoards of the Bronze Age and those of the later 1st millennium AD. Surely their investigation belongs to separate intellectual traditions. In a sense this is true, but it is important to decide whether those ways of working result from differences in the past itself, or the self-imposed limitations of schools of thought in the present.

Even the examples quoted so far reveal some significant faultlines in the discussion of hoards and other deposits. They are both regional and chronological. Perhaps the disadvantage of very detailed studies of individual discoveries is that they overemphasise particular cases at the expense of the broader traditions of which they formed a part. That is hardly surprising when so many artefacts are involved. There are plans to catalogue the deposit of Iron Age war booty from Illerup in Denmark in 14 volumes. Similarly, the German series *Prähistorishe Bronzefunde*, which aims to catalogue all the Bronze Age metalwork in Europe already runs to 180 publications and considers about 140,000 individual objects, both hoard finds and single finds.

Again the clearest contrasts are between the archaeologies of Northern and Western Europe, as they include the greatest quantity and variety of deposits. Despite certain similarities, they are normally considered separately. Why has this happened?

There have been three main influences. The first is an apparent contrast between indigenous and Roman practices which is emphasised by studies of material found within the Imperial frontier. Researchers sometimes suppose that practices that characterised large parts of Iron Age Europe lapsed as a result of Roman occupation in the west but continued unchecked beyond the limits of the Empire. A second factor is the influence of another discipline – numismatics – which has affected studies of the pre-Roman Iron Age and subsequent phases. Another was the adoption of Christianity which happened earlier in Western Europe than it did in the North. Each will be considered in later sections of this chapter.

In their broadest terms hoards, water finds and related deposits extended over a considerable period of time. They were not restricted to the phases in which metals were used. In Northern Europe hoards and single finds are well-known in the Neolithic, and the placing of artefacts and animal remains in water began even earlier, during the Mesolithic period. Once established, these practices had a very long history. In other cases Iron Age and even earlier artefacts are discovered in the same locations as those of the Roman period. That certainly applies to the river finds from Mainz (Kappesser 2012). Similarly, the metalwork recovered from the Thames extends from the Early Bronze Age to the Viking period. What applies to metal objects can extend to other kinds of deposits. In Northern Europe there are similar collections with human and animal remains, ceramics, worked stone and wooden artefacts. The evidence from the West includes occasional finds of similar character, but they are not so frequent.

An obvious faultline can be identified between studies on either side of the North Sea. In one case it is clear that water provided a focus for deposits of artefacts from the Neolithic period and even earlier. The finds include human bodies and hoards of stone axeheads. Until recently, the axes of the same date found in the Thames had been interpreted as chance losses, but more attention was paid to those in Irish rivers (Cooney & Mandal 1988, 34–38). Across much of Western Europe the systematic study of hoards and related deposits began with early metalwork. Thus one faultline divided students of early prehistory who work in different regions, yet they were investigating similar evidence.

A second faultline divides the archaeology of the Roman world from that of its neighbours. It has happened for two reasons. The first is the existence of formal temples, sanctuaries and shrines during this period. Their architecture takes recognisable forms and they are associated with a wide range of votive deposits, some of them made specifically as offerings. They include coins, personal ornaments and figurines. Because they are so readily identified and are associated with sacrificed animals it has been easy to characterise these deposits, but it has happened at a price. It has meant that material found in isolation is treated separately. This is particularly true of hoards of metalwork, coin hoards and river finds. For a long time specialists on the Roman period had a clear conception of the nature of ritual sites and votive deposits, and discoveries that departed from that model were explained in anecdotal terms. The river finds from Mainz are a typical but extreme example. An even more obvious example is provided by large collections of Roman coins associated with springs in Germany, France and Britain, the best known of which come from Bath and Bourbonne-les-Bains. Sauer (2005) suggests that offerings of this kind first developed in Italy and may have been introduced into Europe north of the Alps by soldiers who had been recruited in the Mediterranean. That could be true of the collections he documents in France, but the finds from the Great Spring at Bath include a small proportion of pre-Roman issues that may have arrived there during the Iron Age (Cunliffe 1988, chapter 5).

There are other cases in which the same locations may have been used as sanctuaries and shrines in both the Iron Age and Roman periods. This is especially true of southern Britain and northern France. Their character may have changed, but a common characteristic of the 'Romano-Celtic' temples of lowland England is that they were built in places that had enjoyed a special significance before the Conquest. A well-known example is the 4th century AD temple inside the earlier hillfort at Maiden Castle (Wheeler 1943, 31–35). This relationship is frequently identified, and suggests that such sites retained something of their original significance even after an interval. More important, the desire to return to traditional locations could be understood as a form of resistance and a continuing commitment to the values of the past. If that applied to the construction of temples, there seems no reason to take a different approach to deposits of artefacts in 'natural' places with a history of pre-Roman finds. A telling case is Nico Roymans's (2004) study of the Batavians, an indigenous community whose members were recruited into the Roman forces. He asks why military equipment, especially swords which had been issued by the army, should have ended up in rivers and concludes that after their period of service was over, individual recruits chose to deposit their weapons according to long-established conventions (Roymans 2004, 227–36). This need not have been a public display, but it was an expression of beliefs that still retained their power. A similar argument applies to the Roman weapons found in the River Ljubljanica (Turk *et al.* 2009, 86–92).

By contrast, there is no doubt that specialised deposits had an unbroken history outside the Roman frontier. This is most obvious from the 'war booty sacrifices' found in Northern Europe and especially in Denmark (Pauli Jensen 2009; Nørgård Jørgensen 2009). They consist of the weapons and other equipment of defeated war bands which had been deliberately destroyed together with the ships in which they had travelled. These collections account for an estimated 40,000 artefacts. The weapons had been used in combat before they were deposited, and studies of the artefacts provide some indication of the origins of the invaders. Human remains were not represented and it seems as if the victims of the conflict had been disposed of separately from their possessions. The most important point is the chronology of these deposits which spans the pre-Roman Age, the Roman Iron Age and the Migration Period from about 350 BC to AD 600. The same locations were chosen for such deposits on more than one occasion (Fig. 5). For instance, there were eight successive deposits at Vimose (Pauli Jensen 2009, fig. 2). Although the oldest generally accepted example comes from Hjortspring in the 4th century BC, it is possible that the concentration of human remains and weapons in a river at Tolensee in north-east Germany provides evidence of a similar practice. Although this has been identified as

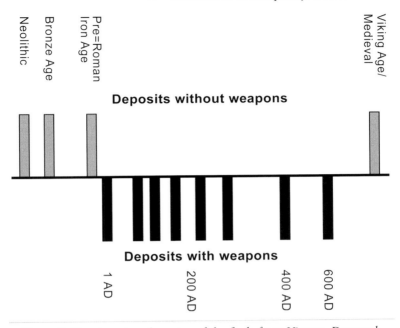

Neolithic

Bronze Age

Pre=Roman
Iron Age

Viking Age/
Medieval

Deposits without weapons

Deposits with weapons

1 AD

200 AD

400 AD

600 AD

Figure 5. The changing character of the finds from Vimose, Denmark.
Information from Pauli Jensen (2009).

the site of a Middle Bronze Age battlefield, it seems as if some of the artefacts had been discarded with a certain formality and that different kinds of metalwork were disposed of separately (Jantzen *et al.* 2011; Krüger *et al.* 2012).

In Northern Europe the main faultline lies not at the end of the Roman Iron Age but between the Migration Period and the Viking Age. As mentioned earlier, one interpretation, advocated by Charlotte Fabech (1998), is that deposits of valuables were no longer associated with natural locations but with new power centres in Scandinavia. Lotte Hedeager (2011, chapter 7) suggests that this simplifies a still more complicated situation, for the metalwork hoards of the Migration Period are in the similar places to those of the Viking Age 350 years later. In this case there is a further complication, for those collections include an increasing proportion of coins. Did this happen as new kind of economy developed – the 'Viking silver economy' of a recent book title (Graham-Campbell & Williams 2007)? Or was the situation even more complex than that?

If there was a faultline between studies of pre- Roman and Roman finds in Western Europe, here is another example of a similar process. In each case the common element is the presence of coins. Like the study of Bronze Age and Iron Age metalwork, the analysis of ancient coins can be cut off from wider developments in research. Again there is a danger of imposing modern notions of human motivation on people in the past, claiming them as 'common sense' when they need be nothing of the kind. Detailed studies of the contexts of Iron Age coins and their associations suggest that they played a specialised role along with other valuables (Haselgrove & Wigg-Wolf 2005). Current research is suggesting a similar level of complexity among Roman coin hoards. This is not to suggest that traditional notions are wrong, but they may be too rigid and should allow for greater diversity. The same applies to the use of gold pendants known as bracteates between the 5th and 7th centuries AD and the first silver coins of the Viking Age (Hårdh 1996). It is unfortunate that this kind of material culture can be studied separately from the other artefacts with which it is associated.

In contrast to Northern Europe, the main faultline in the West separates the Roman period from its successors. In one sense that seems strange as this phase is known as the Migration Period because it was the time when settlers moved from areas beyond the frontier into regions vacated by the Roman state. In Western Europe this signifies the beginning of a new sub-discipline – 'early medieval' archaeology. Unfortunately, it also introduces a fresh set of assumptions, not all of which can be supported. In particular, it has led to an underemphasis on hoards and river finds which have been explained in anecdotal terms. That is surprising as similar deposits in the homelands of the settlers are interpreted in a different way. The situation is changing, but there is scope for a more imaginative approach to the evidence. In Continental Europe weapons were still deposited in rivers during the later 1st millennium AD, but they are seldom discussed; important exceptions are Stefan Wirth's (2000) account of river finds in Bavaria and a review of the evidence from France by the aptly-named Jean-Claude Rivière (2012). Similarly, radiocarbon dating has shown that in middle Sweden human and animal remains were placed in water until AD 1000 or even later. In North-East Europe a study of Jette Anders (2013) showed that weapons and sometimes sickles were deposited in rivers until AD 1200. In Britain the situation is even more confusing. A recent paper has drawn attention to a series of weapons deposited in northern English rivers during the Viking Age. Ben Raffield (2014) claims that this was an unfamiliar practice introduced by settlers who maintained their traditional practices in their new surroundings. John Naylor, on the other hand, has identified a series of early Saxon spearheads from the Thames which predate these finds of swords. Any hiatus in the deposition of metalwork was more apparent than real (Naylor 2015).

Controversy and uncertainty

It is worth exploring these disciplinary faultlines in one specific region: eastern and midland England between the late pre-Roman Iron Age and the Anglo-Saxon period, focussing on three famous finds of treasure: those from Snettisham and Hoxne in Norfolk, and the so-called Staffordshire hoard. They have been selected because their interpretation is controversial. A feature that has complicated the analysis of the finds from Snettisham and Hoxne is the presence of coins.

Snettisham (Fig. 6)

Snettisham is the earliest of the three and probably dates between the 3rd and 1st centuries BC, although there was Roman activity on the site. As many as 14 hoards of metalwork have been found on top of a prominent hill with a view towards the Wash (Stead 1991). The first account of the site concluded that it was where valuable raw materials and finished products were stored together by a smith – a view reminiscent of the traditional interpretation of Late Bronze Age

Snettisham

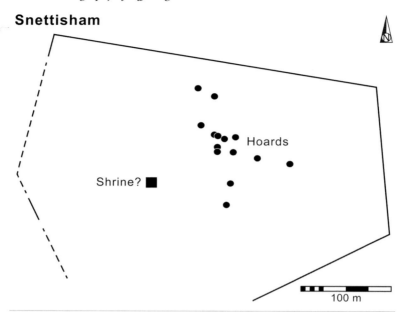

Figure 6. Outline plan of the ditched enclosure at Snettisham showing the positions of the Iron Age metalwork deposits and that of a possible Roman shrine. Information from Stead (1991) and Hutcheson (2011).

hoards in the same region (Clarke 1954, 27 & 70). That became more difficult to maintain as further discoveries were made there. The original finds were mostly gold and silver ornaments, which could be either complete or broken into fragments, but a subsequent discovery was a hoard of about 6000 high value coins inside a sliver bowl. The most recent estimate is that 75 complete torcs or neck-rings have been recorded at Snettisham as well as fragments of about another hundred. In addition there were roughly the same number of artefacts identified as ingots, rings or bracelets (Stead 2014). Three of the 14 hoards were interpreted as scrap metal; there is no doubt that it was being worked at Snettisham. Some of the material used to make gold torcs could have been obtained by recycling coins. One example was concealed within the terminal of an ornament of this kind.

Interpretations changed as more deposits were found. Just as Rainbird Clarke had considered the hoards as metal stored by a smith, they have also been seen as 'flight hoards' – deposits of valuables concealed for safekeeping at the time of Caesar's expeditions to Britain in 55 and 54 BC. That idea was favoured by Warwick Rodwell and quoted in the second edition of Barry Cunliffe's (1978, 72–75) account of *Iron Age Communities in Britain*, but was dropped from subsequent revisions. One reason is that the material is too early in date. It is directly associated with radiocarbon dates of 370–160 BC and 370–110 BC. A more productive approach was followed by Natasha Hutcheson (2004) who observed that in the 2nd century BC similar deposits of valuables in Norfolk were associated with high ground within sight of the Wash. Like the Bronze Age hoards considered earlier, their positions in the landscape were influenced by social conventions. Seen in this light, Snettisham was not a good hiding place.

The principal excavator of Snettisham, Ian Stead, was aware of all these problems. He suggested that so many valuables were buried that they must represent the wealth of an entire community. He rejected the idea that the hoards were votive offerings, arguing that such deposits would have been associated with water – an extreme version of the position followed in studies of other periods. He chose his words carefully, leaving the character of the Snettisham hoards entirely unresolved:

> 'If they were not votive, then Snettisham and other hoards of torcs could have been treasure – perhaps buried in times of danger or possibly an accumulated source of wealth' (Stead 1991, 462).

There has been a more recent development. Stead's excavation showed that all the hoards were inside a large polygonal ditched enclosure. It might not date from the Iron Age, but subsequent fieldwork in its centre found the disturbed remains of a Roman stone building which had plastered walls and a mosaic floor (Fig. 6). Despite its poor state of preservation, it could have been a rural temple (Hutcheson 2011).

Stead (2014) disagrees, but it now seems more likely than ever that Snettisham was a sacred location and that the hoards which were buried there were not meant to be recovered.

Hoxne

In the same county another exceptionally rich hoard was discovered and excavated at Hoxne, but in this case it dated from the 5th century AD, the very end of the Roman period in Britain. Its contents were published in two volumes written by separate scholars (Guest 2005; Johns 2010). One is concerned with the gold jewellery and silver plate, and the other with the coins found in the same deposit. The reason for drawing attention to this division of labour is that the authors of these books cannot agree on why the treasure was buried and why it remained in the ground.

The character of the finds is not in doubt, as it was well recorded. The hoard had been buried in a chest and contained gold jewellery, silver vessels, silver spoons, a strainer and a series of toilet instruments. With them there were nearly 15,000 coins which had probably been in a bag. The hoard was not associated with a settlement but was near a Roman road. Catherine Johns who studied the fine metalwork considered that the chest was a 'strongbox'. She took a resolutely practical approach to its interpretation. The Romans were sensible people who would not engage in irrational activities like the deliberate destruction of wealth:

'I have taken it as read that the Hoxne treasure is a …
safekeeping hoard … buried with the intention of recovery …
I find myself quite unable to believe in the regular, voluntary
or permanent renunciation of wealth as a widespread ancient
custom' (Johns 2010, 202).

The hoard resulted from the 'long-term secure storage of objects that were not in everyday use'. Their deposition was not 'a hasty response to a sudden menace'. Even its location could be explained, for its contents were heavy and it would be easier to recover them because they were close to a road. Why, then, did it never happen?

Peter Guest who studied the coins took a different line. Roman coins could be used in gift exchange between living people but also in their dealings with the supernatural. The Hoxne hoard was by no means unique. In fact it belonged to an established tradition of similar deposits in eastern England. It was unlikely that it remained untouched because of the crisis that accompanied the collapse of Roman authority early in the 5th century AD as the same political situation affected the inhabitants of other regions where similar finds are not known. Nor did peaks in the deposition of coinage correspond with well-defined periods of unrest in the Roman Empire. Instead 'the population in certain areas of Britain buried hoards fully intending them to remain in the ground' (Guest 2005, 32).

The main components of the wooden chest were interpreted in completely different ways.

The Staffordshire Hoard

The same uncertainty attends another remarkable collection of metalwork, but in this case it is considered to date from mid-7th century AD. What is troubling is that discussion follows virtually the same lines as interpretations of Hoxne and Snettisham.

The artefacts were discovered by metal detecting and the initial find was followed by excavations intended to recover the remaining material and to secure the site from damage Leahy *et al.* 2011). Although geophysical survey was undertaken, it found very little, but there is reason to suppose that the metalwork had been located on, or beside, a conspicuous mound which could have been of natural origin. By the Anglo-Saxon period it would have been difficult to distinguish between this feature and the remains of a prehistoric barrow.

Four thousand fragmentary artefacts were recovered (Leahy & Bland 2014). They were made of gold or silver. Two elements stood out from the start. Unlike other hoards of the same period, this assemblage did not contain any coins. It consisted almost entirely of war gear, mainly sword fittings which had been removed from their blades. About 60% of the objects had been mutilated. There was also part of at least one helmet. Despite the size of this collection, no female jewellery was represented. It is obvious that its contents had been carefully selected. The finds are still being studied, but it is already evident that their chronology extends over about 100 years. For that reason it is not certain that they were deposited simultaneously, and a few comparable artefacts come from a second location nearby.

Interpretations differ radically, for it occupies one of the disciplinary faultlines mentioned earlier. Leslie Webster advocates a practical interpretation similar to Ian Stead's explanation for the Snettisham hoards and Catherine John's account of the Hoxne hoard:

> 'It is essentially scrap put together for recycling … which was somehow diverted from its destination' (Webster *et al.* 2011, 222).

Because the finds were beside a Roman road, Watling Street, she suggests that robbers may have intercepted this material while it was being transported. If so, that does not explain why they left it behind.

Patrick Périn has proposed an even more circumstantial version of events. Because the material had been made over a lengthy period, he says it cannot have consisted of war booty. In view of what is known about the inheritance of weapons during the 1st millennium AD, this argument cannot be right. He suggests that:

> 'The best option … is that the collection was amassed as ritual deposition in a pagan sanctuary. This place was subsequently raided, and the collection acquired by a goldsmith who extracted the precious metal and gems before the remains were buried in unknown circumstances' (in Webster *et al.* 2011, 226).

In a field rife with speculation this version has the qualities of farce.

Kevin Leahy, who has studied the excavated material, takes a different line. It is unlikely that the collection represents the stock of itinerant goldsmiths 'because they seem to have been supplied with their metal by their clients' (Leahy & Bland 2014, 52). The fact that certain parts of individual weapons are represented rather than others can also be explained. They were the parts that had touched the warrior's hand and were most closely associated with him. It is surely significant that it was a decorated sword hilt that Beowulf recovered from Grendel's mere. This way of treating Anglo-Saxon weapons may not be a unique instance as Leahy (2015) has identified a similar pattern of selective deposition at sites recorded by the Portable Antiquities Scheme. It has also been identified among finds of Late Bronze Age weapons (Bradley 2005, 155).

The suggestion that there was a mound at the findspot of the Staffordshire hoard gives rise to a different problem. For the proponents of a practical interpretation, it could have marked where the treasure awaited recovery. An equally important point has been raised by Catherine Hills (in Webster *et al.* 2011, 226–29). There is no evidence that the metalwork had been buried in the first place. It may have been placed on the surface and protected by powerful taboos. That seems to have happened with the weapons deposited around a timber building at the Swedish site of Uppårkra. In the circumstances Martin Carver's (2011, 231) summary of the Staffordshire find is entirely apposite: 'We do not even know if it was a hoard'.

The sources of confusion

It is obvious that three issues have affected the interpretation of metalwork deposits.

The presence of coins

Coins did not occur in the Staffordshire hoard, but they were represented at Snettisham before the Roman period began and at Hoxne as it closed. They are an equally important feature of Viking silver hoards. In each case pieces of fine metalwork had been broken up to obtain a set amount of raw material. The result is described by the term *hacksilver*; gold could be treated in the same way.

Hacksilver is sometimes characterised as bullion, but the evidence for an agreed system of weights suggests that it was employed in a similar manner to currency (Painter 2013). Indeed, coins provided one of the main sources of the metal. The designs they carried may have lost their significance, but they were still used in the same transactions. Hoards of precious metal like those at Snettisham illustrate this point as they include decorated torcs, the rings that Stead interprets as ingots, and high value coins. They could be mixed together and it is likely that these coins provided some of the material for making ornaments. They were treated in the same way as the complete and fragmentary artefacts. Something similar happened in the silver hoards of the Late Roman period (Painter 2013) and again in the Viking Age (Williams 2013). Like the Late Iron Age examples, they contained coins as well as personal ornaments and rings. The coins had been imported and were often incomplete; again they provided a source of metal. Still more striking, the arm- and neck-rings were made to standard weights. Detailed examination confirms that they had been worn on the body, but on occasion they assumed another role as ingots and were melted down to provide a particular mass of silver. There is no doubt that the proportion of coins found in hoards did increase over time so that the deposits associated with early Viking towns in Northern Europe could have been used as currency (Hårdh 1996; Graham-Campbell & Williams 2007). The same may be true of Iron Age coins in Britain which continued to circulate after the Conquest together with Roman issues.

That is not to say that Roman coin hoards were always buried for safekeeping. The conflicting interpretations of the Hoxne hoard show how difficult it is to maintain that argument. Sauer's account of spring deposits makes the point especially clearly, for he shows why this phenomenon had been overlooked. In this case ancient coins had been studied for their own sake and numismatists had taken little interest in the contexts in which they were discovered (Sauer 2005).

Another study has shown that late Iron Age coin hoards in Britain were often deposited in the same positions in the landscape – locations that recall the places where other kinds of valuables were buried. The comparison with ornament hoards in Norfolk is especially revealing. Current research raises the possibility that some collections of Roman coins may have been distributed according to similar conventions. In the same way Grane has argued that in Scandinavia deposits of hacksilver changed their character between the Roman Iron Age and the Migration Period. They had originally played a role in transactions between local elites. In that sense they might have been treated as the equivalent of money. During the later 1st millennium AD, however, they could be dedicated to the gods (Grane 2013).

A more sophisticated discussion has taken place in social anthropology, where Maurice Bloch and Jonathan Parry (1989) edited an influential book on *Money and the Morality of Exchange*. They make the important point that the true character of any transaction depends on the *social relationship* between the people involved and not on the specific items that pass between them, whether those exchanges involve the provision of feasts, the giving of marriage partners, the acquisition of rare commodities or the use of coins or bullion. The weight of metal and the quantity of coins provide methods of assessing value, but do not determine the circumstances in which they are used. In some cases the object of exchange is considered as *alienable*, but in other instances it commits the actors to a continuing relationship. In ancient societies the use of coins or hacksilver need not have enjoyed any special status. The question has to be investigated one case at a time.

The impact of Christian belief

There was another powerful influence on human behaviour in the past. The adoption of Christianity has coloured the assumptions that researchers make in the present. Students of the later 1st millennium AD assume that practices like those associated with the pre-Roman period were forbidden by the church and rapidly abandoned.

There are several responses to this argument. It is true that the new beliefs took longer to win acceptance in Northern Europe than they did in the West (Sanmark 2004), but this is not a complete explanation of the evidence. The first point to make is that supposedly pagan practices like the provision of grave goods are found as late as the Middle Ages (Gilchrist 2012, 277–82). In the same way there is some evidence that in Britain fonts associated with Christian baptism were deposited in water when they went out of use (Blair 2010; Naylor 2015, 134–46): a remarkable echo of a long-established practice.

The most important argument concerns the attitude of the church to pagan sanctuaries. There is documentary evidence that they were to be treated in one of two ways. Either they must be taken over and dedicated to the new religion, or they had to be destroyed. The evidence is similar in Western and Northern Europe, but it raises a problem. Roman temples might be converted to Christian churches. There were sacred places in Scandinavia and some examples have been excavated (Andrén 2014, 36–38). Most of them went out of use and a few might have been replaced by structures dedicated to the new religion, but, if the basic thesis of this study is accepted, there were others that remained more or less concealed. These were rivers, bogs, lakes and their surroundings. They could hardly be destroyed as they left no trace in the landscape. It would have been difficult to prevent their use even after the Conversion – a close comparison would be with the deposition of metalwork in rivers across the Roman provinces. It could be read as an act of passive resistance to the changes imposed by the church. There is no reason to suppose that the deposition of valuables ended when new beliefs were adopted. A hint of the tensions that remained is provided by several artefacts in the Staffordshire hoard. They were damaged along with the collection of war gear, but were associated with Christian imagery. One of them featured an inscription from the bible (Leahy & Bland 2014). Christina Fredengren suggests that in Uppland the sacrifice of people and animals assumed a similar importance during the late 1st millennium AD. It may have been a deliberate reaction to the adoption of Christianity in Northern Europe (Fredengren 2015).

Ritual, crisis and concealment

At one time the metalwork deposits at Snettisham were explained as valuables hidden when Caesar invaded England. That argument can be rejected on chronological grounds, but the Hoxne treasure does date from the time when Roman administration collapsed. Although the authors of the definitive study of this material take different views, is there a way of reconciling their distinctive approaches? Were there cases in which the practice of ritual deposition was compatible with the concealment of valuables?

Two recent studies suggest that it is possible to combine these interpretations, although convincing examples are very rare. The first considers the burial of gold hoards in the Low Countries at the time of Caesar's conquest of Gaul (Roymans & Scheers 2012). They contain high value coins as well as fragmentary personal ornaments, and in three cases it is known that they were deposited away from the settlements of the same date; a fourth hoard comes from a possible cult site, while another was outside an Iron Age fortification. Roymans and Scheers (2012) argue that they were buried in order to conceal them during a period of conflict, but make the interesting suggestion that they can still be considered as offerings. The coins, arm rings and torcs had been placed under the protection of the gods even if people intended to recover them when the conflict was over. Alternatively they could have been offered to supernatural powers as a request for victory over the invader:

> 'The assumption that profane [hoards] and sacred votive deposits were mutually exclusive categories is overly simple … Hoards might have been placed under the temporary protection of a deity for safety reasons. The place of burial may also have had supernatural associations or even have been a regular cult site … We can break through the problematical dichotomy between profane [collections] and ritual hoards by making a distinction between the *reasons* for burying hoards and the *form* that depositions took. The immediate reason could be a crisis, but the form may have been ritually determined (Roymans & Sheers 2012, 20; emphasis in the original).

The other study investigates the deposition of five hoards of personal ornaments inside a stone fort at Sandby on the Baltic Island of Öland (Fallgren & Ljungkvist 2016). These collections date from the late fifth century AD or the beginning of the sixth. They included a series of brooches of exceptional quality as well as pendants and beads. All the hoards were inside houses.

Sandby was attacked and abandoned in the early sixth century AD and excavation found the remains of men who had been killed and left unburied. One reading of the evidence would be that valuables were concealed in the buildings as the site was attacked; they were not retrieved because the inhabitants were massacred. There are several problems with this interpretation. The contents of all five hoards were very similar to one another and had been carefully selected. In every case they had been deposited on the right hand side of the doorway. That suggests that they were located according to shared conventions, and for those reasons they may not have been hidden from an enemy. Like the collections studied by Roymans and Scheers (2012), they may have been deposited as part of a ritual, but again they remained intact because political events made them impossible to recover.

At Sandby there is another point to consider. The fort itself has an unusual character. A central block of stone buildings contains 18 houses (or two groups of nine), while a second range of structures attached to the enclosure wall includes three further groups of nine structures, and another perhaps with ten. At least two of these rows of houses are separated from one another by entrances to the enclosure. The emphasis on the number nine can hardly be fortuitous, for it is evidenced at other forts on the island. This could be significant as this particular number plays a special role in Scandinavian cosmology. Anders Andrén (2014, 115) has discussed a comparable monument at Ismantorp and considers that its layout is one of 'the oldest depictions of the Old Norse worldview, as it is known in later texts'.

Fallgren and Ljungkvist (2016, 697) offer an intriguing explanation for the hoards at Sandby:

> 'It is possible to see them as props – theatrical artefacts that belonged to the fort (in the same way as liturgical objects belong to a church). That is why they were deposited in such a uniform fashion … They may have been used in different kinds of ritual dramas … The main reason why the hoards were still in place is likely to be the massacre … and the fact that someone … prevented those living in the area of the fort from burying their dead kinsmen and reusing [the site]'.

Again there is the same interplay between ritual and practical considerations.

Unfinished business

These could be exceptional instances. Practical explanations for the deposition of valuables more often fail as they cannot explain why so many artefacts have survived. Nor have they managed to account for the striking similarities between phenomena associated with different periods or regions. Has the 'archaeological analysis of prehistoric hoards and votive deposits' promised 25 years ago finally reached an impasse, or are there new directions to explore?

It is useful to focus on two issues that have already been mentioned in passing. Each develops directly from the approaches considered here. What may be novel is a change of perspective. The first of these issues is the contrast between studies which analyse prehistoric artefacts according to their *type*s, and a biographical approach which places more emphasis on their *histories*. Published sources show an overwhelming emphasis on the classification of artefacts, their associations and dating, but did their outward forms really determine the ways in which they were treated? It seems more important to consider how they had been used between their production and deposition, and their relationships with people and events during that time. Here an obvious starting point is provided by the deposits of war booty in Northern Europe.

Secondly, it is worth returning to discussions of the siting of hoards and other deposits. The traditional distinction between ritual and non-ritual hoards was based on the feasibility of recovering artefacts after they were taken out of circulation, but little was said about the distinctive character of the places where it happened. Did they share features in common, and have important themes in the siting of specialised deposits been obscured by an inflexible distinction between wet and dry environments? The settings of these finds have been treated as passive *containers* for valuables, yet it is more than likely that they possessed considerable importance in their own right. One example is the deposition of Middle and Late Bronze Age

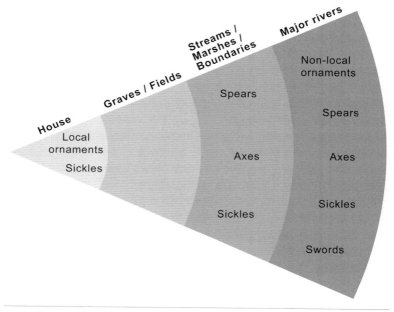

Figure 7. The distribution of Bronze Age metalwork deposits in relation to settlements in the southern Netherlands. Information from Fontijn (2003) and Bradley (2005).

metalwork in the southern Netherlands (Fig. 7). Many of the finds were associated with wet places rather than dry ground, but particular kinds of artefacts were associated *with different kinds of water*. Here axes and spears were found in streams and marshes, whilst ornaments of non-local types and more elaborate weapons were confined to the major rivers (Fontijn 2003, chapter 14). Did those qualities influence the ways in which certain places were used? Questions of this kind are rarely asked.

Public histories

For about a century and a half artefacts have been sorted into classes, and different types have been studied according to their associations with one another. This method is particularly appropriate to the contents of hoards and graves. It is probably more sensitive than projects which consider the dating of ceramics found at settlements. In some ways these two kinds of research have proceeded independently as few burials are associated directly with domestic deposits, and the more complex metalwork usually occurs in isolation. The connections between the artefacts in Bronze Age and Iron Age hoards help to date the single finds, but otherwise they have little impact on field archaeology. The principal objective of many studies – understanding the development of settlement – is frustrated by the structure of the archaeological record.

The histories of ancient objects are written in terms of *types*, and the recognition of those types was one of the first objectives of the discipline of archaeology. That still remains the case, and it is no accident that the past has been subdivided according to the ordering of this material. The Bronze Age in Northern Europe was organised into six periods by Oscar Montelius, using the evidence of hoards and grave goods. His ideas were extended to other regions as local scholars followed his lead (Gräslund 1987). Only where relative sequences could be tied to a historical chronology was there much likelihood of progress. The use of scientific dating has solved that problem, and to some extent has replaced the kinds of studies that preoccupied an earlier generation of prehistorians. And yet a legacy remains. A positive feature is that a scholar like Montelius was right in most of his interpretations. Unfortunately, it means that accounts of the more elaborate artefacts – especially those in hoards and rivers – are still organised by their typology.

One of the paradoxes that have run through this chapter is that the same kinds of artefacts seem to have been employed in radically different ways. Thus neck-rings and similar personal ornaments could be melted down and recycled to make other objects. In the same way, finely worked swords could be deposited intact in rivers during exactly the same periods as they were treated as scrap metal. Whilst tools can be uncommon in watery contexts during the Bronze Age, they are associated with fragmentary weapons in the hoards on dry land. There is no reason to believe that the kinds of swords or spearheads treated in this way were any different from those left undamaged in rivers and bogs.

At one time it seemed possible to explain this contrast (Bradley 1985). During the earlier 1st millennium BC there were cases in which finds of entire objects occurred in one part of the landscape, whilst the hoards in which the same types were reduced to fragments were found in peripheral areas where they were associated with evidence of metalworking. Was it possible that objects that were significant within a particular region could be used as a source of raw material where they did not enjoy the same importance? A few distribution maps did support that notion, but there were too many exceptions for this to provide a satisfactory model.

That example drew on Bronze Age archaeology, but it is the archaeology of the Iron Age that suggests a more promising way forward. The war booty sacrifices of Northern Europe extend from the pre-Roman Iron Age to the Migration Period. There may be even earlier examples of this phenomenon, but that is more controversial. What is generally agreed is that these collections are associated with watery locations and contain large numbers of damaged weapons. They were sufficient to equip an entire war band (Randsborg 1995). Interpretations of this kind are supported by the fact that the artefacts were of non-local kinds and showed signs of combat damage before they were destroyed.

The point is not to suppose that all deposits of weapons were the property of defeated enemies, but to recognise that in this instance the most important issue for archaeologists to study is not the classification of the metalwork – at best it can offer certain clues to the homelands of the invaders – but their *histories*. When a sword was deposited at Hjortspring it entered the water because it had been used by a defeated enemy, and not because it belonged to a particular type. Jos Bazelmans (1999) and Heinrich Härke (2000) have studied the pattern of gift giving and inheritance in the epic poem *Beowulf*. Individual swords had names and biographies, which related them to important people in the past. Surely that was more significant than their formal attributes. The same could be true of earlier examples.

A similar point is made by Nanouschka Myrberg (2009) in her paper 'The hoarded dead: Late Iron Age silver hoards as graves'. Her starting point is the observation that graves often contain a selection of artefacts which were produced at different times and survive in different states of preservation. They had obviously been accumulated over time. Some could have been created for the funeral, but others are likely to have been heirlooms and might have been inherited across the generations. Indeed they might have been made before the dead person was born. These collections would have been composed by the mourners or even by the deceased as death approached, and they record the biography of the dead person. In her term they constitute an 'obituary'.

She observes that virtually the same conventions apply to some of the metalwork hoards of the Viking Age. They were not arbitrary collections of valuables concealed during a sudden crisis. Rather they are carefully constructed assemblages whose contents can span a similar length of time to the grave goods of the same period. Indeed, they may have similar contents to the burials themselves:

> 'The objects accompanying the body in a grave reflect the identities of the dead person in different ways, and may further represent the social relations the individual was involved in … This … applies to the contents of hoards. The objects represent some inherited items, some achieved through the individual's own efforts, and some reflecting the family and external relations of the individual. Coins represent social relations just like other objects do - involvement in bartering and selling, voyaging and inheritance to attain them. Many hoards include several chronologically separated 'clusters' of coins, which might be seen as *the material results of different events, actions and social relations* rather than fluctuations in … [supply]' (Myrberg 2009, 138; emphasis in the original).

As she says, such collections might have served 'to *create* a dead person, independent of the presence of the human body itself' (Myrberg 2009, 138). The same approach has been taken to Bronze

Age hoards containing sets of female ornaments, some of which exhibit different amounts of wear as if they had been accumulated during the life course or had been passed down from a previous generation (Levy 1982).

The argument is convincing, but leaves a question open. Why were collections of Viking metalwork sometimes associated with human remains and sometimes buried on their own? There are many possibilities – they might commemorate Christian converts; they might be associated with people who had died in unusual circumstances, for example in childbirth; or they might have been dowry that could no longer be used. What matters in this context, is that, like the weapons sacrificed in such quantities in Northern Europe, it was their histories and associations that counted as they were removed from circulation.

When artefacts were deposited in the ground or in water, it represented only the final stage in a longer history. To return to a question asked earlier, perhaps it was the objects which lacked such distinguished biographies that could be reused and recycled. This kind of evidence is lost when archaeologists limit themselves to investigating their typologies and associations.

Implements in their places

The previous section suggested that certain artefacts had a special significance in their own right. It was not due solely to their outward forms. Does the same apply to the places where they were deposited?

The title of this section is taken from a collection by the poet W. S. Graham (1977), but it echoes that of an important article by Trevor Cowie (2004), 'Special places for special axes?'. In that paper he studies the findspots of a number of Early Bronze Age hoards in Scotland, concluding that they could be associated with striking features of the upland topography. His thesis is particularly significant because it moves the study of such material away from the practical considerations that have influenced so much writing on this subject. Similar observations were made by the contributors to a recent book on the siting of Bronze Age hoards in Continental Europe (Hansen *et al.* 2014).

Of course it is easier to recognise the distinctive character of findspots in a mountainous landscape, if only because they include locations where it is unlikely that anyone was living. That makes a new study of Late Iron Age coin hoards in England all the more compelling, for it was densely settled. Phillip De Jersey has analysed the locations of a series of well provenanced finds. Again it seems as if the local topography exerted a powerful influence. He observes that in areas with local variations of relief they are not on the tops of hills. Instead they are placed on their brows, as if their positions were meant to be seen from below (De Jersey 2014, chapter 5). This is similar to the false cresting of older round barrows. They have another striking characteristic. They command views across the land to their east and most of them avoid those extending towards the north or west. That applies to 67% of the hoards considered in his study. It is a striking conclusion for two reasons. It is well known that Iron Age roundhouses and the entrances of enclosures and hillforts show a similar preference. It also applies to the few excavated temples or sanctuaries of the same period where deposits of coins and other artefacts show the same emphasis on the east.

Wetland locations raise a different issue. The particular qualities of such places require dedicated research, but they are often overlooked in an attempt to distinguish ritual from non-ritual hoards. There is no doubt that some places retained their associations over a long period of time, so that the great collection of treasure from Skedemosse on the Baltic island of Öland which dates from the 3rd to 6th centuries AD was in exactly the same place as the remains of animals sacrificed during the pre-Roman and early Roman Iron Ages (Hagberg 1967; Monikander 2010). This practice was renewed on a smaller scale after the deposition of metalwork had ended. Similarly the deposits of war booty from Vimose were not the earliest material found there as the site was originally associated with the fertility of the land and its products (Pauli Jensen 2009). The deposits do not seem to have been marked and yet the same locations appear to have been significant over long periods of time. Again almost 5000 finds are associated with

Lake Ejsbøl but they come from four separate locations, each of them associated with a different combination of artefacts. Their chronology extends between the beginning of the 1st century and the middle of the 5th century AD.

In the same vein David Fontijn (2007) has commented on the importance of 'invisible places' of this kind in his study of river finds from Belgium and the southern Netherlands. People used the same locations over a considerable period of time, but, as happened at sites like Vimose, they did so episodically. Often the sequence was punctuated by lengthy intervals which did not feature any identifiable remains. This is illustrated by Fontijn's study which considers river finds whose history runs from about 5000 BC to the beginning of the Christian era. During that time each of the earliest sites were reused on two occasions. Since the sample is so small one might ask whether this was a coincidence, but the same pattern occurs with a larger group of findspots whose history began around 3000 BC. From 2000 BC the number of finds increased again. In eight cases there is evidence of intermittent use for periods of between 500 and 1250 years, but even more striking is a larger group of locations first utilised between 1750 and 1500 BC whose histories extend to the Iron Age. The number of artefacts is so limited that they must have been deposited there only occasionally.

Fontijn compares the histories of these places with those of burial mounds in the same region. They are associated with a different selection of objects, but their periods of use were much the same. In one case their positions in the landscape were clearly marked, but it would be necessary to know the significance of particular sections of the rivers. There might be topographical clues of the kind recognised by Rundqvist (2015), but it would take special skills to read them. They are discussed in Chapter 9. Obviously much depended on the strength of social memory.

The next stage

The examples considered so far illustrate the perils of a practical understanding of hoards and related deposits. They also suggest that the same mistakes have been made by specialists studying different periods and that there are certain points of comparison between assemblages formed many years apart. They might even be considered as variants on one fundamental practice: a kind of behaviour which has few, if any, precedents in the ethnographic record.

The last two sections have attempted to move the discussion in a more positive direction by emphasising the histories of the artefacts that received such distinctive treatment, and the places where that happened. It sets the agenda for the chapters that follow. They focus on the objects that have dominated the discussion so far, emphasising not only their individual histories but the circumstances in which they were produced and the materials out of which they were made. Chapters 9 and 10 provide a more detailed assessment of the findspots themselves, highlighting the peculiar character of many of these places. They bring those separate elements together and suggest a new way of thinking about the ancient landscape.

CHAPTER FOUR

Proportional Representation

The variety of deposits

Most of the deposits discussed in Chapters 2 and 3 were found by chance, and only rarely were they excavated. More often they have been studied in museum collections. That procedure raises two questions which are considered here. Were these assemblages complete, or were certain kinds of material identified or recovered at the expense of others? And to what extent were the contents of such assemblages modified by differential preservation? Those questions are particularly important when the finds are dominated by one category of material. That is especially true of metalwork and animal bone. The discussion begins by considering a selection of sites which have been extensively investigated. Like those considered earlier, they extend across a wide chronological and geographical range. Again one of the starting points is the Broadward hoard which was investigated in 2010. It is compared with a second spring deposit at Röekillorna in the south of Sweden. There follow short accounts of the wetland assemblages from Flag Fen in eastern England, Oberdorla in north-east Germany and Skedemosse in the Baltic. Finally, this section describes the dryland sites of Wartau in Switzerland, Manching in southern Germany, Thézy-Gilmont in northern France and Hallaton in the English midlands. They have been chosen to illustrate the sheer variety of deposits documented by fieldwork.

Excavations at two spring deposits

Röekillorna

Very different collections of artefacts can be found in similar ways. The book began with the discovery of a hoard of weapons when a well was dug at Broadward in 1867 (Bradley *et al.* 2015). Events took virtually the same course at Röekillorna in southern Sweden where another well was excavated 84 years later. In each case a programme of fieldwork followed, but there any similarity ends. The English site produced a substantial group of bronze metalwork, including 50 spearheads and two swords, whilst its Scandinavian counterpart was associated with pottery, stone and wooden objects and a large assemblage of animal bone. It included only four metal artefacts of diagnostic types: three iron knives and a brooch (Stjernqvist 1997). That is ironic as most studies of prehistoric water deposits emphasise the role of metalwork and say little about its associations.

In many cases this is understandable as only the most attractive artefacts were collected, and sometimes wood and bone were not preserved. The spring deposit at Röekillorna provides an indication of what might have been lost. It was excavated on a large scale and all the surviving material was documented. Its history extended from the beginning of the Neolithic period to the Roman Iron Age, although the comparatively small size of the assemblage suggests that it was used intermittently. Among the most distinctive items were four stone axes, four chisels and three daggers. There were also three bone spearheads and about 300 sherds, most of them dating from the Early Neolithic period and the Iron Age. They are overshadowed by a collection of worked wood and nearly 4000 animal bones. Most were identified as horse and dog, with smaller quantities of cattle and sheep. Intriguingly, there were no fewer than 44 human bones, including a number of skull fragments.

The excavator, Berta Sternquist, compared the results of her fieldwork with the finds from other bogs in Northern Europe. Most were chance discoveries, and again the surviving material is dominated by inorganic artefacts. In the circumstances it is difficult to tell whether the contents of hoards and related deposits were restricted to the diagnostic items that entered the public domain. Sometimes they may be all that remain of a more extensive assemblage.

Broadward

That is the implication of the recent excavation at Broadward (Bradley *et al.* 2015). As Chapter 2 has shown, it examined the surviving part of the pit in which a hoard had been deposited. The hole was dug into the side of a spring which, like its counterpart at Röekillorna, was active throughout the prehistoric period. The work also explored its surroundings which had been disturbed by 19th century drainage. Although the site is known for its collection of Late Bronze Age weapons, the sediments contained a series of distinctive artefacts that extended over a lengthy period of time. The earliest was a stone macehead which dated from the Early Bronze Age. It was an unusual find as artefacts of this type are normally associated with burials, but in this case it had been broken in half and may have been burnt. Close to the pit was a sherd of Late Bronze Age pottery and part of a shale bracelet, apparently of the same date. There was also a complete Roman pot. Animal bones were associated with the spring and were virtually absent from the surrounding area. Some date from the Middle to Late Saxon phase and others from the medieval period. The most remarkable deposit was the latest of all. It was a wooden knife or dagger associated with another group of bones including those of a cat. Such deposits are usually seen as a protection against witchcraft and their history is known to extend into the post-medieval period. In this case the deposit has a radiocarbon date of AD 1480–1650.

The contents of the pit were less diverse but were sufficient to show that the weapons had not been buried in isolation. They included pieces of imported quartz which were used to line this feature, a bone gouge which was a century or more old when it was buried, a few pieces of flaked stone, and several tiny fragments of bone which had been burnt to a high temperature. Unfortunately, it was impossible to tell whether they were human. In the past the Broadward hoard has been studied as if it consisted entirely of metalwork. It is a moot point how many other hoards contained a wider variety of material. Only when they are carefully excavated is it possible to answer this question. The remaining finds from this pit would be easy to overlook.

Excavations at other wetland deposits

Flag Fen

Another site where Bronze Age weapons formed part of a larger collection is Flag Fen in eastern England where a wooden causeway crossed an expanse of open water (Pryor 2001; Pryor & Bamforth 2010). It was built and maintained between 1350 and 950 BC, but the deposition of fine metalwork continued for another 600 years or more into the middle of the Iron Age. Excavation revealed a large collection of bronzes as well as other artefacts and animal bones. It is clear how these deposits were organised. Towards the western end of the alignment where it met dry land there was an important concentration of artefacts, but it continued eastwards into an area which was always submerged. It was towards the terminal that most of the Bronze Age material was found, although its distribution did not extend far into a ditched field system which ran up to the water's edge. Iron Age metalwork, on the other hand, could be found further to the east, in an area that remained underwater. As well as weapons of kinds that have been found at other sites in the Fenland – swords, rapiers, spears and daggers – there were axes, awls, razors, bracelets and pins. A few pieces may have been made specifically for deposition, and some of the swords contained casting flaws and could not have been used for a long time.

Most of the metalwork was discovered along the southern edge of the post alignment, while to its north the prehistoric deposits contained faunal remains. A feature of this collection was a high proportion of dogs. There were a few fragments of human bone. The Bronze Age and Iron Age metalwork recalls earlier finds from the Fens, which were normally discovered by chance. It is only because these deposits were excavated that the smaller items were recognised. The same applies to the human and animal bones. Still more important, it was only through careful fieldwork that the excavators could see how this material was distributed. If it had been recovered by chance, the contents of Flag Fen would resemble those from Broadward.

Another point is important. This is the question of differential preservation. Had the sediments at Flag Fen dried out, little would remain of the causeway. The animal bones would be lost, leaving no more than a series of weapons like those on other wetland sites. Something similar would have happened at Röekillorna where there would be no sign of any wooden artefacts. The same could happen to the human and animal bones that make that collection so distinctive. A few stone objects could still be found at the Swedish site, together with a selection of pottery, the majority dating from periods separated by between two and three thousand years.

Oberdorla (Fig. 8)

If Flag Fen can be compared with the spring deposit at Broadward, Röekillorna shares features with Oberdorla in north-east Germany. Berta Sternquist referred to the site in her monograph, but at the time her text was written the results of excavation there had not been published. Now it is possible to consider them in more detail (Behm-Blanke 2003).

The 'offering place' (*Opferplatz*) at Oberdorla consisted of a series of circular wooden enclosures associated with ephemeral features which their excavator interpreted as 'altars' distributed along the edge of a marshy pool. It saw a continuous history from the Early Iron Age to the middle of the Roman Iron Age, with more restricted activity during the late Roman Iron Age and the Migration period. It was used most intensively between the late La Tène and early Roman times. The distribution of the principal deposits shifted from the south-eastern shoreline during the Hallstatt and La Tène periods to the north-west during the Roman Iron Age. Like Röekillorna, Oberdorla was associated with extensive deposits of animal bones which were interpreted as evidence of ritual meals and sacrifices. The main species represented were cattle, sheep/goat and pig. Human remains were also found there and were commonest during the late 1st millennium BC and the Roman Iron Age. They showed signs of injuries and it seemed possible that people had been sacrificed at the site. That is plausible as the bones from Oberdorla are contemporary with the bog bodies of Northern Europe.

A large amount of pottery was associated with the excavated deposits, but the most distinctive feature of Oberdorla was the

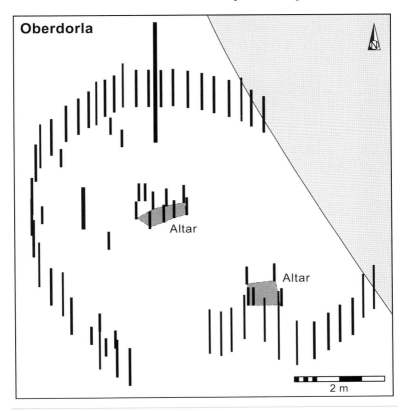

Figure 8. Reconstruction of one of the Iron Age wooden enclosures by the water's edge at Oberdorla, Germany. Information from Behm-Blanke (2003).

presence of 30 or more wooden artefacts which were interpreted as anthropomorphic idols, both male and female. There had been similar claims at Röekillorna but in this case such finds were more common and their identification was more convincing. They were found together with the human and animal remains and were associated with the small enclosures around the water's edge. By contrast, the finds of weapons which are conventionally associated with a wet environment amounted to an iron sword, two wooden swords, two axes and two spears. Metalwork was not important there.

Skedemosse

The evidence from Skedemosse on the Baltic island of Öland is even more complex, for the character of the excavated deposits changed over the course of time (Hagberg 1967; Monikander 2010). During the later pre-Roman Iron Age there is evidence that horses were sacrificed and their remains discarded in a bog. During the following phase human bones were deposited in the same context. They show injuries that raise the possibility that people were sacrificed as well as animals. They were men and women of all ages. Finds of skulls were particularly common. It was in this second period that metalwork featured on the site. In a final period the deposits were smaller and resemble those of the first phase.

There is evidence of feasting at Skedemosse where horses provided the main source of meat. Faunal remains were discovered in great quantities, but were often in local concentrations like those at Oberdorla. There were entire bodies from which the edible parts had been removed; there were individual joints of meat; and there were other bones from which all the marrow had been extracted. As well as horses, cattle, sheep and pigs were strongly represented, but dogs and goats made up a smaller part of the assemblage. The excavators noted that the deer consumed on the site had been unusually large animals.

The site is best known for the exceptional quantity of artefacts deposited during the early 1st millennium AD. The personal items include gold ornaments, belt fittings, rings and combs. There were even a few coins imported from the Roman world. The assemblage also contained an exceptional range of weapons which have been compared with those from the deposits of war booty in Denmark: swords, spears, arrows, shields and horse trappings. Some of the weapons were in 'bundles' similar to the contents of hoards. Other finds were completely unexpected. There were pieces of slag which might have resulted from the production of artefacts on the site. As well as artefacts the bog contained a large number of unworked stones which had been brought there from a distance. Their presence has never been explained. Pottery was absent, but may not have survived due to the harsh conditions at Skedemosse.

Excavations at dryland deposits

Despite the conventional contrast between wetland deposits and those found on dry land, similar collections have been recorded from both environments. They are illustrated by the finds from three Iron Age sites.

Brandopferplätze and the Iron Age site at Wartau

The first example is one of the 'burnt offering places' (*Brandopferplätze*) in the Swiss and Italian Alps (Steiner 2010). Their overall chronology extends from the middle of the Bronze Age into the Iron Age, although there is some evidence of Roman activity on these sites. They are characterised by large quantities of charcoal, ash and animal bones, all of them associated with pottery. The earlier examples formed conspicuous mounds with alternating deposits of burnt material and faunal remains. Sometimes they accumulated over the remains of abandoned houses. Most examples were located within the domestic landscape and there are indications that people lived nearby. The commonest bones are those of sheep or goat. The ceramic assemblage is extremely fragmentary, and in Italy it is thought that the pots were used to bring food from the settlements. The main functions of these places were communal feasting and the sacrifice of animals.

The Bronze Age examples produce finds of metalwork which consist of small personal items, especially ornaments. Weapons are not represented but are associated with rivers in the same region. They have also been discovered in mountain passes and other locations discussed in Chapter 9. A superficial reading of this evidence might suggest that *Brandopferplätze* were integrated with domestic life and should not be compared with deposits of more specialised kinds, but that argument does not apply to developments during the Iron Age. This is shown by the excavated example at Wartau in Switzerland where the main period of use was between the 5th and 1st centuries BC (Primas *et al.* 2001). In this case a greater variety of metalwork was deposited among the bones and broken pottery. Again the finds included large numbers of burnt animal remains, but in this case a wider range of species was represented, including pigs, sheep or goats and cattle. Carbonised plant food was also recovered. The situation changed during a final phase which saw less use of fire. Pieces of glass and Roman coins were deposited at that time.

Again the deposits at Wartau contained some dress ornaments including brooches, but in this case there were also iron swords, metal vessels and an exceptional number of fragmentary helmets. The weapons had been deliberately damaged and were associated with burnt material. One deposit stands out, for it had all the conventional attributes of a hoard. It consisted of 24 objects which had been packed together in a pit. This collection included nine spearheads, parts of five swords and three knives. Had this material been discovered by metal detecting rather than excavation, it might have been studied in isolation.

Hallaton (Fig. 9)

Hallaton in the English midlands belongs to a small group of sites where more than one hoard of Iron Age coins have been discovered (Score 2011). They are usually found by metal detectorists and are rarely excavated on an extensive scale. That is most likely to happen where a Roman temple was built in the same place.

There is no evidence that it occurred at Hallaton where the prehistoric deposits focussed on a boundary ditch which may have formed part of a larger enclosure. It was possibly associated with a settlement, although it could not be demonstrated. The findspot was towards the edge of a ridge and, like those considered in Chapter 3, it was below its summit and faced south east. Dogs had been buried on either side of an entrance leading through the earthwork. A small circular building may have been the earliest structure on the site, but it remains undated although two Middle Bronze Age spearheads were found during the excavation. The oldest coins from Hallaton were

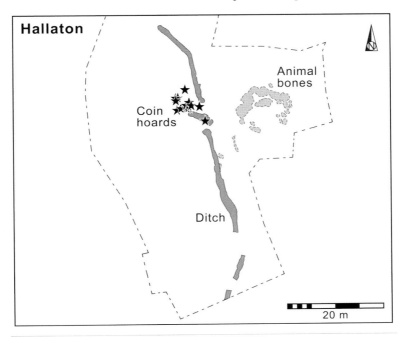

Figure 9. The locations of the coin hoards at Hallaton, in relation to the Iron Age ditch and the main deposits of animal bones. Dogs had also been buried in the entrance to the site. Information from Score (2011).

deposited before the earthwork was built, but most of the others were later. At least 16 separate hoards of gold and silver coins were found outside the earthwork. They were not the only metalwork there, for among the other artefacts were a silver bowl, some bronze ingots and a decorated Roman helmet. The sequence probably started in the later 1st century BC and continued until the middle of the 1st century AD. In that case it would have extended beyond the Roman Conquest.

If the presence of so many groups of coins was one exceptional feature, another was the discovery of large quantities of animal bones inside the enclosure ditch. Most were of pigs and were the remains of meat which had apparently been consumed on the spot. In one case an arc of bones surrounded a small empty area which might have been a reserved space or the position of a low mound. The excavators concluded that Hallaton saw the deposition of valuables as well as large scale feasting. This interpretation is particularly important because only the hoards could be found by metal detection. It required large scale excavation to show that other activities happened there.

The sanctuaries at Manching and Thézy-Glimont

There was a sanctuary in the centre of the famous *oppidum* at Manching in Bavaria. It was possibly the earliest feature on the site and included a series of small square enclosures (Wendling & Winger 2004). The best known example contained a circle of pits and was associated with an Iron Age sword, but not far away there was a similar earthwork. In this case there was a concentration of special deposits between 30 and 50 m away. This material is dated to the later 3rd century BC. Here human and animal bones were found together with damaged weapons, especially swords. Some of the material was particularly distinctive. Pits or wells contained the skulls of cattle and horses, and here the density of human remains was at least four times higher than in the surrounding area (Lange 1983, Beilage 1). Another find was completely unexpected, for associated with all these remains were parts of the statue of a horse. As so often, this species seems to have enjoyed a special status.

Thézy-Glimont in the north of France was another late pre-Roman sanctuary (Le Béchennec 2016). Its siting is most distinctive (Fig. 10). It overlooked what the excavator describes as one of the largest marshes in Europe, and was built beside the confluence of the River Avre and a tributary. The monument consisted of another square enclosure and contained an internal range of wooden buildings surrounding an empty space. Again it was associated with fragmentary weapons – in this case a total of 612 separate pieces including swords. There were also metalworking residues, coins and the bones of 22 people who had suffered fatal injuries. The excavated material is dated between 150 and 125 BC and was later than the deposits associated with the sanctuary at Manching.

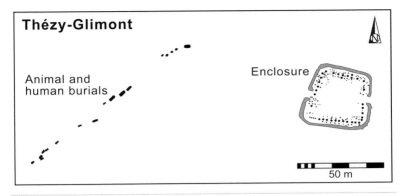

Figure 10. Plan of the Iron Age sanctuary at Thézy-Glimont, France, in relation to the human and animal burials found outside it. Information from Le Béchennec (2016).

Thézy-Glimont is relevant to this chapter because excavation extended for a considerable distance from the earthwork. It found a second series of deposits about 150 m away. The earliest were in disused grain stores which probably predated the sanctuary, but they were followed by a series of rectangular pits closer to the margin of the wetland. They contained a remarkable collection of animal burials – 35 cattle, 12 horses and three pigs. All were deposited as complete bodies. They might well have been sacrifices and were not the remains of feasts. Still more striking, were the bodies of eight young men which were associated with two of those species – cattle and horses. These deposits are dated between about 170 and 40 BC. The most striking feature of Thézy-Glimont is that the formal burials of people and animals *were entirely separate* from the deposits within the sanctuary, even though both included human remains.

A question of scale

It is easy to consider these sites as exceptional, but it would be wrong to do so. Too few votive deposits have been investigated, yet they do share common features. They include large collections of animal bones like those from Wartau, Oberdorla, Röekillorna and Skedemosse. In contrast to those associated with settlement sites, some of them include an unusually high proportion of horses. This is particularly true of Manching, Skedemosse and Röekillorna, but dogs also played a significant role at the wetland site of Flag Fen and the dryland site at Hallaton. In most cases they were deposited in groups, but at Bronze Age sites in Switzerland they formed conspicuous mounds and on the French site they were separated from a ditched sanctuary associated with fragmentary weapons, human remains and evidence of metalworking. At Hallaton they may have defined the limits of a small enclosure. Something similar happened at Oberdorla where the main concentrations of faunal remains were enclosed by rings of posts. There are human remains from most of the same places, in particular Oberdorla, Röekillorna, Manching, Thézy-Glimont and Skedemosse, but they were present in smaller numbers at Flag Fen in the Bronze Age and at Hallaton during the Iron Age. Some of these bones show evidence of unhealed wounds, and the larger collections include a significant number of skulls which seem to have been deposited on their own. Oberdorla and Röekillorna contained wooden idols depicting the human body and a horse was portrayed by a fragmentary sculpture at Manching.

Pottery was found at most of these sites. It was the case at Röekillorna and Oberdorla, and the remains of broken vessels are especially common at 'burnt offering sites' in the Alps where they were sometimes associated with plant foods. The Swiss and Italian sites may seem rather different yet this could be misleading, for some of the other deposits show the importance of fires. It was certainly the case at Skedemosse. Metalworking is among the processes that took place at these sites. It was evidenced at Thézy-Glimont and ingots were found at Hallaton. At Skedemosse there were pieces of slag.

Lastly, there are the deposits of weapons which have dominated discussion for a long time. They were certainly present in six cases: at Broadward, Flag Fen, Thézy-Glimont, Manching, Skedemosse and Wartau, and smaller quantities have been recorded at the other locations. What stands out is how little metalwork of any kind was found at Röekillorna and Oberdorla, or, indeed, at the Bronze Age burnt offering sites in the Alps. Even when fine metalwork, including a helmet and a silver bowl, was associated with the hoards at Hallaton it is well to remember that they were found with a collection of animal bones resulting from communal feasts. In some ways the finds from Oberdorla provide a necessary corrective to accounts of more elaborate objects. Here large scale excavation found only one iron sword, but two others were made of wood. A balanced account of these deposits must account for the full range of evidence.

A question of time

It also needs to consider their extended history. They feature over a longer period in some parts of Europe than others. In the West they are first identified during the Neolithic phase, and by the post-Roman period they play a comparatively limited role. In the North, on the other hand, the earliest examples are Mesolithic, and the collections of metalwork described as hoards retained, or even increased, their importance in the 1st millennium AD.

During that lengthy sequence their character changed more than once. The earliest finds associated with water date from the Mesolithic period and consist of animal sacrifices at sites in Scandinavia, but even before that period ended their character was transformed, with an increasing emphasis on deposits of axes and bone and antler tools (Koch 1998). These developments became more pronounced during the Neolithic phase, but by the end of the 3rd millennium BC they were supplemented by finds of metalwork (Vandkilde 1996). Only then is the Scandinavian material considered in the same terms as deposits in Western Europe, yet faunal remains and copper or bronze artefacts might be placed in separate locations.

In Northern Europe a second development was a closer association between foodstuffs and metal artefacts. In Denmark the number of associations between such objects and food increased in the earlier 1st millennium BC (Matthews 2008) and most of the hoards containing animal bones date from Montelius Period V (about 900–700 BC).

Occasionally they included four or five individual sets of ornaments; other types, including weapon or sickles were less common. The importance of vessels containing meat or plants continued into the early Iron Age when less metalwork of any kind is found. Another change took place in the Migration Period, for this was the time when gold and silver artefacts were deposited in isolation. The same development happened in the Viking Age.

The true complexity of the evidence is illustrated by two more sites investigated in the field. The first is Hindbygården in south-west Sweden where the earliest deposits are late Mesolithic (Berggren 2007). The sequence continues through the Neolithic period but most of the finds predate the widespread adoption of copper and bronze in Scandinavia. They include a variety of artefacts and animal bones and contrast in almost every respect with the hoards associated with the Roman Iron Age and the Migration Period. They are epitomised by a series of finds from the Danish power centre at Gudme. They date between AD 200 and about 600 and consist exclusively of metalwork. Gudme and Hindbygården are positioned towards opposite ends of the history of hoards and wetland deposits.

Hindbygården

Excavation at Hindbygården investigated a peat-filled hollow which had once been a shallow pool. During the course of the Neolithic period the sediments dried out until by the Early Bronze Age it was little more than a damp meadow. It has been compared with the spring at Röekillorna, where the sequence is not so well dated but continued until the Iron Age. The two sites are only 70 km apart. During the same period the setting of Hindbygården changed from closed woodland to a largely open agricultural landscape. There is evidence of houses, pits and mortuary monuments of the same date in the surrounding area which was extensively investigated during the development of Malmö.

The filling of the pool was carefully excavated, with the result that an important sequence of deposits was recorded. Their history extended from the late Mesolithic period to the early 2nd millennium

BC, although the frequency with which the site was used varied over time. There was most activity during the Late Neolithic period. Its contents can be compared with the finds from Röekillorna, but they resemble deposits of stone artefacts, usually axes, in Denmark, north Germany and elsewhere in the south of Sweden (Rech 1979; Karsten 1994). Some were isolated discoveries and others were obviously hoards, but they illustrate the same association with bogs and areas of damp ground. The sediments at Hindbygården contained a series of shafthole axes as well as simpler forms made from flint, antler axes, sickles, daggers and Neolithic pottery. At the beginning of that period entire vessels were deposited, but the later levels contained broken sherds. With them was a wide variety of worked stone of the kind found in settlements, as well as the remains of wild and domesticated animals, mainly cattle and pigs. There were also some human bones. The excavated material included an extraordinary amount of burnt and unburnt stone of a kind that was placed in pits around the water's edge. Only one piece of metalwork was found in the entire excavation.

The Neolithic assemblage can be compared with the contents of a similar feature at Skogmossen in middle Sweden. It was not far from a house of the same date (Hallgren *et al.* 1997). Again fine flint artefacts, such as axes, and decorated pottery were associated with large quantities of burnt stone, perhaps from food preparation. At Skogsmossen the lithic artefacts from the pool were rather larger than those in the adjacent settlement and half of them had been burnt. Complete pots had been deposited in the water and the excavator was able to show that a higher proportion of them had been decorated than the vessels from the living site. Axes which had been broken or damaged by fire were also placed in the water, and the same applies to complete and serviceable querns. Unfortunately, little animal bone survived at Skogsmossen, but the material from Hindbygården contrasts with the collection from Röekillorna which included the remains of horses and dogs. Comparison with the Bronze Age and Iron Age sites mentioned earlier suggests that they may have been deposited in the spring towards the end of its period of use.

The pots placed in the water at Hindbygården and Skogsmossen resemble those from similar contexts in Northern Europe. A study by Eva Koch (1998) suggests that this practice began in the late Mesolithic period, and that most of those in her study area in Denmark were put there before 3000 BC. They could be associated with the remains of plant foods, the bones of domesticated animals and occasionally with human remains. She suggests that they became less common once stone axes were deposited in the same environments. It is curious that the custom of placing food remains in bogs reappeared during the pre-Roman Iron Age when another group of ceramic vessels was deposited in similar places (Becker 1971). Again they were associated with offerings of food, but in this case there were also items of agricultural equipment, particularly a simple form of plough. The two phases were separated by more than two thousand years. During that time copper and bronze artefacts featured in the same contexts.

Gudme

If the Mesolithic artefacts at Hindbygården are among the oldest finds from a wetland context in Scandinavia, the hoards associated with Gudme on the island of Funen characterise the later part of the sequence. Only the Viking silver hoards date from a subsequent period. Both groups are composed entirely of metalwork.

During the middle of the 1st millennium AD Gudme was one of the richest settlements in Northern Europe. In fact it may be misleading to think in terms of a single settlement for it was really an agglomeration of separate farms, some of monumental proportions, connected to a coastal landing place at Lundeborg which was associated with another distinctive collection of artefacts (Nielsen *et al.* 1994). It seems possible that the main nucleus was dominated by three sacred hills, whose special character is recorded by their ancient names. Lotte Hedeager (2011, 150–52 & 159–62) has suggested that Gudme was the location of Asgård, the seat of the Scandinavian gods. Excavation shows that it contained wooden buildings of exceptional size and complexity.

It was associated with some remarkable discoveries, and it was this feature that led to an ambitious programme of fieldwork (Nielsen *et al.* 1994). The most spectacular of the chance finds came from the edge of a wetland at Broholm, but others were associated with living sites. The Broholm hoard contained the largest collection of gold found in Denmark and included bracteates, arm-rings and necklaces. Other hoards were discovered through the use of metal detectors and their findspots were excavated. Their contents were extremely varied, but it is notable that none of them contained anything but metalwork and the equipment for working metals. One included Roman coins dating from the 4th century AD, a gold ring, parts of an imported ladle and a dish. It was associated with a house and also contained a crucible. A second group was associated with another domestic building, but in this case the collection was composed of gold and silver scrap. A separate find on the same site consisted of nearly 300 Roman coins. In a third instance metal detecting located a hoard of bracteates, including coins that had been turned into personal ornaments, a series of gold pendants and a ring of the same material. Again it came from a settlement. Elsewhere in the Gudme complex were two hoards containing neck-rings and scrap silver. Further finds included scabbard mounts and a gold ingot on one site, and gold scrap and sword hilts, on another.

These are only examples of the range of variation, but they provided the basis for a simple classification of these deposits (Nielsen *et al.* 1994, 30–40). Firstly, there were caches of scrap metal, much of it in the form of imported coins. There was some evidence of metalworking. Then there were sets of personal jewellery which may have built up over time. They commonly included bracteates. A third group was characterised as 'untouchable capital' and interpreted as the result of aristocratic gift giving. It includes gold neck-rings, other personal ornaments and decorated scabbard mounts. The Broholm hoard probably belongs in this category. Taken, together they date from about the 3rd century to the 7th century AD.

Several points are worth making here. The first is that the main raw materials – gold and silver – had to be imported and were often worked by recycling foreign artefacts and coins. This may have happened in a domestic setting, although not all the hoards were associated with settlements and those containing gold or silver were sometimes kept apart, even on the same site. Another observation is that the sets of intact valuables must have played a different role from those associated with scrap metal, ingots or crucibles. That may be why the gold hoard from Broholm was associated with a wetland – the kind of environment which had been favoured from the early prehistoric period and retained its significance into the Viking Age. It is a moot point how many collections of scrap metal, especially gold, were used to make finished objects that would eventually be buried together. A final observation is perhaps the simplest of all. The deposits that have been so carefully recorded at Gudme do not contain any animal bones. Instead, excavations at the central places of the later 1st millennium AD have identified accumulations of burnt stone and faunal remains. This suggests that feasting had become a separate activity from deposition of valuables. Sacrifices of people and animals continued and in Northern Europe they are documented until the end of the 1st millennium AD.

Summary

The principal characteristics of these deposits considered are summarised in Table 1. It is clear that there were two traditions that sometimes overlapped. One was the deposition of sacrificed animals and the remains of feasts (Pluskowski 2012) and the other was the deposition of metalwork. In this particular sample the earliest and latest deposits illustrate only one of these practices. During

Table 1. The main associations of the sites discussed in the text

Mainly animal bones and artefacts	• Hindbygården • Röekillorna • Oberdorla	• Wartau	• Flag Fen • Hallaton • Skedemosse • Manching • Thézy-Glimont	• Broadward • Gudme	Mainly metalwork

the intervening period they could be found independently or in combination.

Among these excavated sites the deposition of animal remains began during the Mesolithic period and continued until the Roman Iron Age; in other cases it lasted even longer. They were occasionally accompanied by human remains which were most abundant towards the end of this tradition. Sometimes both groups of bones were accompanied by distinctive objects. The earliest were stone axes, although other lithic artefacts, including flint daggers, have been found in excavation. During the Neolithic period pots containing food or drink were deposited in similar locations, and this practice was followed on an increasing scale during the pre-Roman Iron Age when finds of other kinds are less common.

The deposition of metalwork seems to have run in parallel with most of these practices and it can be no coincidence that axes made of copper or bronze took on the special role that stone artefacts of the same kind had played since the Mesolithic period. Other types of metalwork were equally important and are commonly discovered on dry land and in wet locations. They became less common during the early pre-Roman Iron Age, but their frequency increased again in the following phase and they remained important from then on. Andres Dobat (2010) has drawn attention to the large collections of animal bones, ash and burnt stones associated with some of the 'central places' in Northern Europe during the 1st millennium AD. He interprets them as the remains of sacrificial feasts, although they also include a few human remains. They are a particular feature of the Danish site of Lejre and the Swedish sites of Borg and Uppåkra. At the Viking manor of Borg Dobat reports that the remains of pigs were distributed around a small timber building. The skulls and jaws of female animals were found together with iron pendants, but those of boars were associated with furnaces and deposits of slag. It is obvious that, for all the mass of food remains, these were formal deposits. At the same time the gold and silver hoards from Gudme typify a wider pattern, for they were not found in the same contexts as food remains. That also applies to the metal hoards of the Viking period, but it does not mean that feasting and animal sacrifice were any less important. Rather, collections of human and animal bones were less frequently associated with the deposits of fine metalwork at the same locations.

To conclude, there is more variety among deposits of these kinds than is commonly supposed, and that is why their history has been studied as if they represented two entirely independent phenomena, separated from one another by regional and chronological specialisms. It is because different periods are investigated by different scholars that Mesolithic material is seldom considered in similar terms to those of the Bronze or Iron Ages. It also explains why deposits of human and animal bones are rarely analysed together with accumulations of metalwork, even when they are found together in the same place. The situation is even more discouraging when only one class of material is discovered, for it makes it harder to recognise that they formed only part of a wider phenomenon. The lesson of Thézy-Glimont is most important here. By good fortune the excavation, which was carried out as part of development-led fieldwork, was sufficiently extensive to identify not only an Iron Age shrine containing broken weapons, but also an important series of human and animal burials 150 m away. The two assemblages were contemporary with one another, but their contents were almost entirely different.

That is not to suggest that the composition of such deposits remained constant over time. The earliest predate the first use of metals and were associated with pottery and stone artefacts as well as biological remains. The latest could exclude human and animal bones altogether, although these still appeared in other locations where they were commonly associated with layers of ash and burnt stone from food preparation. They were a particular feature of the later 1st millennium AD, but in between those periods, during the Bronze Age and pre-Roman Iron Age, both the traditions might be combined. Unfortunately, they can all too easily be studied as separate projects. For the reason explained in Chapter 3, Roman deposits raise yet another set of problems, and here there remains a worrying tendency to explain the presence of both artefacts and animal bones in anecdotal terms. Sometimes that may be correct, but it remains to be seen how often it was the case. One way of addressing the problem is to consider the deposits from sanctuaries or temples whose contents span the Late Iron Age and Early Roman periods. That approach is already proving its value in England and France.

One point is already clear. In the archaeology of any period a rounded account of deposits of metalwork, human and animal remains must treat them together. It cannot follow the conventional division of labour in which studies of artefacts are conducted with little reference to the biological remains from the same locations. With honourable exceptions, some of which featured in this chapter, analyses of these collections have not been sufficiently ambitious.

CHAPTER FIVE

The Hoard as a Still Life

'Pronkstillevens'

Every discipline has a language of its own and as a result technical terms can be difficult to translate. The Dutch word *Pronkstillevens* provides a good example. It refers to the pictures described as 'sumptuous still lives', but this name gives little away. They were a distinctive genre of oil painting practised in the mid-17th century.

The contents of these pictures are easier to describe, and the same applies to the context in which they were created. This is important because the paintings share certain features with hoards. They depict arrangements of distinctive and visually arresting objects, sometimes accompanied by flowers, fabrics or food. Among the commonest components are metal vessels and lavishly decorated ceramics. *Pronkstillevens* were painted during the period when the Netherlands saw an unprecedented influx of rare and valuable commodities through the opening of trade routes to Asia. It was a period when the activities of the Dutch East India Company were at their height and it was through the expansion of international markets that new materials, among them lacquer and porcelain, were introduced to Northern Europe. One outcome was the emergence of a distinctive visual culture (Van Campen *et al.* 2015).

These paintings developed out of an older tradition of depicting domestic artefacts and foodstuffs, but they soon provided a medium which allowed rich merchants to celebrate their wealth. The pictures showed their personal collections and complemented the displays of objects in their homes. Of course, there are other ways of interpreting them. They have been seen as allegories illustrating the vanity of earthly possessions. That would be consistent with the strength of Protestant belief in the Netherlands, but most authorities agree with

Simon Schama (1987, 160–61) that the display of *Pronkstillevens* was a form of conspicuous consumption. A useful comparison is with the late Roman period when sets of precious tableware are evidenced in Western Europe (Hobbs 2006). The Hoxne hoard, discussed in Chapter 3, can be considered in this light.

Two points are especially important here. The Dutch paintings portrayed displays – real or imagined – of valuable objects. They emphasised the importance of their owners' contacts with remote countries, with novel materials and even with exotic styles of imagery. In time they came to influence the character of locally made products, but even then it was the reference to unfamiliar locations, beliefs and practices that made them so attractive. The contents of these pictures illustrate the significance of distant places and their products that Mary Helms (1988) describes in her book *Ulysses' Sail*.

If the Dutch term *Pronkstilleven* gives problems, so does the English word *hoard*. It has at least two meanings according to the contexts in which it is used. *To hoard* is to accumulate valuables which are kept together and rarely used. In archaeology, however, *a hoard* is a collection of artefacts which were deposited in a group on the same occasion. As Chapter 2 has shown, opinions differ on why that happened and whether this material was meant to be recovered. In the Dutch example the striking collections of objects portrayed in 'sumptuous still lives' could be the result of *hoarding*, for these paintings document the accumulation of private wealth. Rare and expensive objects were assembled from different sources and arranged in a single composition; but in archaeological parlance they would only be *hoards* if their contents had been buried or concealed. That rarely, if ever, happened.

Accumulation

The objects illustrated in the paintings had been obtained from distant sources. Commodities which had come from different places could be shown together, so that the finished artworks proclaimed the extent of their owners' connections. The same could have happened in the ancient world. The first part of this chapter reviews the contents of three hoards and bog deposits. It features groups of metalwork whose histories extend from the Early Bronze Age to the Viking Age. The second part considers the possibility that they had been displayed on public occasions.

Dieskau

There were three Early Bronze Age hoards at Dieskau in Germany, two of them inside pots (Von Brunn 1959, 55–56 & illustrations 12–23). They were associated with the Únětice Culture. The number of separate artefacts was quite exceptional. There were numerous personal ornaments – both beads and rings – but there were also weapons which must have been deposited as blades. The number of ornaments is remarkable. In one collection there were nine arm-rings and eight other rings of different forms, in addition to 23 bronze beads and another 106 beads made of amber. The hoard also contained a further ten neck-rings which may have been employed as ingots. Tools were much less common, but there were two shafthole axes and another axe which had come from Ireland. By contrast, no fewer than 13 halberds featured in this collection. These objects seem to have been deposited in a prescribed order. Thus the beads were towards the bottom of the vessel, the rings were above them, and the finds of weapons were at the top.

The other hoard inside a pot contained a different selection of artefacts. Weapons and ornaments were present in smaller numbers – there was a single halberd and six arm-rings of various types – but axes entirely dominated the assemblage. Apart from two double axes, there were no fewer than 293 axeheads of a local form. The third hoard contrasted with both these finds. In this case the collection was significantly smaller and contained two gold bracelets and another ring. A striking contrast with the other hoards is that the only axe was made of gold.

The Irish axe was clearly an import, and the gold must also have been obtained from a distance. The same applies to the amber beads. The ingot torcs illustrate a different point, for they were really units of raw material distributed in the form of a personal ornament. The interplay between different forms and raw materials goes even further. Hoard 3 contained nearly three hundred bronze axes, but Hoard 1 included a single example fashioned from gold. There were striking contrasts between the composition of these hoards, and in Hoard 2 the artefacts inside a ceramic vessel had been divided into separate groups.

Llyn Cerrig Bach

The Dieskau hoards were identified as votive offerings from the outset, but the presence of ingot torcs raises the possibility that the people who assembled this material played a role in the metal supply. The great collection of Iron Age metalwork from Llyn Cerrig Bach on the island of Anglesey experienced a similar history of interpretation (Fox 1946). It consisted of a large quantity of bronze and iron artefacts, the most striking of them military equipment. It also included a cauldron, currency bars, agricultural tools, vehicle fittings and horse gear. It seems to have been associated with a lake or bog. From the time of its discovery Cyril Fox saw this material as a votive offering.

He suggested that the metalwork from Llyn Cerrig Bach was placed in the water intentionally, drawing attention to Tacitus's statement that Anglesey played a role in the religious rituals of the Druids. The artefacts had been brought there from different regions and were sacrificed in a sanctuary that was renowned throughout the British Isles. He based his case on stylistic arguments which have not stood the test of time. Even so, the idea remains important. He also observed that the metal finds were associated with large numbers of animal bones, few of which could be recovered.

Philip MacDonald (2007) has published a new assessment of the find which supports Fox's basic analysis without endorsing all the details. The new work suggests that the artefacts and animal remains had been deposited at the edge of a small island, perhaps over several hundred years. It happened in at least two phases. The main group of weapons and complex artefacts dated between the 4th century BC and about AD 50, but decorative items were still being placed there until the late 2nd century AD. Macdonald also studied the surviving animal bones and, on the basis of radiocarbon dating, suggested that Llyn Cerrig Bach may have been employed for animal sacrifices before any metalwork was present – an interesting analogy is with Skedemosse. Among the bones that still survive are those of dogs and horses. Macdonald was reluctant to accept the idea that the finest objects were contributed by people in distant parts of Britain and Ireland, but he did agree that they were made in more than one style and were produced from different ores. Llyn Cerrig Bach might not have been the pan-national sacred site that Fox originally envisaged, but its contents may still have been drawn from a wider area. In that respect they recall the hoards considered earlier.

Hoen

If much of the material from Llyn Cerrig Bach dates from the Late Iron Age of Western Europe, the Hoen hoard comes from the Late Iron Age in the North – in this case the 9th century AD (Fugelsang & Wilson 2006). It was found south-west of Oslo in 1843. The findspot has been investigated more recently and the definitive account of the metalwork concludes that 'the site where the treasure was buried must have been a relatively dry bog' (Fugelsang & Wilson 2006, 70). 'Treasure' is the right world to use for such a rich and varied deposit.

It contained a series of personal ornaments made of non-local metals – silver and, especially, gold. There was a necklace, two neck-rings and three arm-rings, a finger-ring and a brooch made out of a reused strap mount. With them were 54 gold or silver objects, including 20 coins which had been turned into ornaments. There were also 132 beads of glass or semi-precious stone. Both the arm-rings and neck-rings employed exactly the same weight of gold – a simple way of calculating their value. The coins are unusual too, as they predate most of those represented in Viking hoards.

What stands out most of all is the variety of contacts evidenced by the artefacts at Hoen. They also span a period of time which could have been as long as 500 years. The authors of the definitive monograph do not agree on the affinities of all the objects, but that is simply because some of them seem so exotic. Nevertheless their origins appear to be Scandinavian, Byzantine, Frankish, Carolingian and Anglo-Saxon. The coins were Roman, Byzantine, Arab, Merovingian, Carolingian and English. Certain items could have been loot, but that might not explain their multiple origins. The fact that the hoard was discovered in a bog suggests that, however it was acquired, in its final form it can be accepted as a votive offering – one of the latest in a long tradition of such finds.

Common elements

The three sites considered here have common features. The ideal starting point for any discussion is Fox's account of Llyn Cerrig Bach. As so often, his ideas were ahead of their time and have a new relevance today. He argued the votive offerings found in the bog were provided by communities in different parts of the British Isles. Later researchers have questioned the identification of such obvious regional traditions, but the idea that items were brought from far afield might retain some validity.

That is certainly true of both the hoard sites considered here – one of them dating from the pre-Roman period and the other dating from the Viking Age – and they share elements with many other deposits in ancient Europe. Two are particularly important. Like Fox's analysis, the first depends on stylistic considerations. Thus one of the collections from Dieskau contained an axe thought to have been made in Ireland. The finds from Hoen illustrate the same point but date from a much later time. Their original sources map a large part of Europe during the 1st millennium AD.

Stylistic arguments can be vulnerable, as accounts of Llyn Cerrig Bach have shown, and more can be learned from the materials of which the artefacts were made. It is true that Dieskau is in an area rich in metals and that Hoard 2 contained torcs which may have been intended as ingots, but that does not explain the significance attached to gold which could not be of local origin. Baltic amber was also represented there. In contrast, the treasure from Hoen was largely composed of gold and silver which must have been introduced, some of it as coins or other items recycled for their metal content.

These specific examples typify a wider pattern. Of course, hoards of metalwork can be found near sources of raw material, but in every phase they are at least as common at a distance. That was particularly true during the Bronze Age and again in the later 1st millennium AD. Whilst the exploitation of local ores might account for the rich assemblages associated with the Únětice Culture, it cannot apply to the equally spectacular deposits of the Nordic Bronze Age which were almost entirely dependent on imported objects and metals (Ling *et al.* 2013). Similarly, the richness of the Irish Bronze Age may have been influenced by the local availability of gold, but this can hardly apply to the bronze artefacts of the same period, as copper mining virtually ceased in the island around 1800 BC (O'Brien 2014, 125–37). Something similar must have happened in Northern Europe during the Migration Period and the Viking Age when gold and silver became particularly important. As the hoards from Gudme show, many of the richest collections recovered by archaeologists include elements of non-local origin. There seems to have been a predilection for accumulating valuables from distant areas. The same taste for the exotic and rare is illustrated by *Pronkstillevens*.

Display

This comparison with painted still lives has a second aspect, for in many parts of ancient Europe there are depictions of artefacts of kinds that were buried or deposited in water. The clearest evidence comes from Brittany, Scandinavia, Iberia and the British Isles. Further information is available from the French and Italian Alps. These images were extremely durable as they were cut in stone.

Still lives in stone

Two features were widely shared. These petroglyphs showed groups of artefacts which had a similar composition to deposits of artefacts, some of them found in the same regions. A second characteristic was that, unlike most of the other images, such objects were normally shown full size. That was a feature of petroglyphs which were not associated with human figures; otherwise there was more variety. It seems as if these objects were represented for their own sake, as if they were in hoards. A few examples may be helpful here.

Neolithic axes in Brittany

The Morbihan in southern Brittany contains an exceptional variety of Neolithic monuments, some of enormous proportions. It also includes an unusually high density of axes of the same period. These features could be related to one another. A few stones resemble enormous axeheads set on end, and this argument is most persuasive where there is evidence that they had been shaped. They are occasionally associated with hoards or single finds of the objects themselves, and the connection between them is strengthened where these artefacts were set upright in the ground (Cassen 2009).

The axes came from various sources. Many were made in north-west France, but they include a remarkable number that originated in the Alps. The greatest concentrations of imported axes are associated with monumental mounds which date from the late 5th and early 4th millennia BC. They had been brought over a great distance, but there is evidence that they could be reworked into locally acceptable forms. Others were copied by people in the Iberian Peninsula (Pétrequin *et al.* 2012b). The commonest way of treating these axes was to change them into pendants by boring a hole through the butt where they would have been hafted.

The tombs and standing stones in this region were often decorated with pecked (and possibly painted) designs. There was a considerable overlap between these separate structures as there is evidence that standing stones were reused in the fabric of chambered tombs. Even so, depictions of stone axes, with or without their hafts, are known from nearly 20 Neolithic monuments in Brittany, most of them in the area around Locmariaquer where the best evidence comes from the chambered tomb of Gavrinis. Its construction has recently been dated to the period between 4250 and 4000 BC (Cassen *et al.* 2014). Here as many as eight separate panels depict axeheads of the same form as those made of Alpine raw material. Not all are easy to identify as they are incorporated in larger non-figurative designs, but others occupy panels on their own. Their frequency on any one orthostat extends from three to eighteen. None is shown with its haft. They depict collections of rare and valuable objects similar to those buried in the ground.

Early metalwork in Sweden

By contrast, in Sweden the earliest drawings of metalwork show axes together with their handles and cluster at a small number of places near the sea (Malmer 1981). Early swords are also depicted, although they can be found on separate sites. In this case two features are important. Again recent work has confirmed that the raw material was introduced from Central Europe (Ling *et al.* 2013). Even if the artefacts themselves were made locally, the raw material was exotic and had to be brought from a distance. Occasionally both the tools and weapons were shown at more or less their actual sizes. At times the match is so precise that the drawings may have been based on individual objects. That is especially striking as it does not apply to the other elements in the same panels. Humans, animals and boats appear on a diminutive scale, although the artists acknowledged some differences among the seagoing vessels.

The comparison with finds of artefacts goes even further. Among the carved rocks at Simris on the shore of the Baltic, all the axes have hafts and are scattered across the surface of the stone (Skoglund 2016, 71–77). At other sites their distribution is rather more clustered. For the most part the drawings of swords are organised in a different way. Although they can be associated with one another, they are frequently found on their own, widely distributed across an individual panel, as they are at Himmelstalund (Hauptmann Wahlgren 2002). The contrast between both groups of images reflects the contexts in which their prototypes are found. The fact that axes are shown together recalls the comparatively rare hoards of the same period (Larsson 1986), but most weapons occur as grave goods and single finds. In South Scandinavia deposits of tools and weapons complement their distribution in Bronze Age rock art (Malmer 1981, 50–53 & 105–08). Spears are also represented in the drawings, but they are different again because they are usually associated with human figures.

A distinctive feature of the Swedish sites is that virtually all the axes are shown together with their hafts. Recent research has identified a striking exception. This is the famous cist at Kivik which plays an important role in interpretations of Bronze Age religious beliefs. One of the decorated surfaces features a boat together with a schematic representation of its crew, but a new study of this design suggests that it does not show human figures after all, but a row of upright axeheads (Fig. 11). The design makes a striking reference to the exotic

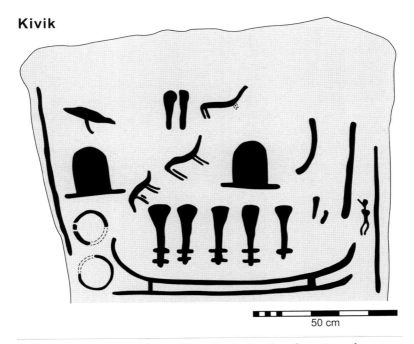

Kivik

50 cm

Figure 11. *Decorated cist slab at Kivik, Sweden, featuring a boat associated with a series of upright axeheads. Information from Toreld and Andersson (2015).*

nature of the metal, which had to be introduced by sea (Toreld &
Andersson 2015).

Early metalwork in Britain

The same feature is found on another well-known monument –
Stonehenge. Recent work has shed new light on the images associated
with the principal setting of monoliths (Field *et al.* 2015). They
were first observed during the 1950s but more examples have been
found since then. At present there are records of three daggers and
115 axes distributed across four of the standing stones. The largest
concentrations amount to roughly 35 and 50 axeheads, none of them
shown with hafts. They were carved long after the monument had
been erected. The number of carved axeheads is extraordinary, as
there are only 200 of these objects in the Early Bronze Age hoards of
the British Isles; the largest groups contain no more than 20 examples.
The rock art at Stonehenge can be compared with other carvings
of metalwork, which occur in small quantities inside burial cists in
western Scotland and on the kerb of a round barrow in southern
England (Bradley 1997, chapter 9). This mound, at Badbury, is another
place where daggers and axeheads appear together. It is significant as
weapons were normally deposited in graves whilst tools are found
in hoards, but at Dail na Caraidh in the Scottish Highlands three
separate deposits were identified (Barrett & Gourlay 1999). One
contained nothing but axes, but the other two contained more daggers
or knives. This site is considered again in Chapter 10.

   In the same way the Scottish site of Ri Cruin includes a cist with
a panel of axes at one end and a drawing of a halberd at the other
(Needham & Cowie 2012). In Britain all the axes are shown as units
of metal, as none of them has a handle. Andrew Meirion Jones (2015)
has compared them with the stone moulds used to make them. The
number of carved axeheads at Ri Cruin is similar to the quantity in
Scottish hoards of the same date. These drawings were of uniform size,
yet it did not apply to those in a nearby cist at Nether Largie where
there were significantly more examples. As was the case at Stonehenge,
the largest were roughly four times the dimensions of the smallest.

Like the axeheads associated with the carved ship at Kivik, these were displays of metal rather than tools which were ready for use.

Early metalwork in Iberia

Displays of a rather different kind feature in petroglyphs of the same date in the north-west of the Iberian Peninsula. In this case it is not only the contents of these drawings that matter but the relationship between the objects on the decorated surface. Although there are some exceptions, daggers and halberds were grouped together in compositions which look like a display of spoils (Bradley 1998). Although similar artefacts were buried with the dead, they occur singly in graves. In the rock drawings, on the other hand, they are present in significantly greater numbers. Some are associated with other images – diminutive people and animals – but they were often set apart and appear on steeply sloping surfaces where they confront the onlooker (Fig. 12).

The same combination of weapons is found in the metalwork hoards of this region, and in one case, at Rianzo, these elements are represented in both media. Here there are drawings of halberds and daggers, as well as an actual deposit containing artefacts of the same kinds. Another Galician site, Auga de Laxe, is unusual because here

Coto das Laxas

Figure 12. A panel of rock art at Coto das Laxas, Spain, featuring a series of halberds and daggers. Information from Fábregas Valcarce et al. *(2009).*

the weapons are drawn on an extravagant scale. There are enormous halberds, daggers whose blades were more than two metres long, and a series of enigmatic motifs which have been interpreted as some kind of shield or possibly a vehicle. It is the organisation of these drawings that strikes the observer, for the entire panel has been composed so that it resembles an exhibition of trophies (Bradley 1998, 134–44). Perhaps the collections of war booty of the Northern Iron Age took a similar form before they were destroyed.

Summary

There are striking contrasts between these regional groups, but there are also common elements. Like other rock drawings in Europe and beyond, they depict collections of metalwork of the kind deposited in hoards, watery locations and graves. These artefacts are drawn full size but are rarely depicted in use. Instead they are presented to the viewer as static displays. It makes no difference whether the metal could be obtained locally or whether it had to be imported; it seems to have been significant in its own right. That was particularly true where axes were depicted without their handles and would have represented units of a valuable material. It cannot be a coincidence that drawings of this kind have been identified at two of the best known prehistoric monuments in Europe – Kivik and Stonehenge. Neither is in an area with evidence of metal extraction.

How were these collections of objects related to the human body? The following section considers the rock art of the southern Alps and compares its composition with the organisation of inhumation burials.

Exhibitions of artefacts

Rock drawings in the Alps

The rock art of the Alpine valleys occurs in several different settings. Its currency extends from approximately 3300 BC and it was made during both the Copper Age and the Early Bronze Age. Geoffroy de Saulieu (2004) has studied these designs in relation to the places where they are found and distinguishes between two traditions which he calls 'art discret' and 'art monumental' respectively. Neither term is self-explanatory. 'Art monumental' is represented on anthropomorphic statues, stone settings and chambered tombs, but it is also a feature of conspicuous rock outcrops, where it could be pecked into vertical or steeply sloping surfaces. A characteristic of these panels is that they were often altered by superimposing new drawings on older ones or even by defacing existing images. 'Art discret', on the other hand, does not occupy conspicuous positions. It could be created on horizontal panels and might have been difficult for people to locate. The designs developed over a long period of time but their positions respected one another.

The monumental compositions combine at least two different elements: the human body, which is sometimes shown life size, and a variety of weapons and ornaments which are placed around it, frequently in considerable numbers. They might have depicted particular people or supernatural beings. The weapons resemble those found in smaller quantities in graves, and it is this connection that establishes their chronology. 'Art discret' also features impressive displays of weapons – sometimes many of them – but in this case people are not represented (Fig. 13). Like the petroglyphs in Sweden and Spain, these are displays of metalwork but, apart from those in graves, the objects that were shown are rare or absent in the same region, although they do feature in hoards in northern Italy.

De Saulieu's research has identified a striking chronological pattern. 'Art discret' appeared at the beginning of the Chalcolithic period and became less common between 2900 and 2400 BC when 'art monumental' developed and was practised on an extensive scale. From 2400 to 2200 BC it was the only kind of rock art in the Alps. The situation changed after that time (the beginning of the Early Bronze Age). Then all the designs were 'art discret'. On one level this illustrates the interplay between panels in which ornaments and weapons were depicted together with human bodies, and those with self-contained collections of metalwork. During the principal phases in which metal

Arco   **Valcamonica**

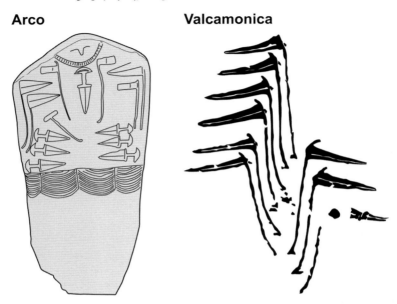

Figure 13. Left: Statue menhir at Arco, Italy showing a human figure wearing halberds, daggers and a series of ornaments. Right: A panel of halberds in the rock art of Valcamonica (Italy). Information from de Saulieu (2004).

items were accompanied by human figures, other pictures of artefacts were rare or absent. Once statues and related images went out of use, 'art discret' reappeared.

This sequence recalls a pattern that extends far beyond the early Metal Age and is found in other parts of ancient Europe. Many writers have recognised an interplay between hoard finds, single finds and burial assemblages which runs from the Neolithic to the Migration Period. The same kinds of objects were buried with the dead during one phase and were deposited singly or as groups in another. Alternatively, similar objects might be represented in both these contexts, but in different regions. This was the key finding of Walter Torbrügge's study of river finds published in 1971.

Grave finds and other deposits

The usual way of explaining this relationship is to suppose that finds of the kind that otherwise appear in graves represent an alternative form of funerary offering. Rather than associating them with the corpse – or burying them with the body when a grave was closed – they were removed from circulation at a different location. One of the strongest advocates of this interpretation is Lothar Sperber (2006) in a study of the artefacts from a former channel of the Rhine at Roxheim. Although their history extends over a considerable period of time, most of them date between the 11th and 9th centuries BC when formal burials disappear from the surrounding area. The finds include broken weapons, but the collection also includes smaller items like razors, sickles, knives and decorative fittings, many of which had been in a fire. There was no burnt bone, but this approach has been particularly influential in studies of periods when cremation was the principal mortuary rite. Perhaps objects that might have accompanied the body to the pyre were removed before, or even after, its remains were burnt. This is a plausible argument, but it cannot account for all the deposits of valuables deposited in water or dry ground. This argument does not explain the complex relationship between the deceased, the mourners and the artefacts associated with the dead. Were these objects personal possessions? Were they provided by the mourners and possibly made for the occasion? Or were they parts of a distinctive funerary costume – a more colourful equivalent of a shroud? Each of these interpretations could shed light on individual cases, but they share a common element. For however short a period, they were put on display to be viewed by the participants in the ritual.

The contents of inhumation graves can be extremely stereotyped. This applies not only to the selection of artefacts but, equally important, to the ways in which they were distributed around the body. Both were obviously influenced by local norms. Two important studies shed some light on this issue. The first is concerned with a famous Early Bronze Age burial at Leubingen in north-east Germany which dates from the 20th century BC. It would have been contemporary with some of the petroglyphs considered earlier. The other is Frands Herschend's analysis of a boat grave at Valsgärde in middle Sweden which is dated between AD 560 and 630.

Leubingen

According to Marie Louise Stig Sørensen (2004), Leubingen is among the richest graves in Early Bronze Age Europe. It was one of a small group of barrows constructed at a time when the production of metalwork expanded. It appears in the same cultural context as the hoards at Dieskau.

The burials were inside a timber building, roofed with thatch and buried beneath a cairn and then a mound. Sørensen suggests that it was designed in the image of a house. On its floor was the body of an old man. A second corpse, probably that of an adolescent or a child, was placed across it.

With the earlier burial was a series of gold ornaments which may have formed a set. They were on the right hand side of his body, and other artefacts were further away. Here there were axes, a halberd and three small daggers. At a greater distance were three chisels that could have been for working wood. Still further removed there were stone artefacts: a kind of pickaxe and a cushion stone for metal working. All these items might have stood for different attributes of the dead person. By contrast, the only object on the left hand side of his body was a pottery vessel surrounded by stones. If the mortuary structure was based on the plan of a house, then this was the position of its hearth.

The items represented in the grave were carefully organised. Sorensen (2004, 173) observes that:

> 'The objects were grouped according to their materials, with gold the furthest into the grave and also the only material associated with the upper part of the body. Bronze is found around the middle of the body, while stone objects and ceramics are placed towards … the feet'.

Although these burials were eventually covered by a cairn, this was a display in which both the artefacts and the bodies played a part. The mortuary house was precisely rectangular. Its entrance faced the head of the principal burial which was laid out along the middle of the chamber. The addition of another corpse created a second alignment crossing the interior at right angles, and the juxtaposition of these two burials is echoed in the configuration of the tools and weapons. Just as the child or adolescent was positioned at right angles to the remains of the man, a halberd with its staff was superimposed on one of the metal blades; the other two knives or daggers were placed across one another in a similar manner. These objects observed two alignments, each running parallel to a chamber wall.

Sørensen comments on these characteristics of Leubingen. The most obvious is the positioning of the bodies, one of them associated with artefacts, and the other unaccompanied. All these elements could have been imbued with meanings that escape the researcher today, but there can be little doubt that such an orderly arrangement of artefacts and human remains was carefully contrived and must have created a powerful impression. Even after the mortuary house was hidden beneath the cairn it would have left an image in people's minds. It might have been like the more tangible pictures that were so important in the Alps.

Valsgärde boat-grave 8

A second example is Grave 8 in the Swedish cemetery of Valsgärde (Herschend 2001, 68–91). It has been chosen precisely because it is remote from the Neolithic and Bronze Age examples considered so far. This is one of a series of boat burials associated with a long lasting cemetery.

The boat-grave was just under 12 m long. After an interval during which the vessel started to decay, it was covered by a mound which overlooked a river. In that sense it was perfectly located to represent a journey to the Otherworld. The monument had three distinct elements. The vessel was divided into compartments, and on the ground outside it were the bones of sacrificed horses. Little trace remained of the person buried there, but he seems to have been laid out on a bed, surrounded by swords, drinking vessels and – in a curious echo of Leubingen – some woodworking tools. This was a private space. As Herschend says, 'he would have seemed to be asleep in his boat, in a makeshift chamber ... It [was] a tidy room' (Herschend 2001, 70).

By contrast, the other room, which was situated towards the prow, was far less orderly and contained a wider variety of artefacts. There was his helmet, a spear, a series of shields and another drinking horn. There was also a dinner service made of wood and a gaming board together with its pieces. This part of the assemblage celebrated the consumption of food and drink. Not surprisingly, the artefact assemblage included a cauldron. Here there were the remains of meals.

Herschend (2001) suggests that the layout of the boat-grave was based on the organisation of a domestic building of the kind excavated on dry land. That interpretation is supported by the artefact assemblage. It displays the material equipment associated with high social status, and its distribution within the buried vessel evokes the kind of monumental buildings associated with sites like Lejre. Although it represents such structures in miniature, it contains an exceptionally rich assemblage of grave goods. Moreover, they were laid out in a way that would have evoked the life style of the dead man and his followers. Herschend considers that during the later 1st millennium AD other mortuary monuments refer to the domestic domain. They share this characteristic with Leubingen.

The comparison with hoards and related deposits

There is little evidence that hoards themselves were intended as displays, but there are problems in making this assertion. Many ancient burials have been recorded by excavation, whilst nearly all the other discoveries were made by chance. Only a few have been carefully recorded, with the result that little is known about how their contents were organised. Numerous graves are investigated in the excavation of barrows, but other deposits of the same date are in isolated positions where they are found by metal detectors. Even when their contents are recorded in the ground, they may have been disturbed. Even worse, fieldwork conducted around the findspot is usually designed to recover additional artefacts and is not sufficiently extensive to place the deposits in a wider context. All these factors bias the available record.

Even so, there seems to be less order in the layout of hoards than there is in the structuring of burials – especially those of the Bronze Age when both these features were common. Only occasionally is there any indication that isolated groups of metalwork were laid out with much formality. Most collections show little or no sign of order. Of course there are certain exceptions. Artefacts could be placed inside a ceramic vessel, as happened at Dieskau; they might also be stacked, or organised in layers, as they were on that site. They could be contained in a box or a bag; individual items could even have been kept in a pouch; and on rare occasions objects might be placed inside one another.

There is some interesting evidence from Ireland and Britain. In one case a series of Early Bronze Age axeheads were placed in a circle on a hollow rock by a stream. All their blades faced outwards. They enclosed a deposit of deer bones and ash and were covered by a slab (Needham 1988, 232). Similarly, during the Late Bronze Age George Eogan (1983, 55) records a hoard in which up to 50 bronze rings were arranged in a semicircle in the ground. In another case a sword, a spearhead and a socketed axe were placed side-by-side and shared a common alignment from north-east to south-west; perhaps coincidentally, these are directions of the midsummer sunrise and midwinter sunset respectively (Eogan 1983, 98–99). At sites in Northern Britain swords stood upright in the ground, with their points driven into the subsoil; in another case shields were arranged in a circle (Coles 1960, 104 & 106–07; Colquhoun & Burgess 1988, 94). There are poorly documented examples of similar type.

Such finds are certainly intriguing, but they attract attention because they are comparatively rare. More is known about finds of personal ornaments. In Britain individual pieces could be threaded on a wire, and others could be stacked vertically in the ground (Roberts 2007). Something similar happened in the Danish hoards studied by

Janet Levy (1982). She recognises only three kinds with any semblance of order. Again occasional examples were inside pots. There were a few cases in which objects lay parallel to one another, but a number of neck-rings encircled other kinds of object. This arrangement accounts for a quarter of those deposited during Period V. Elsewhere sets of personal ornaments feature in formal displays in combination with weapons, sickles, axes and bronze vessels.

Tudor Soroceanu has shown that other kinds of metalwork were laid out with the same formality, but this was by no means common. Swords could be placed on end or sunk vertically in the ground. They could also be arranged in striking patterns. His studies have been concerned mainly with finds of weapons between the later 2nd millennium BC and the beginning of the Iron Age (Soroceanu 2011) and with collections of Late Bronze Age date containing metal vessels (Soroceanu 1995). In the Carpathians such patterning extends to finds of tools, especially axes and sickles. Again certain objects might be arranged in a circle before they were buried. Otherwise they might be placed across one another to form a cross or a star-shaped design. In one case swords were organised in parallel rows, their tips facing in opposite directions (Fig. 14).

Such deposits have a wider distribution, but are by no means common. Soroceanu (2011) shows that they are mainly a feature of Central, Eastern and Northern Europe. They are rare or absent in France, Iberia and the British Isles. Their chronology is restricted,

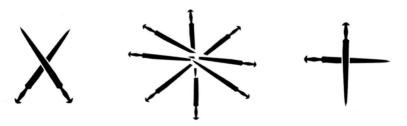

Figure 14. The formal organisation of deposits of swords in hoards from Central and Eastern Europe. Information from Soroceanu (2011).

too. They are primarily a feature of the later Bronze Age and are rarely evidenced before that time. For that reason their history does not overlap with the displays of metalwork depicted in rock art. What may have been a similar idea was manifested in distinctive ways in different contexts and at different times. Again these collections show only a limited overlap with the grave goods of the same period.

The Viking Age

In the Viking Age the contents of burials were much more varied and quite unlike those of the Bronze Age. In this case they were the outcome of public events that Neil Price (2010) compares to a theatrical performance. It might have involved acts of violence, the sacrifice of people and animals, eating and drinking on an extravagant scale, and the conspicuous deployment of valuables. Even more important, these events included the performance of tales that were illustrated by the deposits placed around the corpse: 'Many, perhaps the majority, of Viking funerals involved the material manifestation of stories' (Price 2010, 146). In fact the graves may have been left open to allow these displays to be viewed for some time, for in his term Viking burials were 'theatres of death'. He suggests that some of the stories acted out at the funeral were recorded in the literature of later centuries. The link is extremely plausible. As Price observes, another narrative set down during the 1st millennium AD – *Beowulf* – is also structured around funerals. If he is right, the artefacts, human bodies and slaughtered animals formed only part of the drama, but they were the element that had the most striking visual impact. By contrast, there was a clearer structure in the composition of Viking hoards. Chapter 3 explained how they have been reinterpreted.

In between these extremes there were other ways of handling valuable objects. The striking display in the boat-grave at Valsgärde 8 recalls the ship burials at Sutton Hoo in eastern England, and the most recent excavator of that site, Martin Carver (2005), has commented on how their contents were organised in the ground. Those associated with Mound 1 were in four distinct groups: a putative coffin including a body, clothes and textiles; a sword and a helmet associated with the role of the warrior; a pair of unusual objects connected with leadership – a sceptre and a standard – and, finally, a group of cauldrons evoking a feast. The objects were organised as separate displays and had been obtained from an extensive area. Carver (2005, 313) interprets the assemblage in these terms:

> 'The Mound 1 burial is a composition, a poem, a statement composed of objects in a theatrical setting, in which a warrior, a leader, an ambassador, a mariner and mortal man were sent off in a ritual display'.

The main cemetery at Sutton Hoo dates from the 7th century AD, which means that its use could have overlapped with the formation of the Staffordshire Hoard; certainly, they were close together in time. There is a striking contrast between the two assemblages. Although there are problems in understanding the contents of the graves, there is no doubt that they were clearly structured. They provided a powerful spectacle until the mounds were built. The finds from the Staffordshire Hoard differ in almost every respect. Despite the circumstances in which they were first discovered, they show little sign of order and there is no question that they had been severely damaged before their deposition. Whether or not this was strictly a hoard, it was the result of a different process from the grave gifts at Sutton Hoo.

Like the contents of the Viking burials considered by Price, the artefacts found in Staffordshire were the outcome of violent activity (Leahy & Bland 2014). Two points seem to be agreed, and both have interesting implications for this discussion. The finds were predominantly of war gear and are interpreted as the spoils from a battle or battles. At the same time all the weapons had been stripped of their blades, so that only their gold accoutrements remained. The sequence of events is important. The weapons were first used in combat. Then the possessions of the defeated army were appropriated. It is not clear whether they were confiscated from the survivors, stripped from corpses, or whether they were left behind as their owners escaped. In any event it would have taken some time to remove the gold from the blades and to reduce it to fragments. It seems unlikely that it happened on the battlefield. Perhaps it occurred when these objects were deposited in the 'hoard', but this is equally improbable as not a scrap of iron is present in the collection. It raises the possibility that the victors' spoils were exhibited before they were destroyed. They might have provided a public spectacle; the deposition of small pieces of broken metalwork would have had a smaller impact. It suggests that the Staffordshire Hoard was not a display in its own right, but simply the end result of a longer process.

Comparable displays

There is evidence that a comparable sequence was followed at late pre-Roman sanctuaries in Gaul. In this case there is archaeological evidence that the arms of defeated war bands – and sometimes their bodies – were put on show before their remains were taken away and deposited in pits, ditches and rivers. When that happened the weapons might be broken or damaged and the corpses were decapitated. Something very similar is described by Julius Caesar in his account of the Gallic War:

> 'When they have decided to engage in battle it is to Mars that they will dedicate most of what they may take in the fight. When victorious, they sacrifice the animals they have captured and gather all the rest of the spoils in one place … One may see mounds made out of such objects in holy places, and rarely does it happen that anyone … dares to hide away his spoils at home, or steal them away once they are placed on the mound' (*The Gallic War*, 6.17, 3–5).

Similarly, the German defeat of the Varus and his legion in AD 9 was commemorated by what Frands Herschend has called 'an installation … of defeat … exhibited with slain men and officers … as well as disgraced symbols of power *and small altars composed of spoils*' (2009, 365; my emphasis) His description paraphrases an account by

Tacitus. The idea of such an installation would have been familiar in the Classical world where a victor's triumph would feature a display of captured weapons. A comparable sequence could apply to the deposits of war booty in the Iron Age of Northern Europe, but in this case the dead of the defeated army must have been treated separately from their possessions. As Chapter 2 has shown, there is literary evidence for practices of this kind. The spoils were put on show before they were sacrificed as a thanks-offering to the gods.

These examples suggest a new way of thinking about earlier deposits, especially those containing Bronze Age metalwork. But this can be no more than an analogy that extends the interpretations of these deposits. Its virtue – if it has one – is that it raises some possibilities that could be explored by traditional methods. In this case it may help to explain two observations made in an earlier part of this chapter. The first is that rock art in a number of different areas shows metal artefacts in unfamiliar configurations. Such images are found in so many regions that they must record a widely shared phenomenon. The objects in these drawings are readily identifiable. So are their associations, yet they do not conform to similar patterns when they are discovered in the ground. Either these scenes – and there are many of them – were drawn from imagination, or they show a stage in the histories of these objects that left no other trace. The simplest explanation is that they depict displays of valuables that were shown for a finite period before they were buried.

A second clue is provided by Bronze Age rock art in the Alps. Here weapons and ornaments were displayed in two different settings depending on whether they were linked to the human body. Thus statue menhirs and related images can be compared with inhumation burials accompanied by the appropriate gifts. If that comparison is acceptable, there seems every reason to compare weapons portrayed on their own with hoards and single finds. That is an assumption – as it must be – but again the details of these scenes show that such artefacts were not displayed at random. They could be arranged with some formality as if the pictures illustrated some kind of ceremony. Could it be that such exhibitions of valuables provide the missing term of the equation: the stage at which precious objects were assembled and displayed before they were removed from circulation? Their exhibition might have provided a public spectacle as much as their final deposition, and both involved performances that could have been recalled long after these collections had been destroyed (Rowlands 1993).

Summary and conclusion

This chapter began with a short account of some distinctive paintings in the Netherlands. It suggested that ancient deposits of artefacts provide evidence of similar concerns.

The paintings had two features. They emphasised the attraction of exotic artefacts and materials, unfamiliar technologies and beliefs. At the same time they brought these objects together in a series of striking displays which offered a new way of engaging in conspicuous consumption. This account has considered both these features but has placed the main emphasis on depictions and deposits of metalwork, particularly those of the Early Bronze Age. It has identified some striking similarities: hoards whose contents combine exotic objects and metals; collections that brought together elements which were widely distributed over space and time. It also made a more tentative suggestion that many of the collections that still survive are the residues of displays of valuables with significant historical and geographical connections. How and why they were treated in particular ways is the concern of the following chapters. All this account can claim is that it provides one way of harmonising the pictorial evidence from earlier prehistory with the artefacts that are still being discovered today.

CHAPTER SIX

The Nature of Things

Technologies and myths

In 1948 W. H. Auden published *The Age of Anxiety*. The title of his 'baroque eclogue' referred to a long tradition in European thought in which the past was subdivided into separate 'ages'. Such schemes were necessarily a product of their times. For another poet, the Greek writer Hesiod, history had gone through four phases: a Golden Age, an Age of Silver, an Age of Bronze, and an Age of Iron (Montari *et al.* 2009). Nineteenth century scholars adopted a comparable approach when they devised the Three Age System used by archaeologists today (Rowley-Conwy 2007). On one level this division into Stone Age, Bronze Age and Iron Age recalls the kind of history discussed by ancient writers. In another respect it is entirely different.

Each scheme had its own agenda. The framework adopted by Classical authors was metaphorical. It was recorded in the 8th or 7th century BC and charted the degeneration of society from an initial state of perfection during the Golden Age. Despite the reference to metals, it was not concerned with technology. The Three Age Model had another emphasis. It began as a way of placing artefacts in order, but eventually it came to reflect the political concerns of the day. It identified successive ways of working raw materials, but in the background there was the idea of 'progress'.

The most obvious contrast between these schemes is in their treatment of metals. In the Classical world gold, silver, bronze and iron were employed as symbols; this scheme took little account of specific objects. The system devised by archaeologists started as a way of organising a museum collection and only later was it linked with social evolution. Ironically, these hypothetical sequences ran in opposite directions to one another and the mythical history described by Hesiod can actually be reversed. Although the use of bronze preceded that of iron, gold was most important in the Migration Period, and silver in the Viking Age. In terms of the Three Age Model, the use of stone came before that of metal, but bronze was used together with copper and gold. The adoption of iron came later and, in the West, that was largely true of silver.

The artefacts considered in this book have been characterised according to the conventional terminology, but it can cause confusion. The first metalwork in the North is assigned to a Late Neolithic period, but other regions had a Copper Age or Chalcolithic. In Scandinavia, the Late Bronze Age ended when iron had been known for some time, and here the Iron Age itself lasted longer than in other regions. The confusion can be resolved by absolute dating, but it does nothing to address the problems created by these terms. What was the original significance of the materials on which these schemes depend? Was technology the only important factor? And, if not, were others equally significant? This is especially relevant to the selection of artefacts for deposition as hoards or single finds.

Hesiod lived in a very different world from 19th century prehistorians, but his perspective may be as relevant as the ideas on which the Three Age System was founded. Perhaps ancient materials had qualities apart from their mechanical performance, yet this feature has dominated thinking since the Industrial Revolution. The language of archaeology is revealing. Stone artefacts were made in 'axe factories'; metalwork hoards show how the bronze 'industry' was organised; and metalwork might be hidden to encourage its 'exchange value' to rise. The four ages described by Classical writers may have been a poetic conceit, but it was a product of one of the periods considered in this book. It is obvious that the two schemes have different emphases, but a rounded account of ancient materials and technologies must treat them together. The discussion that follows reflects on the relationship between the practical uses of objects of the kinds deposited in land and water, their treatment over the course of their histories, and the more arcane characteristics that influenced their final destinations. To limit this discussion to the commonest materials, it focuses on the properties of stones and metals.

Stone

The first stone artefacts deposited in water date from the Mesolithic period. Those in Scandinavia can be found with Ertebølle ceramics (Koch 1998). This practice intensified during the Neolithic phase when they were also incorporated in hoards and graves, and continued on a smaller scale in the Bronze Age. It has been easy to infer their special character from the places where they are found, but fieldwork at the production sites adds another dimension.

One of the main influences on studies of prehistoric quarries is the work of Pierre Pétrequin who has observed contemporary axe-making in New Guinea and emphasises the importance of extracting the stone at remote locations which only a few people are allowed to visit. It is a measure of the special importance of the products, which can be used to acquire status through gift exchange. They are also employed in death and marriage payments. The raw materials were formed by 'Primordial Beings' and play a part in rituals connecting people with the spirit world. Pétrequin applied the same principle to a study of Neolithic stone extraction in eastern France and, on the basis of his ethnographic research, was able to locate the sources where prehistoric axe blades were made (Pétrequin *et al.* 1995).

A similar lesson comes from fieldwork at the main group of Neolithic quarries in Britain. They were in the Cumbrian mountains and were the principal supplier of non-local axes in the country (Bradley & Edmonds 1993). Again the most prolific quarries were in inaccessible places on the mountainsides of Pike o' Stickle and its neighbours; the stone source on Scafell Pike is very near the highest point in England. Their siting is especially remarkable because rock with the same physical properties could be obtained from outcrops in more hospitable locations. It would have been easier to work there and simpler to remove the products, but these exposures of raw material were little used. The special significance of the rock is equally apparent from the later history of its source. During the Bell Beaker period material of the same kind was chosen for the production of archers' 'wrist guards' (Woodward & Hunter 2011, 29 & 35–36). They were not heavy duty tools and may have been a kind of ornament. The mechanical performance of the stone must have been important, but it cannot explain the significance of its products.

The Great Langdale complex was in the middle of the Lake District mountains, some distance beyond the settlements in the surrounding lowlands. It was not the only way to restrict access to the quarries. Others were on offshore islands – Lambay Island, and Rathlin Island are well-investigated examples – and further stone sources were most easily reached by sea. One was the mountain of Tievebulleagh – the most prolific source of Irish axes which overlooks a sheltered bay – and another was Graig Llwyd which occupies a similar location (Bradley in press). Such evidence is not restricted to the British Isles, as one of the most dramatic axe quarries in Northern Europe was on another offshore island, Stakanset off the west coast of Norway which can only be reached in good weather (Bruen Olsen & Alasker 1984).

One might suppose that different considerations would apply to flint mining which was widely practiced in Europe, but even here there are problems. There is no doubt that large numbers of axes and other artefacts were made there, yet suitable raw material could sometimes be obtained from cliffs or surface deposits; such places assumed more importance during the Late Neolithic period. It is easy to suppose that the scale on which mining took place was related to the adoption of farming and the clearance of woodland. It is true that most mines belong to an early phase (Kerig *et al.* 2015). At the same time the extraction of flint deep underground could have restricted access to a valuable raw material. There is a further problem as this does not explain why so many of the deposits of axes in rivers, bogs and hoards date from subsequent phases. The importance of mining may have diminished, but the social importance of stone tools remained the same. Did they become more valuable because mined flint was less common? Or were some of the objects deposited during the Late Neolithic period actually heirlooms made many centuries before? Again a purely functional model is insufficient.

What applies to axe blades is true of other artefacts. One type with a special significance was the flint dagger, and in Northern Europe these objects shared an unusual characteristic with axes (Van Gijn 2010, chapter 7). In some cases even the finest examples retained a tiny patch of cortex so that people could identify the source of the raw material. Flint might be moved over long distances. Blades in the form of daggers were brought to Northern Europe from Grand Pressigny in the west of France. In this case they had been ground and polished so severely that all trace of human workmanship was eliminated. By contrast, it would have been easy to distinguish between polished flint axes and those made by pecking other kinds of rock. At times they were treated in different ways from one another. Per Karsten (1994, 129–33) has observed that an increasing number of ground stone artefacts in southern Sweden were deposited as hoards and single finds, especially in areas where local flint was available. In this case more distinctive artefacts were favoured for these kinds of deposit.

Such interpretations depend on two features: the types of objects found in unusual locations, and the character of the sources from which they were obtained. A further factor may be even more informative, but until recently it had been overlooked. Chapter 3 suggested that objects were selected for deposition because of their distinctive histories rather than their outward forms. What was true of Iron Age war gear may apply to stone tools and weapons. That is not to suggest that studies based on typology are unimportant. Rather, they can be supplemented and enriched by another kind of analysis.

Most accounts of stone artefacts have assumed that their forms were directly related to their functions. An obvious example is the making of axes to fell trees. Another interprets the production and distribution of flint daggers as evidence for warfare and social inequality. Perhaps certain individuals were considered as warriors, so that when they died this role was emphasised in the funeral rite.

A recent development has been microscopic analysis of both kinds of artefact. It has led to exciting results.

Stone axes are normally associated with land clearance, just as flint daggers are interpreted as weapons. Both have been found in hoards where they can be unusually well preserved. It makes them especially suitable for laboratory analysis. This has been particularly informative in the Netherlands where detailed examination of a sample of large flint axes has had an unexpected outcome. Instead of documenting the microwear associated with woodworking or carpentry, there was evidence that they had been wrapped in fabric and were repeatedly removed and displayed. Still more striking, it is clear that they were painted with red ochre (Wentink 2006). It follows that these objects were employed in a special way. They took the form of tools, but that was not how they were used.

Something similar applied to a sample of flint daggers deposited as single finds in bogs. There was evidence of polishing on their blades, suggesting that they were repeatedly withdrawn from their sheaths. That might be consistent with a role in combat, but there was no sign of any damage to their edges or tips. They might have been used occasionally and on special occasions as this would not leave microscopic damage, but the evidence suggests that they were meant to be seen rather than used (Van Gijn 2010, 186–89). Something similar happened to Grand Pressigny daggers which also retain traces of microwear (Plisson *et al.* 2002). On that basis they had been interpreted as sickles, but again these traces were probably left by a sheath.

Purely practical arguments have their limitations, but in this case there is another factor to consider. This kind of analysis can only produce results on objects in good condition. Those recovered from hoards, graves or bogs are particularly suitable for this purpose, but this raises a problem. Were the items selected for laboratory analysis typical of the wider uses of axes and daggers, or had the objects studied been selected for formal deposition precisely because they had an exceptional history? There seems no doubt that they were used in special ways before they entered the archaeological record, but there is no way of knowing whether other objects of these kinds had different biographies. Since they can be less well preserved, it may be impossible to answer the question.

Stone and metal

If stone artefacts present problems, what can be said about their relationship with the metalwork of the same date? Early daggers made of flint or metal raise this question, but an even better illustration concerns the relationship between copper and the group of Alpine rocks commonly treated together as 'jade'; the term is employed in the same sense in a major research project, *Projet Jade*, conducted by Pierre Pétrequin and his colleagues. Its findings are relevant here. As mentioned in Chapter 5, it is clear that stone axes of exceptional character were obtained from sources in the Italian Alps and distributed across large parts of Western and Southern Europe during the 5th and early 4th millennia BC (Pétrequin *et al.* 2012a). The concentration of finds in southern Brittany illustrates this point. Here imported axeheads could be modified to conform to a distinctive local type. It was in their new form that they were depicted inside chambered tombs like that at Gavrinis. Some were also changed into personal ornaments. At the same time the distribution of Alpine axeheads extended eastwards as far as another famous site: the rich cemetery at Varna on the Black Sea. Again raw material that came from the Alps was reworked, but in this case it was used to make axes of another local kind. The graves at Varna also contained objects of copper and gold.

The use of non-local material at Varna raises another issue (Fig. 15). The wider distributions of 'jade' and copper axes are almost mutually exclusive (Klassen 2004), but there are signs that ideas passed between these regions. In Italy and Denmark Alpine axeheads were imitated in copper, and the same applies to the shapes of metal axes in central Germany and on the Adriatic coast. The axes studied by *Project Jade* were generally a feature of the south and west, while their counterparts in copper are found in Eastern, Central and, to some extent, in Northern Europe (Pétrequin *et al.* 2012a). The pattern is so striking

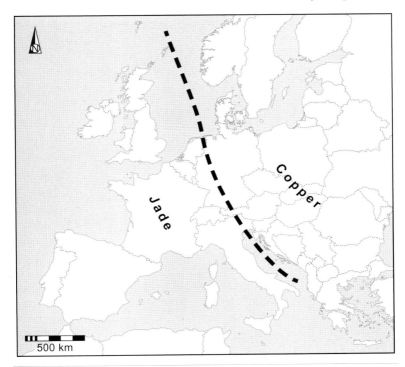

Figure 15. The main areas within which jade axes circulated in Western Europe, compared with the region within which their copper equivalents are found. Information from Klassen (2004) and Pétrequin et al. (2012a).

that it seems possible that objects made in stone and metal came to share a similar significance. In fact they have occasionally been found together. The copper axes were made before the production of Alpine axe blades began and they may have been one source of inspiration for these objects.

A functional explanation of this relationship is unsatisfactory. Like some of those mentioned earlier, the Alpine quarries were located in remote and inaccessible positions. They were discovered by systematic fieldwork, and again the project was inspired by

Pétrequin's investigation of modern axe production in New Guinea. The main source of Alpine axes was Mont Viso, the highest point in the southern Alps, which accounts for about two-thirds of the larger axeheads – those studied in his research. More came from the Mont Beigua massif, and both sources were situated above the local tree line at heights of between 1500 and 2400 m (Pétrequin *et al.* 2012a). Many of their products had been polished to such an extent that they were unsuitable for practical tasks, suggesting that their value was influenced by their attractive appearance. Their exotic origins were another factor. People had to make long journeys to reach the sources of the stone and many may not have known where it originated. These places were well outside the ancient pattern of settlement and would have been inaccessible in winter. Field survey has located shelters and working areas close to the sources of the rock. In recent centuries these places have been exploited by seasonal transhumance, and that might have been the case in the prehistoric period.

Most Alpine axes with adequate provenances are single finds from lakes, pools, bogs and rivers. They have also been discovered in rock fissures and beside large outcrops and waterfalls (Pétrequin *et al.* 2012a). Of the large examples which provided the focus for *Project Jade*, 79% were associated with water, 18% with natural rock formations, and 8% with standing stones. Others were 'planted' in the ground with their blades uppermost, as if they were living organisms. This practice is recorded in the Morbihan and elsewhere, but it has also been recognised at the stone source on Mont Viso. The artefacts also appear in hoards whose distribution is mainly in northern and north-western France, or inland from the north shore of the Mediterranean. Few of these collections contain more than two examples, but a remarkable hoard from Svoboda in Bulgaria included 31 examples, some of which had been repolished. Similarly, the first copper axes are also found in hoards, although they are comparatively rare. Burials associated with Alpine axes are distributed more evenly across North-West Europe, and copper and gold feature alongside 'jade' in the graves at Varna. In the Early Bronze Age it is significant that a few of these stone axes were reused as metalworkers' hammers.

Finally, some of these Alpine axeheads have a distinctive colour – green – but their frequency can be exaggerated. It may be more than a coincidence that the same applies to their metal counterparts, which change their appearance as a result of patination. This phenomenon has been recognised in different cultures:

> 'The contrast of colours between the pure … metal and its watery blue and green salts was felt to be significant … This embodiment of opposites was regarded as symbolic in cultures as diverse as the Aztecs and the Dogon of Mali, for whom the accretion of green corrosion … symbolised the return of vegetation after rain' (Aldersey-Williams 2011, 239–40).

That is why the anthropologist Mary Helms (2012) has suggested that copper and bronze might have been thought of as living substances. Perhaps these distinctive materials were associated with the fertility of the earth that provided the ore.

For all these reasons neither the copper axes nor those described as 'jade' should be interpreted according to a strict technological model. This seems obvious from the character of the Alpine sources and their products, but the observation that they were the regional equivalents of metal tools has serious implications. Whether or not Helms is correct, it would be wrong to interpret either group of artefacts in wholly practical terms. The relationship between the objects made in these materials is so close that they should be treated together, and in each case some of these artefacts were deposited in similar circumstances.

Metals

Like the Three Age System, Hesiod's conjectural history depended on the sequence in which metals were worked in the past. For 19th century thinkers it illustrated the dominance of technology over nature. In ancient Greece, however, these materials were ranked according to their values and were used to illustrate a story of cultural decline. Both involved assumptions that were rarely questioned.

Like the audience for Hesiod's poem, people in Northern Europe looked back to a golden age, but in the 1st millennium AD it had special connotations. The possession of gold was a source of honour as well as riches, and in the past the gods themselves had worked metals. Later this role was assumed by dwarves, yet a connection with otherworldly powers still remained (Hedeager 2011, 144–45). Odin could to see all the precious metal in the ground and only he commanded the sorcery needed to recover it. Those who could make fine objects owed their skills to supernatural forces. In early sources the smith was a master craftsman, but he was also dangerous

The comparison between Greece and Scandinavia suggests that different metals were valued in the same way, but that was not always true. There have been instances in which iron was regarded at least as highly as other materials. In the New World precious metals could be less significant than those with unusual properties:

> 'The Taíno …. assigned distinct roles to gold and silver, and also to a range of coloured alloys … [They] placed more importance on *guanín*, an alloy of copper, silver and gold. What pleased them about it was its reddish-purplish colour and most of all its peculiar smell … Both gold and *guanín* were associated with power, authority and the supernatural world, but *guanín* carried the greater symbolic charge' (Aldersey-Williams 2011, 20).

There are other cases in which the differences between materials were important. Particular problems arose in comparing bronze with iron, because the 19th century idea of progress prevented a dispassionate analysis. It is obvious that iron was not a direct substitute for bronze as there was a phase with little sign of ferrous technology during which metal was scarce. To some extent the problem was influenced by patterns of deposition, but most of the difficulties faced by prehistorians were of their own making. If one material replaced the other as the Three Age Model prescribed, it followed that the latest bronze hoards must date from a period of transition.

An example of this confusion is provided by the last collections of bronze axes in northern France and southern England. These objects were alloyed with lead and were too soft to use as tools; they were simply units of metal. Recently their chronology has been reviewed (Milcent 2012) and it is obvious that they do not date from a 'Late Bronze Age' after all; they were made more than 100 years afterwards, during the 'early Iron Age'. Technological arguments can be misleading and another factor might have been important. Perhaps objects made of bronze could be buried, while iron was more suitable for other roles. If so, these metals were not equivalent to one another. They were different kinds of substance. Marie Louise Stig Sørensen (1987) has taken a similar approach to the metalwork hoards of Period VI in South Scandinavia.

Certainly these materials were worked in distinctive ways. Bronze objects were made by heating rock until it melted, and they were shaped inside a mould. Iron, on the other hand, was worked in a solid state. The methods used by smiths may have had as much influence as the materials they employed. In Britain during the pre-Roman Iron Age objects made by casting were generally deposited on land. They included brooches, arm-rings, collars, chapes and horse gear. Those formed from sheet metal, such as cauldrons, buckets, bowls, shields and helmets, could also be placed in water (Garrow & Gosden 2012, 97–100). In Iron Age Scotland a comparable distinction extends to collections of ironwork. Artefacts made by techniques favoured by the Roman army occur in terrestrial locations. Those produced according to local methods come from water (Hutcheson 1996).

Similar issues arise with late pre-Roman Iron Age metalwork where the most valuable artefacts were those of gold and silver. In each case the raw material had to be introduced from outside. In the sanctuary at Snettisham one of the deposits of valuables was buried in a pit in which the personal ornaments made of silver were kept completely separate from those of gold (Stead 1991). Gold artefacts remained important in the Migration period and again they could be deposited in different hoards from those containing silver. The distinction became more pronounced in the Viking Age. Even when both metals featured in the same collections, Birgitta Hårdh (1996, 132) observes that gold objects remained intact while the others were reduced to hacksilver – they were not mutually convertible. Gold was also deposited in hoards where it was the only material. There were single finds too, some of them associated with water. By this time silver coins were taking on an important economic role and gold may have been more suitable for votive offerings.

The interpretation of Neolithic axe quarries was influenced by ethnographic evidence. The same is true of ancient metalworking, although analogies have been sought in other parts of the world – Central and South America in the case of copper, silver and gold; Africa in the case of iron production. There is an interesting contrast between these studies. The evidence from the New World emphasises the properties of particular materials and raises the intriguing suggestion that metals were organic substances that grew beneath the ground (Helms 2012). Here the main emphasis was on the powers of the ores and those of the beings who controlled them. In the Andes certain mountains are the guardians of the local population. Here spirits, known as *apus,* determine the success of food production and protect people and their animals in return for offerings. At the same time the peaks on which these spirits live contain plentiful deposits of gold. These are dangerous places and the power of the *apus* means that mining the ore is a hazardous undertaking. It is surrounded by prohibitions and depends on appeasing the supernatural forces associated with the metal (Sallnow 1989).

The African example concerns the rituals associated with iron production. The process involves a restricted number of people – always men – and takes place out of public view. The furnace in which the iron is smelted is considered as a female body and sometimes it is provided with anatomical features. The creation of the metal is compared with parturition (Barndon 2004; Haaland 2004). This is a secret process, undertaken on special occasions and, like the extraction of gold in the New World, its success depends on achieving the right relations with otherworldly powers. As in South America, metalworking is associated with the fertility of nature.

Such observations have inspired work in European archaeology. Two examples are particularly striking. In Spain and Portugal the extraction of copper has been related to the depiction of artefacts on natural outcrops. The raw material for making these objects was taken from the rock, and was returned in the form of petroglyphs illustrating the finished products. In this case metal finds come from screes and even from a few sites with prehistoric images (Alves & Commendador 2009). The relationship between ironworking and fertility documented in the African example is also recognised in the pre-Roman period. Melanie Giles (2007) has studied an unusual deposit inside a settlement in north-east England. Here a blacksmith's tool kit, consisting of a paddle, a poker and pair of tongs was packed in straw and covered by a deposit of threshed barley. Ore was taken out of the ground in order to make iron, but some of its products were given back to the earth. That was similar to the treatment of cereals at a time when grain storage pits contained specialised deposits.

Further possibilities are suggested by excavated evidence for the production of bronze and iron. This is only a sample of an extensive literature but it makes a similar point to the earlier discussion of axe quarries. The mechanical performance of materials was of real importance, but their other properties must be considered too. One line of argument is illustrated by stone and ceramic moulds, and another concerns the places where metalworking was carried out.

Bronze Age moulds have been studied in some detail, and the contexts in which they are found raise several points of interest. They can be recovered from waterlogged deposits which also include finished objects and human remains. Thus clay moulds for making swords were found in a kettle hole on a site in lowland England which was also associated with cremated bone (Timby *et al.* 2007, 38–45). Similarly, an artificial pool outside Haughey's Fort – a defended enclosure in Ireland – included the moulds for making Late Bronze Age swords (Lynn 1977). Here they were associated with pieces of human skull. In other cases clay moulds were buried with as much formality as their products. For example, they were associated with the entrances of a Late Bronze Age ringwork in lowland southern

Britain (Needham & Bridgford 2013). Stone moulds have been found in hoards where they may be the only kind of artefact. They can also be associated with their products. A particularly striking example is where a bronze axe was buried after a significant period of use; in this case it was accompanied by the mould that had made it. These artefacts were reunited when their use lives were over (Webley & Adams in press).

At the same time it is clear that such deposits of moulds provide a biased picture of the kinds of metal in circulation. Here there is a problem, for those made of stone could have been used more than once, whilst clay moulds had to be broken when a casting was complete. Kurt Rassmann (1996) has studied a series of metalwork deposits in South-East Europe which date between about 1300 and 1000 BC. During one phase the ratio of hoard finds to those of moulds varied between different kinds of objects, and those for making ornaments outnumbered finds of the artefacts themselves by a ratio of 4:1. In the case of spearheads the equivalent figure was 1.5:1. In other instances finds of axes outnumbered their moulds by 3:1 and with bronze sickles the disparity was even greater and nine examples were found for every mould that was preserved. It is obvious that, like other artefacts, those associated with bronze working were carefully selected for placing in the ground.

Quite different associations are recorded in Northern Europe where moulds have been found on the same sites as burial mounds and cult houses (Fig. 16; Jantzen 2008). In both cases they occur together with cremations, leading Joakim Goldhahn (2007) to suggest that smiths were ritual specialists whose skills at achieving high temperatures allowed them to transform both bodies and raw materials. That is consistent with the evidence from the Swedish site of Hallunda where the largest group of Bronze Age furnaces identified in the country was associated with metal production and deposits of burnt bone. Similarly one of the most extensive workshops in Norway was associated with a cemetery at Hunn (Melheim *et al.* 2016). Bronze was also worked at specialised monuments in the British Isles – Scottish stone circles, a timber circle in Wales, a round cairn in south-west

Sandagergård

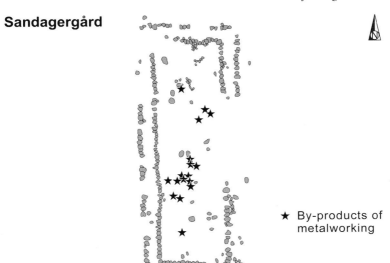

Figure 16. Plan of the cult house at Sandagergård, Denmark, showing the distribution of by-products of bronze production. Information from Jantzen (2008).

England and several megalithic tombs. It may be no accident that all these locations were connected with the dead (Bradley 2000, 156–57).

Comparable arguments apply to the production of iron. For all its practical advantages, it had specialised connotations too. The point is illustrated by pre-Roman ingots. Such 'currency bars' assumed several forms but were modelled on the shapes of artefacts with a particular significance: ploughs in one case, and swords in another (Hingley 2005). Some may even have copied the spits for cooking meat. They can be found in wet locations like the River Thames or the island bog at Llyn Cerrig Bach, but are more common in dry land hoards in Britain (Hingley 2005) and Continental Europe (Berranger 2006). In England they were generally buried at the entrances to enclosures or hillforts, or towards their outer limits. Others were associated with land boundaries, and one example comes from an Iron Age temple.

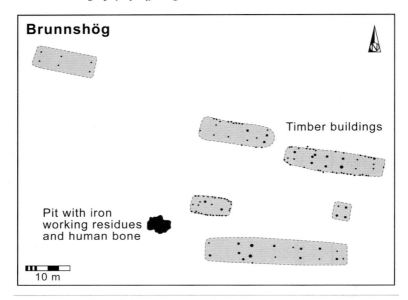

Figure 17. Plan of the Iron Age settlement at Brunnshög, Sweden, in relation to a pit containing human remains and the residues of iron production. Information from Carlie (2012).

There is different evidence from Brunnshög in the south of Sweden where iron was worked in a settlement (Fig. 17). With the domestic buildings was a pit containing the waste from metal production. It was directly associated with cremated human bone (Carlie 2012). Not far away were other deposits of slag, each of them associated with an area of wet ground of the kind selected for offerings. Another example was summarised in Chapter 4. At the Swedish site of Borg, which is interpreted as a Viking manor, the skulls and mandibles of boars were directly associated with the remains of furnaces and deposits of slag, but the remains of sows had a different distribution and were not associated with the working of metal (Dobat 2010). The same connection is illustrated by Late Iron Age cemeteries where pieces of iron slag were frequently deposited in graves (Burström 1990). In

Africa the furnace is compared to a living being. Medicines can be placed in the furnace itself, and sometimes slag and iron filings are added to other potions intended for human consumption (Insoll 2015, 375–77). In all these cases the by-products of metalworking may also have been endowed with life.

A similar interpretation is favoured by Terje Gansum (2004) who suggests that in Scandinavia human and animal bone was incorporated in sword blades in order to give them life. That is credible since there is literary evidence from the 1st millennium AD that certain weapons had personal names and were thought to exert their own agency. A similar idea was expressed by placing metalworking tools in graves. Perhaps these were not the burials of smiths. Instead the ability to transform the raw material identified 'leaders, who … secured the prosperity of their community'; these objects had become 'symbols of elite standing' (Ježek 2015, 121). A useful comparison is with Thor's hammer which was apparently associated with fertility, iron working and a Nordic god (Davidson 1964, 80–84).

These examples do nothing to reduce the importance of metals in farming, warfare and exchange, but they do suggest that in certain circumstances the production of bronze and iron was accompanied by rituals. They gave the finished artefacts their power and at times they even imbued them with life. In that way they played practical, social and religious roles at the same time. It is why it is so important to think about how these objects were treated when their careers came to an end. That is the subject of Chapter 7.

CHAPTER SEVEN

A Kind of Regeneration

The final act

The previous chapter had one principal theme. Some of the materials from which ancient objects were formed could have possessed special qualities. Their acquisition and production cannot be reduced to a simple question of technology. Sometimes artefacts could be treated like human beings. That is why in the 1st millennium AD swords had names and histories of their own. Of course the idea can be taken too far as their importance depended on the people who made and used them, and it cannot explain why so many items received special treatment when they were taken out of circulation. Here an appropriate analogy is with a funeral ceremony. How were these objects prepared for their removal from the world?

A useful comparison is with the well-known burial at Hochdorf in south-west Germany (Planck *et al.* 1985). It is rightly famous for the richness and variety of the funeral gifts and for the distinctive way in which they were organised in the ground. Less attention has been paid to small items with a longer history, some of which may have belonged to the dead man himself. They were not among the offerings provided by the mourners, yet they were covered in gold before the grave was sealed. In other words these comparatively insignificant artefacts were transformed as their histories came to an end. Much the same had happened during an earlier period when flint axes were deposited at Dutch chambered tombs. They were re-sharpened when they were provided for the dead (Van Gijn 2010, 129–32). In each case the character of the objects changed as they entered a new state. The same must have happened to human remains. Hoards and single finds are rarely associated with bones, but if certain artefacts shared attributes with people, it seems possible that they underwent a similar process. Chapter 6 considered the insights provided by lithic microwear. A similar approach can be taken to finds of metalwork.

This work has important implications for the interpretation of hoards and other deposits, but until comparatively recently scholars had been more concerned to define the types of metal artefacts and to study their associations. It was on that basis that chronologies were established and regional styles were defined. The distinction between hoards and burials was not important here; what mattered is that items entered the ground together. Nor was it of much interest whether an object was damaged or incomplete, provided its original form could still be identified. This was a method that by its very nature could not extend to single finds. Researchers even complained about the poor condition of some of the surviving material. It had been treated so badly when it was deposited that it was no longer suited to this kind of analysis.

The fact that objects survive in so many states provides a clue to their original significance. Two kinds of study have been especially revealing. The first is an investigation of how different forms of artefact had been used in the past. For example, weapons that had been thought to play a purely ceremonial role show the kinds of damage that result from combat. Early Bronze Age halberds are the obvious example (Brandherm 2011). Bronze Age swords have been studied by similar methods, and here Kristian Kristiansen (2002) has recognised an important contrast in the ways in which two distinctive types were used, one with a solid metal hilt and the other where the hilt was of organic material. In one case they could have played a role in public events. Their blades were in good condition, but there was evidence that they had been repeatedly withdrawn from their scabbards, as if to demonstrate their fine quality. Other swords had 'duelling scars' – the kind of edge damage caused by fighting. There was evidence that they had been repaired. He suggests that they might have been used by different groups of people. Some were displayed at ceremonies but others were weapons of war. Anthony Harding has shown that these basic types appear in different contexts. In Central Europe those with metal hilts can be found in watery environments, while the others were placed in graves (Harding 2007, 129–31). Their contexts vary in other parts of the Continent, but the contrast between them follows regional lines.

A second approach concerns the working of metals. Studies of hoards investigated the state of their contents. It was thought that they had been deposited by smiths, and where these collections contained moulds, slag, ingots or casting jets, the idea was difficult to refute. The problem was that it could be pursued in an intellectual vacuum and other issues were less often raised. Why did the contents of these hoards vary from one region to another (Maraszec 2006)? Were particular kinds of artefacts treated in particular ways? Why were the same kinds of objects divided up differently in neighbouring areas (Turner 2010)? And why was so much material left in the ground? Only where newly made pieces remained intact did the evidence seem easy to interpret, for such collections were understood as products that had been stored and lost before they could be distributed to the customer.

There are certain limitations. These approaches work better on some materials than others. Iron corrodes and for that reason this chapter is restricted to Bronze Age metalwork (Fig. 18). It is treated in some detail in the hope that it will illustrate more general patterns, but at the moment such information is quite limited and there is scope for a fuller project. In the past important sources of variation were overlooked. In particular, the distinction between hoard finds and single finds is misleading and will not be followed here. Instead of focusing on individual instances, this discussion will consider the sheer variety of treatments applied to artefacts as they were prepared for deposition.

A basic distinction is between those that were complete when they entered the archaeological record and others which had been damaged or broken.

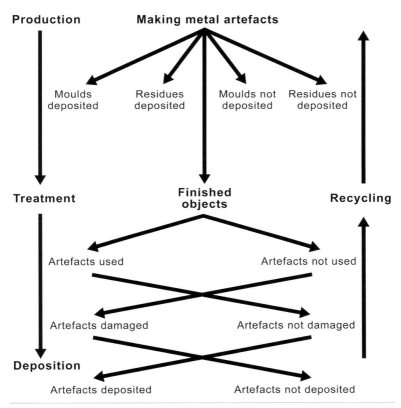

Figure 18. Possible pathways for the treatment of Late Bronze Age metalwork. On the left the sequence extends from production to deposition. On the right it considers the possibility that metals were recycled.

Whole and undamaged artefacts

Both hoards and other deposits include complete and undamaged objects, but this is rather unusual. At one time it was assumed that artefacts were intended as offerings from the outset and would have been deposited in fresh condition. This view was seldom questioned. In fact it applies to a comparatively small number of pieces, for instance some small rings associated with the causeway at Flag Fen (Pryor 2001). In other cases artefacts had physical defects that might have prevented their use. That could explain their deposition, but it may not have been the intention from the outset. A telling example is provided by a few swords from that site which had such severe flaws that they could never be employed in combat.

In the Netherlands studies of microwear reveal that the Late Neolithic axes were work tools, but they were painted before they were placed in the ground (Van Gijn 2010, chapters 6 & 7). This pattern remained much the same during later periods. Helle Vandkilde (1996) has shown that the first copper and bronze axes in South Scandinavia had played a practical role before their deposition. The same point is illustrated by the tool marks that survive on waterlogged wood in the British Isles (Brennand & Taylor 2003, 22–30). Here a few axeheads were embellished with designs like those on pottery. In this case the decoration may have been added after these objects had been damaged in use (Moyler 2008). Some received a coating of tin which enhanced their surface appearance and gave it a silvery sheen (Close-Brooks & Coles 1980).

Personal ornaments, especially arm-ring and neck-rings, also show signs of use but they generally remained intact (Sorensen 1997). These objects are usually found together in hoards. In Northern and Western Europe individual items can show different amounts of wear. For example, the arm-rings in Danish hoards are divided into three distinct groups according to their sizes, forms and weights (Levy 1982). This suggests that they were acquired at different stages in the lives of the people who wore them (Sofaer Derevenski 2000). The rings were often deposited as sets and were sometimes arranged in formal patterns in the ground. They are like the artefacts that accompany the body in a grave, but in this case it is clear that items associated with several people could be buried together. Other kinds of ornaments had extended histories. The clearest evidence comes from Early Bronze Age Ireland where Mary Cahill (2005) has demonstrated that the decorated gold collars known as lunulae were repeatedly rolled up or folded. At times they were opened out again, as if to put them on display.

Similar evidence is provided by weapons. Swords, spears and shields were all damaged in combat. Jill York's (2002) study of the metalwork from the Thames suggests that it applied to between 75% and 86% of those dating from the Late Bronze Age. Bénédicte Quilliec (2007) provides similar figures for swords of the same date in other parts of Europe. In common with those in south-east England, many of the swords in north-west France and the Iberian Peninsula showed signs of use. In south-west France, northern France and the remaining parts of Britain the equivalent figures are not much lower. Research of this kind is important as it provides some of the best evidence for armed conflict during the prehistoric period.

Lorraine Bourke's analysis of finds associated with water in Ireland arrived at a similar conclusion, but it considered the different parts of the weapons (Bourke 2001). The blades of dirks and rapiers could be damaged, yet approximately a third of these artefacts showed little indication of use. The evidence was not the same for swords. In the large sample of Class IV (the latest type) half of those examined had damage on the hilt, and virtually the same proportion of the blades showed evidence of use. There were similar patterns within the largest groups of spearheads. In one case 40% of their sockets remained intact, and 48% of the blades. Another variety provided a different result, for in this case half the sockets were well preserved, but the same applied to two thirds of their blades. Weapons could deteriorate during a battle, but the condition of the socketed spearheads might result from removing their shafts. A similar approach applies to the butts of dirks and rapiers. In each case it could have happened when these artefacts were taken out circulation.

In other cases it seems to have been essential to maintain the integrity of an object. Just as large flint axes in the Netherland had been wrapped in fabric, metal tools and ornaments could be kept inside boxes, pouches or bags. That was certainly true of the lavishly decorated bronze mirrors of the late Pre-Roman Iron Age (Joy 2009, 550–51). Something similar applied to weapons. The discovery of chapes among the river finds of the Late Bronze Age suggests that certain of the swords were deposited within their scabbards. Many more examples can be identified in the pre-Roman and Roman Iron Ages. Something similar applies to those spearheads which retain traces of their shafts. They are usually represented by small fragments of wood inside the sockets, so it is not clear whether they were snapped off as the weapons were decommissioned. Even so, there can be a contrast with the objects in dry land. David Fontijn (2003, table 3.2) has shown that artefacts were separated from their hafts in the hoards of the southern Netherlands.

Just as certain objects retained at least parts of their shafts there is evidence that others were re-sharpened immediately before they were deposited. The traces can be so fresh that it seems unlikely that they were ever used again. It is true of both tools and weapons. In the Netherlands it applies to axes whose chronology spans the whole of the Bronze Age and also to the spearheads made from the middle of that period onwards. The same practice is evidenced in the early Iron Age. Throughout these phases it was less common with swords and has not been identified among the contents of burials. Fontijn (2003) suggests that such objects were prepared as if for use. That provides an important clue to their interpretation.

Incomplete or damaged artefacts

Breaking or damaging objects was a very different process. By disabling or destroying them they were put beyond use. Again the nature of the evidence varied across space and time.

In some respects this procedure was the opposite of the practices described so far. Weapons could be removed from their hafts so that they were no longer serviceable. They could also be bent or broken. Individual examples were fractured using exceptional violence, a characteristic highlighted in studies by Louis Nebelsick (2000). It is particularly obvious in the case of sword blades which might be snapped or bent, for this would have been difficult to accomplish; after all, they would be virtually useless if they were liable to break in the course of battle. A detailed study of the Bronze Age weapons from the Thames provides another dimension. Like those studied by Kristiansen, many had been damaged in combat, but at a later stage in their histories these artefacts were decommissioned, often with considerable force (York 2002). The two types of treatment shed new light on the swords and spears in the river. The proportion with evidence of use remained at a more or less constant level, but during the later Bronze Age weapons were disabled at an increasing rate. Between 1300 and 1100 BC it applied to only 39% of these artefacts. During succeeding periods the figure rose to almost 70%.

The results of Jill York's analysis can be compared with the work of Bénédicte Quilliec (2007), whose study showed that most of the Late Bronze Age swords in northern and north-west France had been deliberately destroyed. The same was true in Britain, but even in her study area it was not a universal pattern. In the Iberian Peninsula it was comparatively rare. It is obvious that practices varied from one area to another. A related phenomenon was the division of Late Bronze Age sword blades into segments. Incomplete examples have been found in rivers, but they are mainly a feature of dry land hoards. Again it took considerable force to achieve this. Another development is the demonstration by laboratory analysis that some seemingly intact weapons had been weakened by exposure to a fire (Bridgford 1998).

Most accounts have focussed on the treatment of Bronze Age weapons, but the condition of ornaments and tools is equally important. Again it shares some common features with what happened in other periods. Victoria Fischer (2011) has examined a large number of finds from the waters around Alpine lake settlements. Her work shows that they were deliberately deposited there between 1050 and 800 BC; that would make them broadly contemporary with the swords investigated by Quilliec. In this case the artefacts are mainly personal ornaments, especially pins and rings. Tools are also represented. Two types of treatment were identified by Fischer. Objects might have been exposed to fires, or they could have been divided into fragments. Burning was not apparent in every collection, but, where it was observed, it accounted for up to 16% of the deposits.

The breaking of artefacts, mainly ornaments, accounted for between 20% and 48% of the material.

Friendly fire

One of the most striking characteristics of Late Bronze Age metalwork hoards is that so many of their contents have been exposed to fire. It also applies to a smaller number of intact weapons found in rivers. The commonest explanation is that broken or discarded objects were melted down and the raw material was recycled. On one level this is probably true, but it does not provide a complete answer. There is compelling evidence that metals were reworked from a much earlier date, and it is possible to document the circulation of raw materials for a long time before their products entered the archaeological record.

It may be more than a coincidence that during the Late Bronze Age the use of fire was important in other spheres. The most obvious example is the treatment of the dead, for this was a time when the cremation rite achieved a new importance. Not only were bodies burnt as part of the mortuary ritual, their remains were reduced to fragments in a similar fashion to the metalwork found in hoards (Brück 2001; 2006). Not all these 'burials' contained a full set of human remains, and some fragments may never have been recovered from the pyre. As Svend Hansen (2016) has observed, the amount of burnt bone in the grave can be surprisingly limited. It raises the possibility that some relics of the deceased never entered the ground but circulated among the living. A graphic example of this practice was the funeral of the English poet Shelley, who drowned off the coast of Italy in 1822. When his body washed ashore his friends, including Lord Byron, burnt it on the beach (Holmes 1972, 730). His ashes were interred in the Protestant Cemetery in Rome but the mourners kept small pieces of bone as mementos of their dead companion. A similar practice may explain why so many metalwork hoards contain incomplete artefacts. The residue could have been melted down, but it could also have passed from hand to hand.

Fire was important at the burnt offering sites of the same date in the Alps (Steiner 2010). It also played a significant role at the petroglyphs of south Scandinavia, where considerable deposits of burnt stone accumulated near to the decorated surfaces. There is even evidence that fires were ignited on the outcrops themselves (Bradley 2009b, 182–85). In some cases they damaged or destroyed existing images, but in other instances these drawings were concealed beneath a deposit of fire-cracked rocks. Similar accumulations have been found in isolation in Northern Europe and can be associated with human bones.

If bodies and artefacts were modified by fire, what was the connection between them? There is little to suggest that metalwork affected by heat had been taken from a pyre. Anders Kaliff (2007) has suggested that the burning of a corpse and the fragmentation of the remains allowed the spirit to escape, so that the dead person could be regenerated. The idea has been discussed in relation to Indo-European literary evidence, but by its very nature the connection is tenuous. On the other hand, the same notion could easily apply to the melting of raw material and the making of new artefacts out of the remains of old ones. The problem is created by the way in which archaeologists think about the past. Cremation is considered as a ritual and connected with cosmologies and religious beliefs. The recycling of objects, on the other hand, is thought of as a technological process that has to be discussed in economic terms. Similar problems affect other aspects of Bronze Age metallurgy.

Fragmentation

Like burning, fragmentation is not a normal feature of Bronze Age hoards until the later 2nd and earlier 1st millennia BC. It is first found in Central and South-East Europe and subsequently in the North-West. Many of these collections contain fragmentary artefacts which cannot be refitted, meaning that other parts must have been removed.

They feature in studies by Oliver Dietrich (2014) and Svend Hansen (2016). Several points are especially important. Hoards containing broken metalwork were a largely new development in Europe. Their predecessors were composed of a restricted set of objects – often axes or rings – which usually remained intact. From as early as 1600 BC such collections ran in parallel with deposits made up of fragments which frequently included a wider variety of types. They have seldom been studied in detail, but Hansen's work in South-East Europe shows that their composition can vary from one period to another and also along regional lines. Some objects are represented by a single fragment. Certain types of artefact may have been fractured according to shared conventions. This was certainly true of sickles, and Christoph Sommerfeld (1994) has suggested that their parts were treated as a form of currency.

The fragmentation of artefacts reached a peak during the Late Bronze Age when they were broken especially violently, but Hansen has shown that some hoards in his study area contained a mixture of types that accumulated over several hundred years. Within the larger collections there are examples of what he calls 'miniature hoards', where the socket of an axe or a spearhead was used as receptacle to hold a series of smaller pieces. Sometimes these were inserted with considerable force. According to Dietrich (2014), the distribution of these deposits extends from South-East Europe in the 13th and 12th centuries BC to the North-West during the 10th and 9th centuries BC.

Drawing on the evidence from Classical sanctuaries, Hansen (2016) suggests that incomplete items can be interpreted as votive offerings, following the principal of *pars pro toto* which allows just part of an artefact to stand for the entire object. In that case it seems possible that the large collections of broken metalwork that typify the Late Bronze Age were votive deposits assembled by more people than the earlier hoards. He describes this process as 'democratisation'. If so, the 'miniature hoards' concealed within these larger collections might have been provided by particular individuals.

This does not explain why so many hoards of broken metalwork in Northern and Western Europe contained ingots, moulds, slag or casting waste, and here the traditional interpretation that associates them with the activities of a smith may have more to commend it.

These collections provide the clearest evidence for the use of fire. Late Bronze Age hoards contain certain pieces of objects at the expense of others – particular parts of these artefacts had to be retained when others could be recycled. An example mentioned earlier is the breaking of swords. It was the hilt that seems to have been preserved where part of the blade is absent. The evidence is similar for single finds and hoards. It is clear that this is not related to the mechanical performance of these weapons or to the likelihood of their breaking during use. In different parts of Late Bronze Age Europe the ratio of the hilt to the lower blade ranges from 1.1:1 to 5:1. It also varies over time within particular regions (Bradley 2005, chapter 5). Perhaps the explanation is found in Kevin Leahy's (2015) interpretation of the broken weapons in the Staffordshire Hoard where he suggests that the hilts of swords were preserved because they had been held in the warrior's hand.

Since the missing pieces rarely turn up as single finds, the simplest explanation is that they were melted down. The material that survived was buried by the smith. On a practical level that interpretation may be correct, but this procedure could have been problematical. One of the paradoxes identified in this book is that objects of exactly the same types were treated in very different ways. Swords of the kinds deposited as complete objects in water are also represented by broken pieces in hoards. Ornaments that might have been buried as a set can be represented among these fragments, although it is less common. How could this happen? Chapter 3 made the suggestion that the selection of objects for special treatment depended on their histories rather than their outward appearance. Two weapons might be assigned to the same type, but one had been used in a battle or inherited from a famous hero. That might be why it was left intact. The other had a less distinguished history and for that reason it could be destroyed.

The argument is too neat. Chapter 6 made the point that the transformation of metals was not a straightforward transaction. It resembled the treatment of the human body and might have been accompanied by mystery or have taken place in secret; it is true that in many parts of Europe hoards, like cremation cemeteries, were outside settlements, although their locations need not have been far apart. Perhaps by combining the metal obtained from particular objects, whether they were complete or fragmentary, the smith was uniting their separate histories. That would be the case if those objects were compared with living beings. The merging of artefacts with different biographies was not necessarily a simple procedure.

Weights

It is not a new idea that some Bronze Age artefacts contained prescribed amounts of metal. This approach has been taken to the distinctive *Ösenringe* made from Alpine copper. Their characteristic forms resembled those of personal ornaments, and they have been claimed as unfinished examples of that type. Although they can be found in graves, it seems more likely that they were ingots – standard units of metal whose value would be immediately apparent (Innerhofer 1997). Many intact examples occur in hoards, suggesting that they were assembled with some formality. The weights of entire collections could have been as significant as those of their individual components. A similar approach has been taken to artefacts of the Middle and Late Bronze Ages, particularly the complete and broken sickles of Central Europe (Sommerfeld 1994) and the last socketed axes in North-West Europe (Briard 1965, 270–71). Both have been interpreted as a kind of primitive currency. Mats Malmer (1992) took the same approach to a series of anthropomorphic figurines in south Scandinavia.

Robin Taylor (1993, 54–57) has calculated the average weights of Middle and Late Bronze Age hoards in southern England. They were similar in the Thames Valley, Wessex and the south-west, but in East Anglia such collections were twice as heavy. These figures can also be broken down by period. Most of this material was deposited during two separate phases. The mean weight of metal in later Middle Bronze Age hoards was about the same in Wessex and south-west England and roughly twice that found in East Anglia and the Thames Valley.

At the end of the Bronze Age it was virtually unchanged in Wessex, but had increased four times over in East Anglia, and a little more than that in the south-west. The average weight of a single object was similar in three of these regions. That is important as the compositions of the hoards were not consistent. Some of the objects in these collections were incomplete.

There is a problem with such estimates, as many objects in these assemblages were broken. It is impossible to reunite the remaining fragments because certain parts of these objects are over-represented and other elements are missing. Nor is the evidence consistent from one region to another – for instance, Louise Turner (2010) has shown that the character of the surviving fragments varied between opposite sides of the Thames Estuary. The best way of harmonising these observations is to suggest that particular parts of these artefacts had been recycled, so that no trace of them survived. The others were preserved and might have circulated among the living. They could have played many roles, but some were obviously selected for deposition in the ground. Approximate weights are available for the fraction represented in hoards, but it is impossible to estimate the amount of metal that was lost. On the other hand, the weight of the material that survived would be one way of calculating the value of particular offerings before they entered the ground.

Numbers

Another important factor was the number of objects in hoards. It is clear that in particular parts of Europe people followed specific conventions. Again this implies that these collections were not accumulated by chance. This question is discussed by several authors. Eugène Warmenbol (2010) has identified a series of deposits containing armour and sheet vessels. He observes that these collections are characterised by nine components, and less frequently by 12. In the same way Dirk Brandherm (2007) has investigated the representation of weapons and other artefacts in hoards, where they often appear in pairs. Examples of these types include helmets, buckets and shields. Other collections contain three items, in which case two of the artefacts are similar to one another, whilst the third takes a different form. There is some evidence that these conventions changed over time, so that in Iberia and Denmark hoards containing three objects in the Middle Bronze Age were replaced during the following phase by collections with only two. In the same way Regine Maraszec (2006) has identified a series of Late Bronze Age hoards containing pairs of similar artefacts: two axes, two torcs or two swords. Where a pair of axes were found together they could be of different sizes, types or weights. There was also some regional variation. Maraszec's research showed that pairs of axes appeared frequently in British hoards, but in the Middle Rhine the commonest numbers of artefacts were three or four. In Denmark, seven items were preferred.

The last act

Most studies that investigate the deposition of Bronze Age metalwork begin at the same point. As Chapter 2 explained, the emphasis has always been on practical considerations. Might particular artefacts be recovered, or were they taken out of circulation permanently? Those buried in the ground could be dug up again, especially if their positions were marked. For the most part those in wet places would be harder to find. It might be possible in the case of bog deposits, but it would be more difficult with a lake or a fast-flowing river. Because these objects were irretrievable, they were interpreted as offerings.

Such studies have provided plausible results, but in a sense they are incomplete as less attention was paid to the treatment of the artefacts themselves. The situation will change as wear analysis influences Bronze Age studies in the way that it has already informed Neolithic research. Is it possible to revisit the debates surrounding water finds and terrestrial deposits with the results of this work in mind? The question is important and is considered again in Chapter 8 which extends the discussion to the archaeology of later periods.

There was a difference between two ways of treating artefacts that were largely independent of their contexts. Whole and undamaged objects might be placed either in land or water. They could have remained in use, but for some reason it was not permitted. The argument applies to tools, weapons and ornaments. One clue is provided by wear analysis, but the same point applies when spears retained their shafts and axes kept their handles. The evidence is more compelling when these objects were sharpened as they were discarded. They were made ready for a use that never happened. A clue is the identification of a similar practice at Neolithic tombs, for here the maintenance of these objects can only have benefitted the dead. It follows that where undamaged artefacts were taken out of circulation they may have been destined for use in another world. That was particularly true when they were repaired just before they were deposited. Analysis of Bronze Age metalwork suggests that such practices were comparatively rare. Few pieces lack any signs of use and many weapons were allowed to keep the scars they had sustained in battle. Perhaps these marks were retained as an indication of their histories.

On the other hand, it was common for objects to be reduced to fragments. Again their biographies were important, for they could be objects of the same types as those that remained intact as they entered the archaeological record. There are obvious examples of deliberate destruction – the burning of individual swords, the snapping or bending of their blades. The removal of a spearhead from its socket might have been another example, or the separation of an axehead from its haft. In every case the effect of this distinctive treatment was to prevent their further use. That is the exact opposite of the procedures that applied to whole objects. They were also different from grave goods, most of which were complete.

A variant of this practice was the recycling of objects for their metal content. It has something in common with the process just described, but its objective cannot have been quite the same. Far from preventing an artefact from circulating, it allowed it to remain in existence but in a different form. Interpretations of the evidence are complicated by uncertainties over the role of smiths.

The issues are comparatively simple. The connection between hoards and metallurgy might be an artefact of modern ideas about artefact production, but the presence of metalworking residues in so many hoards in the North and West suggests that in most instances the traditional interpretation is correct. On the other hand, it does not mean that the smith was simply a technician. There are two ways of dealing with this assumption. The first is to compare Bronze Age metalworkers with those in traditional societies and to draw on literary evidence from the ancient world. In each case smiths occupy a specialised role and their work is accompanied by rituals and associated with danger. Those issues were considered in Chapter 6. The second approach is to focus on the peculiar character of the artefacts associated with their activities. The same kinds of objects were broken into different fractions from one area to another, and some of the pieces supposedly reduced to scrap metal were too large to fit in a crucible (Turner 2010). Certain parts of individual artefacts such as axes, sickles and swords are over-represented whilst others are rare or absent. That was a widespread practice, although the precise details vary between different parts of Europe. The same applies to the number of intact objects in particular hoards. Again the weights of individual pieces may have been significant, and so may those of entire collections. These are comparatively new elements in the study of hoards, and some are more fully developed than others. Taken together, they undermine any attempt to establish a 'mundane' interpretation of this difficult material.

It is more helpful to combine both strands. If smiths played a role akin to alchemy or magic, they could have engaged in rituals as part of the production process. If some of the metal was retained when the remainder was recycled, there is every reason to consider it as an offering in its own right. The anthropologist Mary Helms took this view in a recent article on the Bronze Age in which she suggested that because the raw material had been obtained from the natural world metalworkers returned a certain part to ensure a successful outcome (Helms 2012). Alternatively, the metal was buried as a thanks-offering when the task was accomplished. The fact that the composition of some hoards was determined by weights and numbers was one way of establishing the values of such offerings.

It is ironic that the most important evidence of all never survives, for it was the raw material that went on to make other things. A neutral description would characterise this as recycling, but again the process of making and using these artefacts brought them back to life. In that case the conversion of discarded objects could be regarded as a second birth: a kind of regeneration.

CHAPTER EIGHT

Vanishing Points

Sinking treasures

Imagine a sequence of operas that runs for 15 hours and follows the history of a piece of river metalwork. The proposition is absurd, but that is the premise of *Der Ring des Nibelungen* by Richard Wagner, which was first performed in 1876 (Spencer & Millington 1993). Several elements recall features already considered in this book.

The cycle commences with *Das Rheingold*, and its opening scene takes place in the river where a great treasure is kept. The Rhinemaidens who look after it are approached by the evil Alberich. As guardians they are hopeless. Without foreseeing any of the consequences, they inform their visitor that the gold beneath the water has special properties:

> 'Great wealth would come to anyone who made a ring from the Rhinegold. It would give him unlimited power. Our father instructed us to guard the hoard so that no one would steal it' (*Das Rheingold*, Scene 1).

Predictably, Alberich gives in to temptation. He removes the gold and forges the ring from which the drama takes its name. The four operas trace its subsequent history. Over the generations it passes between the actors – assorted heroes and gods, giants and dwarves – until everyone who controlled it is dead. In the end it is held by the warrior Siegfried, who becomes another victim of the conflict. When his lover Brünnhilde joins his funeral pyre the ring is returned to the Rhine and the river bursts its banks. Wagner's stage directions describe the end of the story:

> 'The three Rhinemaidens are carried on the waves and appear over the scene of the fire … They swim towards the back of

the stage, holding the ring aloft in a gesture of jubilation. A red glow becomes increasingly bright … By its light they can be seen swimming in circles and playing with the ring in the waters of the Rhine which has gradually returned to its bed' (*Götterdämmerung*, Act 3, Scene 3)

Another epic tale is *Egil's Saga*, which was set in the Viking Age but written down in Iceland somewhat later. It tells how the protagonist Egil Skallagrimsson buried his valuables shortly before he died. The narrator considers where he might have put them, but does not say why it happened, although that might have been apparent to the original audience – Egil's treasures were to provide him with wealth in the afterlife:

'He told [his slaves] to fetch him a horse … When he was ready he went out, taking his chests of silver with him … But neither the slaves nor the chests of treasure ever returned, and there are many theories about where Egil hid his treasure … It has been noticed that … coins have been found in the gully where the river recedes after floods caused by sudden thaws. There are large and exceptionally deep marshes … and it is claimed that Egil threw his treasure into them. On the south side of the rivers are hot springs with deep pits nearby, where some people believe that Egil must have hidden his treasure because a will-o'-the wisp is often seen there … In the autumn Egil caught the illness that eventually led to his death' (*Egil's Saga*, 88).

Giving and taking

Wagner wrote his own libretto for *The Ring*. Unlike *Egil's Saga*, his 'mythological farrago' (Abbate & Parker 2012, 355) drew on a variety of sources which were only distantly related to one another. They came from separate traditions, supplemented by German folklore. The most important was the Nordic *Volsunga Saga*, but another was the medieval *Nibelungenlied* which described the riches deposited in the river. It may have inspired the composition of the drama, but its account of the treasure was very different from the operatic version. In the original poem the valuables were assembled as dowry and were not just precious metals, although one small piece of gold did have special powers. This provided Wagner with his point of departure:

> 'It was as much as a dozen loaded waggons could carry … in four days and nights, coming and going three times a day. It was entirely of gems and gold … *Among the rest was the rarest gem of all, a tiny wand of gold, and if anyone had found its secret, he would have been lord of all mankind*' (*The Niblungenlied*, chapter 19; my emphasis).

The riches allowed Queen Kriemhild to bestow lavish gifts on her followers, but again longstanding feuds eventually led to conflict. As the tensions increased her brother insisted that the treasure must be destroyed:

> 'Rather than be plagued with the gold let us sink it in the Rhine so that no one will possess it' (*The Niblungenlied*, chapter 19).

But before that could happen, the entire collection was stolen. By a strange coincidence the thief, Hagen, concealed his spoils in the same river. As the poem explains, this was a temporary expedient. He meant to recover them, but in vain:

> '[He] took the entire treasure and sank it in the Rhine at Locheim imagining he would make use of it some day; this was not destined to happen' (*The Niblungenlied*, chapter 19).

Taken together, these sources illustrate most of the reasons for depositing valuables in water. They also extend to the burial of hoards. Unfortunately, they also create confusion. That is not surprising since they were recorded at a time when most of these practices had lapsed. At best they record a distant memory of what had been done in the past. They may have been influenced by chance discoveries, including finds of prehistoric and Roman metalwork in the Rhine itself.

They do not present a consistent picture and there are contradictions even in the same account. For example, in the *Nibelungenlied* Queen Kriemhild's dowry is a source of both wealth and danger. Her brother thinks that the threat can be averted by destroying the treasure. It had been intended for a special purpose and should not be used in other ways, yet that was exactly what Hagen intended when he stole it. The original plan was to sink the valuables in the river to prevent their circulation, but this was precisely where the thief chose to hide them. Different characters in the story considered the Rhine as a place to abandon prestigious objects, or as somewhere from which they could be recovered.

Egil's Saga is equally ambiguous. Egil Skallagrimsson is represented as concealing his treasure shortly before he dies, but he does so in a distinctive location. It might have been a river, a marsh or a spring, but again there is the same association between valuables and water. It is obvious that the site was to remain a secret, as the servants who helped him take them there must have been killed. The account implies that the treasure could still be discovered and even refers to finds of coins. On the other hand, the Law of Odin had allowed people to store their riches for use in the Otherworld (Gullbekk 2008, 164). That would explain the close relationship between Egil's death and the burial of his wealth. The valuables were not meant to be retrieved as they were destined for the afterlife.

Der Ring des Nibelungen concerns the history of a single object made of gold taken from the bed of the Rhine. The ring is the principal actor in the story. Again it was a source of power and one of danger, and over successive generations every attempt to control it resulted in disaster. That is why it was taken back to the river. People wanted to end its circulation and to remove the threat it posed. Although they agree on little else, most researchers accept that river finds result from deliberate deposition. As Hagen found to his cost, the Rhine was not a suitable place for storing valuables.

For all their internal contradictions, these sources suggest at least three different ways of accounting for deposits of precious objects:

1. They could be hidden and stored for later recovery, but for some reason they were never collected.

2. They could be removed from circulation to protect (or even extinguish) their special powers. In that case it was important that certain objects should not become private wealth.
3. They were intended for transmission to another world, either as gifts to the supernatural or to provide for the dead in an afterlife.

Artefacts with attitude

Why are the first written sources so ambivalent about the reasons for depositing exceptional items? And why do those texts offer more than one explanation for the same phenomena?

It is not enough to say that they referred to events in the past. Nor can the confusion be explained by the adoption of a new religion, although Christian belief would have affected the ways in which pagan practices were interpreted. More important was a gradual change in the very nature of wealth. The end of the Viking Age saw some new developments in the relationship between people and things. Coinage became more important as a standard unit of value. With these developments came a new understanding of possession (Myrberg Burström 2015). Of course, there had been rather similar developments in the past, especially during the Roman period, and currency had circulated together with other metal artefacts from the pre-Roman Iron Age onwards; in different forms it remained significant for much of the 1st millennium AD. Nevertheless most scholars would argue that with the emergence of the Viking silver economy developments took a new turn. Water finds were still important, but dryland hoards were increasingly made up of coins and hacksilver and were organised according to a widely agreed system of weights (Graham-Campbell & Williams 2007). Some of these deposits may still have been intended as offerings, but the strongest evidence that they played a role in everyday transactions comes from their representation on urban sites involved in international trade. It is clear that coinage provided an increasingly important medium of exchange.

That is not to say that the giving and receiving of complex artefacts ended altogether, but it may have changed its character in subtle ways.

The social importance of exchange might have remained the same, but with the increasing availability of money the balance between gifts and commodities could have shifted. But gift exchange was never a single process. Sometimes an object passed between people in one transaction, but in other instances the parties were caught up in a relationship that would extend across the generations. In Marcel Mauss's *Essai sur le don*, the giving and receiving of gifts was vitally important to the workings of traditional society. Every gift invited a counter-gift and it was on that basis that relationships could be established, contested and maintained (Mauss 1925). Not surprisingly, the process was open to manipulation, so that the giving of gifts on an extravagant scale could easily lead to debt and might become a cause of social inequality (Strathern & Stewart 2005). A very different model has been proposed by Annette Weiner (1992) who writes about 'keeping while giving'. In this case the essential feature is that some gifts are inalienable – even after they change hands they retain a link to the original donor. Such relationships can extend across lengthy periods of time and endow the objects of exchange with a special power over people. In that way gifts are inescapably connected to their source of origin.

This approach has important implications, for it means that contemporary notions of ownership or property need not apply to prehistoric societies (Kevenäs & Hedenstierna-Jonson 2015). Moreover possession does not involve a permanent relationship between people and things, as it could have been short term and by no means exclusive. It also seems that certain objects carried, or came to acquire, powers and associations as they moved between one stage in their history and another. For those reason modifications to individual objects had to be made with care. They could reflect the processes that affected the people who controlled them – changes of status or the formation of new alliances. That could explain some of the ways in which those objects were altered. Well documented examples of such relationships abound in the historical period. They might be the gifts between lords and their retainers, or *vice versa* (Bazelmans 1999; Härke 2000). Another possibility is that the movement of special objects was governed by rules of inheritance. For example, famous swords might pass from generation to generation, accompanied by accounts of how and when they had been used. In such cases it would be quite wrong to consider them solely as personal property. Indeed, losing or giving away an inherited weapon could mean the loss of social position.

Many of these issues have been discussed by Franz Theuws and Monica Alkemade (2000) who describe a similar process in Frankish society. At a particular age people were 'invested' by the presentation of weapons. These artefacts might be gifts between a lord and his followers and, wherever possible, it was important that the objects should have had a significant history. They must have been used before and could have been taken from a treasury. They could even be composite pieces made out of parts of older weapons; in the case of swords they might not be in their original scabbards. A similar argument applies to the weapons described in *Beowulf* where wealth was not considered as something that could be measured or counted but was equated with more nebulous qualities of honour, worth and fame. These concepts expressed the relationship between a warrior and the society to which he belonged. The giving and receiving of such artefacts was essential for the reproduction of an aristocratic lineage. According to these authors it was an essential component of 'cosmological order'. They also suggest that the deposition of valuables should be considered as one way in which wealth could be *used*. It may be wrong to think of it as *destruction*.

As the last two chapters have shown, objects of this kind literally took on lives of their own. Sometimes that was the outcome of a distinguished history, but it might also be due to their unusual composition, their fine workmanship or their exotic origins. They could be given names and embellished with anthropomorphic decoration (Fig. 19; Pearce 2013). All contributed to the idea that they were animated: they had special powers and for that reason required special treatment. Examples could include insignia or ceremonial weapons which were held in temporary custody while people performed particular roles, but when those roles were at an end such objects would be reclaimed. David Fontijn has suggested that this principle applied to some of the most elaborate Bronze Age artefacts in the Low Countries. In that case they were not personal possessions but powerful objects which helped to define the identities and roles of specific people on particular occasions. They were acquired at important stages in the life course and might have been relinquished when their period of use was over. That was not necessarily the case when someone died (Fontijn 2003, chapters 11 & 12).

It follows that in the past artefacts may have had characteristics which do not feature so prominently in the modern economy. They possessed attributes which could not be measured by their values as items of exchange. Treasures

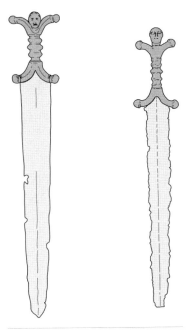

Figure 19. Two Iron Age anthropoid swords found in England. Information from Stead (2006).

might include worn and broken objects as well as newly made ones. Taken together, they signified the social positions of the actors, or their relationships to other people, extending back into the past. They might have possessed them on a temporary basis and their uses could even have been restricted to certain social transactions. In the *Nibelungenlied* an obvious example is the use of Queen Kriemhild's dowry which was assembled for a marriage that had ended when her husband died.

At the same time objects could be imbued with a kind of animation, so that they might have been considered as agents in their own right (Descola 2003, 6; Gosden 2005; Alberti & Marshall 2009; Myrberg Burström 2015). They shared some of the attributes of living creatures.

During the later 1st millennium AD the spirits of the gods and dead were considered to own all material possessions (Androshchuk 2010). The earthly roles of such objects were the result of a covenant between people and the supernatural. The obvious instance of such an artefact is the ring that occasions so much destruction in the course of Wagner's operas, but this was the composer's own interpretation of a variety of ancient sources. A better example is the power exerted by the dragon's treasure in the epic poem *Beowulf*. Its importance was due to its history rather than its fine condition, for the poem emphasises the point that the metal in the hoard was rusty and old. It had been kept intact for many generations, but when its contents were disturbed the consequences were so severe that they led to the hero's death.

In each case these problems drew the same response. The objects had to be taken out of circulation. This could happen for several reasons. It might have been done to curtail their powers and to contain any threats they posed: the ring that Alberich made is one obvious example. It could have happened to prevent artefacts brought together for special purposes from entering the wider economy and circulating as portable wealth. Valuable metalwork could have been melted down; that was clearly a risk with Kriemhild's dowry. Her treasure would have made Hagen rich, but for the queen and her brother its special character would only be protected by taking it out of circulation. For that reason they planned to dump it in the Rhine.

If the principle is easy to understand, it does not explain the different ways in which it was achieved.

Profiting from loss

Strictly speaking, casual losses are impossible to study by archaeological methods, but groups of artefacts hidden or stored together are another matter. In this case the essential feature is that they were never retrieved, but a recent study by Mats Burström (2012) takes a novel approach. His book *Treasured Memories* investigates the personal possessions buried by refugees from Estonia at the time of the Soviet invasion. Some of these people could be traced and recorded their recollections, and in certain instances – but by no means all – it was possible to rediscover the deposits they had left behind many years before. One obvious finding of this research is that it was difficult and sometimes impossible to locate their property after such a long period had elapsed. Memories were not so sharp, drawn and written records were harder to understand, and often the local topography had altered since the deposits were hidden. Buildings had been demolished and new ones had taken their place.

That was hardly surprising, but what did emerge from this research was the distinctive character of the things that were concealed, for few bear any resemblance to the kinds of valuables discussed by archaeologists, which are usually coins and precious metalwork. Among the things that did receive special treatment were history books written in Estonian, diaries and sporting trophies, but far more common were domestic items associated with the everyday practices of consuming food and drink – cooking utensils, pots and pans, glasses, cutlery and china. As Burström argues, they recalled the routines of family life. These items also stood for the friends and relatives who had been dispersed. It was understandable that the obvious place for people to deposit such collections was the soil that provided their livelihood. 'One reason may be connected with a desire to demonstrate a true depth of belonging' (Burström 2012, 110). The title of his book is particularly apt. These items may have been treasures, but they were most important as a source of memories. The attachment between people and things was much more powerful than an economic interpretation of such collections might suppose.

His study is unusual because it can demonstrate a direct relationship between political events, the hiding of valuables, and the character of the things that were concealed. It is based on first hand testimony, where most arguments of this kind must depend on inference, for example the correlation that is often suggested between episodes of warfare and the burial of coin hoards in the past. That is not to say that such interpretations need be wrong – it is the best explanation of the deposits of goldwork in the Low Countries which date to the time of Caesar's invasion of Gaul (Roymans & Scheers 2012) – but in periods about which less is known this approach can lead to a circular argument by which periods of crisis are identified from peaks in the deposition of valuables. At the same time these crises are used to explain why so many items were hidden.

The texts referred to earlier suggest a difference between two other reasons for depositing distinctive artefacts. One was that 'they could be removed from circulation to protect (or even extinguish) their special powers'. In that case 'it was important that certain objects should not become private wealth'. Alternatively, 'they were intended for transmission to another world, either as gifts to the supernatural or to provide for the dead in an afterlife'. Is it possible for archaeologists to apply this distinction in their research, or could these practices have overlapped?

One important distinction applies to the artefacts deposited in water as well as those in dry land. Certain objects were broken with unusual force and may be represented only by fragments. Others remained intact and could even have been repaired or re-sharpened immediately before they were discarded. On a superficial level this would suggest that some items were prepared for use in the Otherworld, while the remainder were disabled in order to bring their lives to an end. There are difficulties with both these positions.

The maintenance of particular objects certainly suggests that their careers were not yet over. They could still be used – and used to even greater effect than before. But who were the beneficiaries? Where such objects were deposited in graves it is tempting to say that they would accompany the deceased to the afterlife, yet the same treatment extended to objects that were deposited in isolation or in hoards accompanied by other artefacts. One possibility is that they were offerings to be used by supernatural beings. Another is that they retained an association with particular people but did not accompany their bodies to the grave. That might explain why river metalwork retained its importance in regions with little evidence of a normative burial rite (Fig. 20). Just as important, these objects may have been employed in mortuary rituals but were separated from the

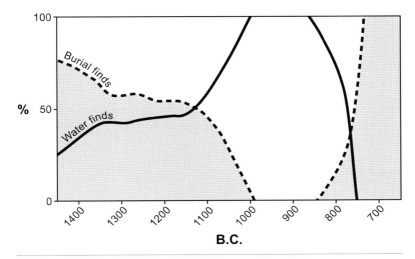

Figure 20. The changing contexts of metalwork finds from the Rhine at Roxheim, Germany, and the surrounding area. As fewer artefacts were associated with the dead, more were placed in water. The relationship changed again at the beginning of the Iron Age. Information from Sperber (2006).

corpse before it was burnt on the pyre. This argument has the virtue of explaining why finds of intact weapons and ornaments play such an important role in the archaeology of the Urnfield period when cremation was widely practiced in Europe (Sperber 2006).

This is not a new idea, but it misses an important point. As Chapter 5 has suggested, furnished graves were themselves a kind of deposit, albeit one which might contain a different selection of artefacts from those associated with terrestrial hoards or with water. It may be a mistake to treat these gifts to the dead as a separate field of study. It happens because researchers privilege human remains above other kinds of evidence. Their presence identifies certain features as 'mortuary deposits', while their absence is the defining characteristic of separate classes of material (Brück 2001). That distinction would lose much of its force if researchers were to follow

Stuart Needham's suggestion in an unpublished series of lectures to the Society of Antiquaries of Scotland that during the Early Bronze Age furnished burials were a way of presenting exemplary individuals to the ancestors. Similarly, if certain artefacts were animated in their own right they might share characteristics with the people who had used them. Assuming that artefacts had personalities and exerted a kind of agency, the distinction between funeral assemblages and other groups of objects would lose its central role in archaeological writing. So would the distinction between graves in which a body was buried wearing ornaments, and hoards in which a similar set of artefacts was deposited.

The same applies to the distinction that is sometimes made between votive offerings and sacrifices. This is a more difficult point as neither of these terms is defined in a consistent manner. At one time it seemed as if sacrificial deposits had to include living matter – that was the position advocated in *The Passage of Arms* – whilst votive deposits were inanimate. The field evidence makes that position untenable. Portable artefacts are often found with human and animal remains, but the argument is weakened even further by the possibility that certain artefacts had been imbued with life. A more important characteristic is that sacrifice can involve the use of violence as living beings are removed from this world to make the transition to another one (Insoll 2012). If particular artefacts were considered in the same terms, their destruction need not have been intended to prevent their use. Instead they could have been killed just like people and livestock. That would explain their violent treatment. The best example is provided by the deposits formed after Iron Age battles, for it is clear that enemy weapons were destroyed in similar ways to the bodies of defeated warriors. Classical sources represent this as a sacrificial act (Grane 2003). No distinction was made between the treatment of the artefacts, their owners or their animals. At the same time any object that became a sacrificial offering was necessarily removed from circulation, so that it could never have become private wealth.

For Marcel Mauss sacrifice was a form of exchange between people and supernatural powers (Mauss 1925). It would be conducted in the hope of a return. In Northern Europe at the end of the 1st millennium AD a further element was probably important. Androschuck (2010) has argued that during the Viking Age the gods were the true owners of all the portable wealth on earth. It follows that people had only temporary custody of valuable objects. By sacrificing them to supernatural beings they were actually returning them to their source. This is similar to the more mundane principle of *heriot* in Anglo-Saxon England which was important between the 9th and 11th centuries AD (Härke 2000). It ensured that a lord would equip his followers with weapons, but in time they must be given back to him.

Sometimes these changes of status took place at public events that provided an opportunity for conspicuous consumption. Chris Gregory (2015) has suggested that the provision of gifts to the gods offers a source of prestige that is harder to achieve through the normal process of exchange. When particular gifts pass between the actors over time, there is usually a degree of reciprocity. Unless one of the parties trumps the others by an exceptional display of generosity a balanced relationship is maintained between them. That is because the gifts must be returned, providing little scope for competition or unlimited accumulation. On the other hand, where people make offerings to otherworldly powers there is no expectation that they will be returned in the same form. Certain items are taken out of circulation in perpetuity. It presents an opportunity for acts of lavish consumption without the risk that balance will be restored as each gift is matched by an appropriate counter-gift. That is one way of converting valuables into prestige.

Again there are problems with this argument which was probably over-emphasised in *The Passage of Arms* (Bradley 1998[1990]). The first is that most calculations of the rate at which complex artefacts were deposited arrive at very low numbers. Such processes took place only occasionally and probably on quite a small scale. The idea of a public spectacle has probably been taken too far. On the other hand, that is not to deny that there were some significant exceptions. The deposition of large collections of artefacts in dryland hoards may have made a greater impact, especially if their contents had been displayed before they were buried – a suggestion which was discussed in Chapter 5. The Iron Age sacrifices of war gear in Western and Northern Europe provide another instance as they seem to have taken place after a battle, but such lavish destruction of artefacts, animals and human bodies can hardly represent the norm. For that reason they do not provide any basis for a wider model. Most hoards and water finds would have been the outcome of less dramatic events.

Exquisite corpses

The point of departure for this chapter was a series of literary references to the disposal of valuables written down in the early Middle Ages. While they may shed some light on broader questions of interpretation, they leave out many elements. The best way of redressing the balance is to focus on information from a much earlier period. Some insights are provided by the Classical writers whose accounts were reviewed in Chapter 2, but in this case it is the archaeological evidence that is decisive.

As Chapter 4 has shown, deposits of weapons, ornaments and other artefacts are sometimes found together with human and animal bones, although just as often they appear in apparent isolation. In the same way there are the remains of people and their livestock in contexts that include few, if any artefacts. That evidence is especially striking in the case of a site like Skedemosse. It is rightly famous for its deposits of metalwork, but in an earlier phase it was where horses were sacrificed. Recent work has shown that it was used in the same way once the deposition of valuables had ceased (Monikander 2010). It was not alone in this respect (Pauli Jensen 2009). Such evidence suggests another perspective on wetland and dryland deposits. Perhaps their longest running feature was the sacrifice of living creatures, and the accumulations of metalwork which have attracted so much attention were merely episodes in a longer history.

That is consistent with the chronological evidence which shows that deposits of metal declined during the period between the end of the Bronze Age and the principal collections of war booty that date from the early years of the 1st millennium AD. During that interval wetland deposits were by no means absent. Perhaps the best known are the bog bodies whose history focuses on the period between 500 BC and AD 200 (Van Der Sanden 1996; Ravn 2010; Aldhouse-Green 2015). Both literary and archaeological evidence show that these were the remains of people who had been killed in unusual ways. Their heads could have been shaved; they could have been stripped of their clothes; and considerable effect was made to weigh down the corpses in the water. It is not known how the victims were selected. Tacitus says that they were transgressors or outcasts (Grane 2003), but in other cases they could have been selected for different reasons. They may have possessed unusual physical features, and not all their bodies showed the usual signs of manual labour. They may have been carefully chosen from a wider community – exquisite corpses indeed.

It seems possible that the bodies placed in Iron Age storage pits played a similar role and, taken together, the distributions of these phenomena extend across large parts of Northern and Western Europe (Fig. 21; Williams 2003). The comparison is especially apt as these features were directly linked with the productivity of the land. Grain was gathered from the fields, processed and buried underground. It grew again after the winter. This provided an obvious metaphor for regeneration. It may be no accident that bog corpses could be placed in abandoned peat cuttings (Christensen 2003). Perhaps these were convenient places in which to dispose of a corpse – for many years that same argument was applied to grain silos – but it might be no accident that peat provided building material and fuel and was remarkably fertile. It may be why Tacitus emphasised the role of Nerthus as the goddess of fertility and why bog deposits of the same date contain pieces of agricultural equipment such as ploughs (Glob 1951). They are often found with pots containing food (Becker 1971). The same concerns were already evident in the Bronze Age when many hoards in Central and Northern Europe contained standard units of metal in the form of sickles.

The implications of these arguments are clear. There seems little doubt that the people who were killed so violently and by unusual

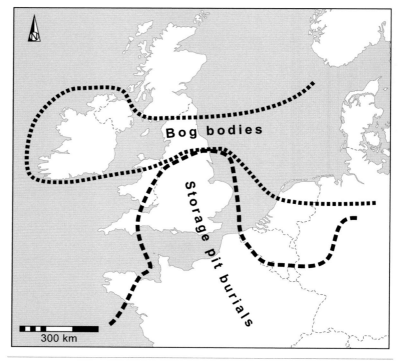

Figure 21. The distributions of Iron Age pit burials and bog bodies in Northern and Western Europe. Information from Bradley et al. (2016).

methods were sacrificial victims. If that is true, the same argument should apply to the animals whose remains were deposited in similar locations. It makes no difference whether their flesh had been consumed before that happened or whether entire bodies were placed in the water. It is logical to regard the agricultural equipment found in bogs as part of the same system. Such practices continued alongside more spectacular deposits of valuables and occasionally went on after those episodes were over.

What of the origins of these distinctive practices? Here the evidence is much more limited, but in Northern Europe Mesolithic and Neolithic deposits in wetlands share several features in common with those of the pre-Roman and early Roman Iron Ages. They include deposits of animal remains, stone axes, querns and amber beads and, as Chapter 4 has shown, again there are pots containing food (Koch 1998). Even the oldest deposits contain ceramics and axeheads. Perhaps less well known are a number of bodies interpreted as those of human sacrifices (Bennike & Ebbesen 1986). These collections predate the general currency of metalwork, and it is unfortunate that it is that category of material that has attracted the attention of prehistorians at the expense of the wider phenomenon of which it was only one part. The remains of people and animals were at least as important as the objects they used and provide a very different perspective from the operatic behaviour with which this chapter began.

CHAPTER NINE

A Guide to Strange Places

Naming places

Susan Möller-Wiering's (2011, 3, note 1) study of textiles from deposits of war booty in Germany and Denmark contains an interesting comment:

> '[Their] names do not refer to settlements but to landscape elements – a hill (Thorsberg), a pond (Nydam), a bog (Vimose) and a valley (Illerup Ådal)'.

It is obvious that local topography assumed a special importance in the past. Thus the names of significant locations near Gudme included 'the home of the gods', 'the hill of sacrifices', 'the hill of gatherings', and Galbjerg, 'the hill of magic' (Hedeager 2011, 173). Elsewhere in Northern Europe there are *theophoric* place names which link such features with supernatural beings. Among them there were parts of the domestic landscape such as meadows or arable land. There are references to human constructions – ancient monuments, cemeteries and heaps of stone – but the majority describe natural elements. The commonest are mountains, hills, islands, rivers, lakes and springs. Their special significance is obvious because so many of these places were associated with divinities (Jakobson 1996, 91–93; Brink 2008; Forsgren 2010, 117–19). Examples include: Tissø, 'the lake of Tyr'; Odensjö, 'the lake of Odin'; Gudingsåkrarna, 'the holy fields of the gods'; the islands named after Njärd and Frö; the Norwegian river Gudå, which was 'consecrated to the gods'; and the Danish Gudenå, which is also 'God's river' (Frost 2013). Similarly, the element 'Ull' refers to a spirit associated with lakes, bogs, bays, islands and bridges. Christina Fredengren (2011) has suggested a more direct relationship between such places and the character of the offerings made there. Thus places associated with Odin were characterised by flowing water and contained male equipment like swords. By contrast, female ornaments were deposited in areas of still water, so that the Swedish name Gullrings Kärret refers to 'the marsh of the golden rings'.

Archaeologists have been less sensitive to the natural topography, preferring to consider it as the background to other elements which they are better equipped to study. Thus monuments like megalithic tombs might be aligned on mountaintops; springs are important as places for hunting animals; and hillforts are generally investigated in preference to hills. There are many reasons why this has happened, but perhaps the most important is that people who live in a densely inhabited modern landscape are losing the ability to recognise subtle differences in the world around them.

Again names provide some of the clearest indications of which elements are overlooked. In his new book *Landmarks* Robert Macfarlane (2015) discusses the work of a number of authors who have written about the natural world, juxtaposing his account with nine glossaries that record terms for places and processes that are rarely observed today. He documents 2000 examples, yet his lists are restricted to Britain and Ireland. They draw on local dialects and languages as well as more technical vocabularies and describe many of the same elements as theophoric names in Northern Europe.

Four of Macfarlane's glossaries of local terms are particularly relevant here. In his scheme they refer to 'Flatlands' (a total of nearly 200 entries), 'Uplands' (another 180 or so), 'Waterlands' (almost 300 words), and a smaller sample that he associates with 'Underlands'. The details of these lists are important, although some of his categories overlap. Thirty five percent of the entries in the text describing 'Flatlands' refer to areas of wet ground. Another list concerns what the author calls 'Waterlands', and here his scheme has something in common with the perception of the environment documented by Scandinavian place names. The surface of the water accounts for just 17 entries, but no fewer than 83 describe flowing water. Pools, ponds and lakes account for 30 more entries; there are 27 terms that refer to riverbanks; and a further 11 describe springs and wells.

Macfarlane's list of words for 'Uplands' contains 72 terms describing hills and peaks, 31 describing slopes and 28 for valleys and passes. There are fewer entries in his glossary for 'Underlands', but it includes 32 words referring to pits, caves and holes. All the lists contain other elements which relate to human constructions, but the sheer number of overlapping terms, many of them almost forgotten, must shed some light on how landscapes were perceived in the past. One element certainly stands out. The features that were most closely observed are similar to those that attracted attention between the Neolithic period and the Viking Age in Britain. Allowing that the lists are a personal selection by the writer, the commonest components in descending order of frequency are: moving water, wet ground, hills, slopes and, finally, pools, ponds and lakes. Valleys, passes and riverbanks are also important.

This discussion helps to explain how I chose the title of the chapter. *A Guide to Strange Places* was originally the name of an orchestral piece written by the American composer John Adams in 2001. It is appropriate here since the principal subject of my account is the variety of locations selected for votive deposits. It soon becomes obvious that some of them were very strange indeed. A good place to begin is the cave system at Han-sur-Lesse.

Going under

According to its website, the system of underground caves at Han-sur-Less near Namur is one of the main tourist attractions in Belgium, and as a natural curiosity it attracts half a million people a year (www.grotte-de-han.be/enthe-tour). Visitors are taken there on 'a century old tram'. From the entrance they follow the course of the River Lesse as it passes beneath a limestone hill. Their guided tour involves a *son et lumière* which exploits the spectacular formations within the caverns. Some of the chambers have evocative names – the Hall of Weapons, the Mysterious Room, the Trophy and the Styx. Finally, after 2 km the visitors emerge into daylight. At this point the website says that they 'will relive a scene of an offering from the lives of our ancestors and feel the vault vibrating to the sound of [a] famous and indispensable gunshot'.

The gunshot adds a theatrical element to the display, but the reference to ancestral offerings is based on reliable information, for the underground river and its margins are associated with one of the largest and most thoroughly researched collections of prehistoric artefacts in Belgium (Fig. 22; Warmenbol 1996; 1999). Although the

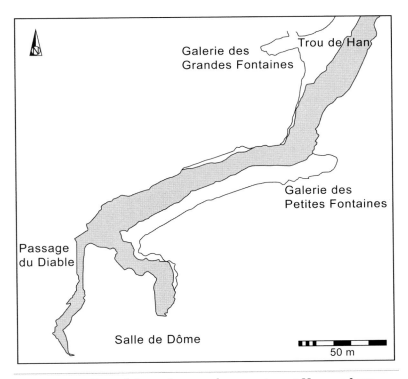

Figure 22. Part of the underground cave system at Han-sur-Lesse, Belgium, showing some of the main locations in which artefacts have been discovered. The shaded area represents the present course of the river. Information from Warmenbol (1996).

caves are best known for their Late Bronze Age phase, this material had a longer history, extending from the Neolithic to the Iron Age and Roman periods, and some of the artefacts dating from those episodes are as notable as the prehistoric metalwork found there. In an early phase this was the findspot of an axe imported from Mont Viso in the Alps and a Grand Pressigny dagger from western France. Somewhat oddly, the end of the sequence was associated with a Roman military diploma.

The underground river has changed its course over time. Some archaeological material has been recovered from dry land at the edge of the channel, but the majority was found by divers. At one time it seemed possible that this was the site of a settlement or a place of refuge, but the character and variety of the artefacts make this most unlikely. The same applies to the idea that the Late Bronze Age metalwork was stored underground by a smith. One reason for suggesting that the cave system played a more specialised role is the presence of human remains, the oldest of which date from the Neolithic period and may have been contemporary with a series of distinctive artefacts. The argument applies to other human bones found in excavation which radiocarbon dating shows were placed there in Late Iron Age and Roman times. That method also investigated a sequence of deposits left exposed a hundred years ago. The new dates raise the possibility of a continuous human presence extending over three millennia from about 3000 BC; that is a minimum estimate as sediments contemporary with the Roman use of Han-sur-Lesse did not survive (Warmenbol 2012). The results of this study are particularly striking since the finds of dateable artefacts cluster in just three phases: the end of the Neolithic, the Late Bronze Age and the Late Iron Age and Roman periods.

The artefact assemblage from Han-sur-Lesse is very unusual, and never more so than in the Late Bronze Age. Large numbers of objects have been recorded by diving and by excavation, but, taken as a whole, the assemblage has few close counterparts in Belgium or elsewhere. Many of the smaller items are broken and burnt. There are finds of tools, and weapons including a few swords and spearheads and 100 metal arrowheads. There are about 15 knives, 20 axes, and artefacts associated with metalworking. The jewellery, some of which is made of gold, is even more distinctive. It includes small discs, hair ornaments, a considerable collection of rings, and over 200 pins.

Their contexts are revealing. Intact weapons were found in the river, but swords and spears were comparatively uncommon there. Arrowheads – some of exceptional quality – occurred in remarkable numbers, but at other sites they are rare. At Han-sur-Lesse the water contained a quantity of tools. The ornaments present more of a problem. In this case the best parallels come from other caves in the region where they occur together with human remains, but their findspots were different as those places were dry. In any case the sheer variety of ornaments discovered in or beside the underground river is altogether exceptional. By comparison the later artefacts are fairly ordinary. Among them are brooches, but there was a fine decorated disc or *phalera* dated to the early La Tène period. The Iron Age and Roman objects included pieces made from glass and amber, as well as coins. There were also the jaws of young people who had been decapitated.

Eugène Warmenbol emphasises the importance of such discoveries of human remains. Unburnt bones were present in the Neolithic, Iron Age and Roman phases on the site, but, with a single exception, they have not been identified in Late Bronze Age contexts. That is hardly surprising as the dead were cremated during this period. As he says, it is most unlikely that their ashes would survive if they had entered the river together with the artefacts – they would have washed away.

He discusses the interpretation of Han-sur-Lesse in a series of articles with evocative titles. In translation, they include: 'The sun of the dead' (Warmenbol 1999), and 'Gold, death and the Hyperboreans: the mouth of hell at Le Trou de Han' (Warmenbol 1996). He observes that the principal concentration of artefacts is found where the river goes underground and the light of the sun disappears. There is circumstantial evidence that there had been a wooden platform at this location, but, if so, its date is not known. The finds associated with the interior, at least during the Neolithic and Late Bronze Age phases, include the kinds of objects buried with the dead. For Warmenbol this was an entrance to the Otherworld.

Although the cave system at Han-sur-Lesse lacks an exact parallel, there are features that recall wider interpretations in archaeology. Warmenbol rightly focuses on the unusual collection of gold ornaments from the site. Like other scholars, he suggests that these distinctive objects might have referred to the sun: a connection that is obviously supported by their distinctive raw material and their curvilinear decoration. The same argument should apply to the Iron Age *phalera*. He is not alone in suggesting that the movement of the sun was important in ancient belief and in a new study of the scenes depicted on Bronze Age razors in Northern Europe (Warmenbol 2015) he considers how the solar cycle was understood. During the day the sun moved across the sky drawn by a horse, and then it returned to its starting point so the process could begin again. During the hours of darkness it was hidden from sight and travelled underwater. Is it possible that the topography of Han-sur-Lesse was understood in a similar way, for it combined solar symbols with the same three elements: darkness, light and water? There is the additional point that the river itself disappears. It would have added to the mysterious character of this place.

Going further

Han-sur-Lesse is obviously an unusual and spectacular location, just as its prehistoric and Roman archaeologies are exceptional, but was it entirely typical of the strange places where offerings were made? That question is difficult to answer, for, rather unexpectedly, the caves combine the most striking attributes of sacred sites in Northern Europe, where water was important, with those in the South, where mountains and rock formations played an equally significant role. That contrast is explored in the discussion that follows.

One reason why it has been so hard to widen the debate from matters of detail to more general issues is that studies of ancient artefacts outnumber any analyses of the places where they were found.

They can be restricted to individual collections or to comparatively small regions. Worse still, they are generally written by, and for, period specialists so that the most important issues are not considered at an appropriate scale. Although there have been detailed studies of the siting of hoards within small parts of Europe, it remains a challenge to establish how widely the same conventions were observed (Hansen *et al.* 2012). The best solution is to offer a broad review of the information from two contrasting parts of the continent and to observe any similarities and differences between them. In each case the emphasis should be not on the details of individual periods but on the existence of a longer sequence.

Following the account of Han-sur-Lesse, it is logical to begin this review with recent work elsewhere in Northern and Western Europe. How far do its results document similar practices? And did they remain consistent over time? The opposite pole in such studies is provided by research in Southern Europe where similar questions have been asked by archaeologists investigating the deposition of artefacts, human remains and animal bones. One reason for making this comparison is that there are obvious contrasts in the makeup of the archaeological record, but another issue is highlighted by the discussion of place names with which this chapter began. The landscapes in these parts of Europe do show certain contrasts and as a result distinctive types of locations might have been given special meanings in one region where it may not have happened to the same extent elsewhere. A simple example is the significance of high mountains, passes, caves and rock fissures in the South. While similar features do occur in other areas, the range of topographic variation is not the same. By contrast, the extensive lowlands and bogs of Denmark, the Netherlands and the North European Plain occupy a more prominent position than they do in the geography of Southern Europe; the obvious exception is the Po Valley. This is not an absolute contrast but a matter of degree. Nonetheless such differences probably were significant, and this is surely reflected by the distinctive sequences identified in these two areas. The focus on those regions does not mean that others can be overlooked. Their archaeology may resemble either or both of those models.

In theory this section ought to provide a straightforward chronological narrative, following the history of various kinds of offerings from one phase to another. In practice that is scarcely feasible and there is a good reason for taking a different approach. This is the surprising discovery that *the locations where deposits were made hardly changed over time*. Despite lengthy intervals in which they might have been neglected, the same kinds of places were used again and again. In some instances the gaps were so long that it must have been the distinctive character of those sites that attracted attention – it seems unlikely that their original significance could be remembered in detail. There may have been important differences between aquatic and terrestrial contexts, but they are not sufficiently subtle to show why particular locations were selected. Wherever possible, this account considers material introduced in earlier parts of this book.

Such considerations have already featured here. Chapter 2 not only compared the anecdotal explanations that were offered for a Late Bronze Age hoard and a Viking hoard in a similar setting, it took the same approach to the Iron Age metalwork from the lake edge at La Tène and the Roman artefacts from the Rhine. In the same way, the Broadward hoard was associated with the very same spring as a series of later deposits. Another excavated spring at Röekillorna was used on at least two occasions, during the Neolithic period and almost three thousand years afterwards in the Iron Age. In the light of such comparisons, the best procedure is to highlight the features that identified suitable places for making special deposits. It seems as if they remained much the same from the Neolithic period (or even earlier) through to the Viking Age.

Northern lights

These deposits had a lengthy history in the North and West, but their character was by no means uniform. To some extent the nature of votive offerings changed within the Roman world and here traditional practices gradually resumed during the later 1st millennium AD. Beyond the frontiers of the Empire, they show more continuity. In each case they overlapped with the adoption of Christian beliefs and remained important until about AD 1000.

The starting point for this discussion was the Belgian site of Han-sur-Lesse which combined a river and a series of caves, but it was water that seems to have been the main characteristic of votive deposits in Northern and Western Europe. As Chapter 2 has observed, distinguishing between aquatic and terrestrial finds is not a simple matter. For a long time it seemed that the difference between artefacts from water and those discovered on dry land would have a bearing on how they should be interpreted, but recent work has shown that this contrast is not sufficiently subtle. It does not take into account the sheer variety of wet locations, nor does it pay enough attention to the relationship between the findspots on the ground – many of the discoveries were made close to water but not within it.

Nor did the conventional contrast pay enough attention to the distinctions between *different kinds of water*. This question has been addressed in a series of studies from Scandinavia to Ireland (Fontijn 2003; Yates & Bradley 2010b; Fredengren 2011; Becker 2013). Consider the case of rivers containing valuables. They had distinctive characteristics. They originated from springs, bogs and lakes and eventually discharged into the sea. They could have been joined by tributaries and crossed by bridges, causeways or fords. All these places can be associated with concentrations of finds. Their channels might flow through marshy ground where different objects from those in the main channel were deposited, and in rare cases they were confined to a narrow valley or a gorge. Occasionally they passed over cataracts, or disappeared underground as happened at Han-sur-Lesse. Sometimes archaeological material was confined to their upper reaches and in other cases it was commoner as they approached the sea. It could also happen where the burden of sediment meant that the colour of the water changed.

Beyond the principal channels there might be bays and lakes, or pools that marked the position of an earlier river course. These were also areas of still water. Over time some of those environments changed their character as waterborne sediments dried out. Bogs and marshes developed and the position of the riverbank moved. All these features were important in discussing finds not only from water but also those from the land beside it. From at least the Neolithic period local areas of raised ground might offer vantage points over confluences, pools and springs (Fig. 23). They could also indicate the positions of offerings beneath the water.

These distinctions were recorded by place names and seem to have been significant. They are obviously reflected by the character of the archaeological record. For example, Christina Fredengren's (2011)

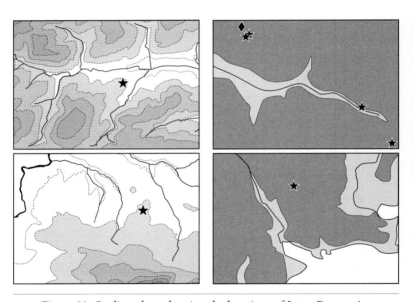

Figure 23. Outline plans showing the locations of Later Bronze Age metalwork hoards in south-east England (stars), and position of a nearby settlement (lozenge). In the two maps on the left the artefacts were deposited on spurs overlooking lower ground or a confluence. Contours are at 50 m intervals. In the maps on the right they are shown in relation to areas of dry ground (darker shading) and alluvium (lighter shading). In this case the findspots were more directly associated with streams. Information from Yates and Bradley (2010b).

suggestion that weapons were associated with major channels and ornaments with still water is supported by independent observations in Germany (Kubach 1979), Ireland (Becker 2013) and the south of England (Yates & Bradley 2010a). What is striking is that this contrast is not restricted to one phase. In the same way, the importance of confluences as a focus for votive deposits has been recognised by separate studies in Britain (Yates & Bradley 2010a), Denmark (Frost 2013) and the Netherlands (Fontijn 2003). Springs were another feature selected for offerings throughout Northern and Western Europe. As the finds from Röekillorna showed, they could be used more than once and not necessarily during a single period (Sternqvist 1997).

Bogs and marshes might have been subject to flooding which made them difficult to access for parts of the year. They had distinctive contents which could be quite different from those of major rivers and their tributaries. In Ireland, for example, the first copper and bronze artefacts were placed in bogs, while later examples are in rivers (Needham 1988). Many collections come from the dry ground close to the water's edge. That is clear from Rundqvist's work in Middle Sweden. He also emphasises the importance of the ancient coastline and the places where freshwater entered the sea (Rundqvist 2015). The margins of lakes and pools were important too. The clearest illustration is the excavated sanctuary at Oberdorla where a series of wooden enclosures and altars followed the water's edge (Behm-Blancke 2003).

Islands were equally significant, for example the famous site of Helgö whose name suggests that it possessed a sacred character (Arrhenius 2011), or the Welsh votive deposit of Llyn Cerrig Bach (MacDonald 2007). The same could apply to artificial islands like Irish crannogs which are sometimes associated with deposits of metalwork and finds of human remains (Fredengren 2002). On a still smaller scale the argument applies to wooden constructions and marker posts in areas of ancient wetland which are occasionally associated with animal bones and human skulls (Schulting & Bradley 2013, 54–59). Iron Age bog bodies are found in similar environments and so are finds of agricultural equipment and pots containing food (Glob 1951;

Becker 1971). Still more examples can be found by wooden trackways leading through treacherous wetlands. Their positions might be indicated by anthropomorphic sculptures like those found in votive deposits (Brunning & McDermott 2013, 369–70).

Some features associated with special deposits bring together the elements of land and water. Examples include ponds and wells, both of which played a prominent role from the later Bronze Age onwards. As Chapter 10 will explain, bridges were equally important from that time and assumed even greater significance during later periods. Early examples include those at Eton Rowing Lake which were found with human remains (Allen *et al.* 2000). Even clearer evidence comes from the Viking Age when their construction was commemorated by runestones (Lund 2008). Causeways like the example at Fiskerton in eastern England may have had a similar importance (Field & Parker Pearson 2003).

The details of many of these deposits have featured in earlier chapters. What is important is to emphasise the distinctive nature of these settings. It is not enough to characterise their contents as 'water finds'. In fact they come from a comparatively limited range of places. That is true from Neolithic deposits of pots and axes to the Late Iron Age weapons in rivers, and it may be no accident that so many discoveries occur in similar locations. That is surely why successive deposits of war booty are frequently found together and why a few of those sites, like Skedemosse, had already been used for sacrificing animals (Monikander 2010).

The common elements seem to be these. The main findspots are where the water changed its character. They included areas that were subject to seasonal inundation, springs, eddies, cataracts, confluences and estuaries. They could also feature places where it had unusual physical attributes. It might change colour; it might contain unusual minerals; or freshwater might be mixed with saltwater towards the coast. At least as often it created an obstacle that needed to be crossed. The water might be deep or shallow, still or fast-moving, but the distribution of archaeological material, from at least the Neolithic period to the Iron Age focused on certain favoured locations. The simple distinction between water finds and terrestrial deposits does not explain why that happened.

Many of the dryland finds in Northern and Western Europe were near to water, but others were in more remote locations. One series followed the seashore and emphasised the importance of promontories and cliffs. They became particularly important from the end of the Bronze Age to the Viking Age. Other specialised deposits were further inland. This is especially obvious in southern England where finds of Middle and Late Bronze Age metalwork are recorded along watersheds (David Dunkin & David Yates pers. comm.). Other finds were more directly associated with hills, although the evidence from the late pre-Roman Iron Age suggests that they were not necessarily on their highest points. Their positions on the brow might have been identified from below, and sites like the sanctuary at Snettisham commanded a vista over the surrounding land. Such views may have favoured certain directions – towards the east in the case of coin hoards (De Jersey 2014, chapter 5), and northwards towards the Wash for hoards of fine metalwork in part of East Anglia (Hutcheson 2004).

It had happened before. In Early Bronze Age Scotland a few collections of axes, knives and daggers were buried in places with dramatic views. These hoards were associated with prominent boulders, outcrops and natural mounds (Cowie 2004). Other deposits of metalwork are found at older barrows, and with the passage of time it may have been difficult to distinguish between them and features of the natural geology. The same applied to the relationship between conspicuous rock formations, caves and the sites of megalithic tombs. All these places were associated with deposits of metalwork extending from the Early Bronze Age to at least the Migration Period, but, compared with the situation in Southern Europe, the choice of such locations was comparatively rare.

A weakness of this analysis is that some of the most significant locations can only be identified from literary evidence. That is particularly true in the case of sacred groves in Northern Europe, where they have been recognised from place names. In one case, at

Lunda in Sweden, this has been substantiated by excavation which revealed a series of small stone settings associated with burnt deposits, arrowheads, knives and beads together with fragmentary bones that had obviously lain on the surface (Andersson 2006). They were not far outside a high status settlement. There is another case in which sacrifices might have taken place at special locations. Eamonn Kelly (2006) as suggested that Irish bog bodies were placed on territorial boundaries which can be reconstructed from documentary evidence. Of course those corpses survived because they were recovered from wet ground, but their broader setting in the landscape is even more important. Both examples suggest that the finds from terrestrial locations may be more difficult to analyse than their counterparts in water.

Southern comforts

In Southern Europe similar deposits had a different history. Here the finds of artefacts began during the Neolithic period, but after a hiatus during the Early Bronze Age their numbers increased and reached a peak during the later years of the Iron Age and the Roman period. Weapons and dress accessories featured prominently. Their deposition continued into the 4th to 6th centuries AD, and there were more finds from the River Ljubljanica between the 8th and 11th centuries AD – the overall range is like that in the North and West (Teržan 2005; Turk *et al.* 2009). Finds of swords, some of them inside their scabbards, were especially common, but their frequency diminished towards the end of this sequence. Among the latest are medieval examples which carry enigmatic signs that may have been thought to protect their owners. Again artefacts dating from several different phases can be represented in the same locations. By contrast, the dryland finds, many of which came from mountainous regions, extended from the Neolithic period to the Roman era. There were fewer of them after that time (Turk *et al.* 2009).

In common with Northern and Western Europe, special deposits in the South focused on water, but in this case there was an almost equally important emphasis on upland contexts (Bianco Peroni 1979; Fischer 1997, 85–95; Höck & Sölder 1999; Zemmer-Planck 2002). The findspots associated with water have similar characteristics to those considered already. For the most part they were springs, river channels, lakes, pools and swamps. A few were close to domestic sites in the wetlands, but, like those in the North and West, other collections of artefacts can be found at confluences away from inhabited areas. More have been identified at crossing places. There are some exceptional occurrences. For example, at one point the character of the metalwork was different on either side of the Ljubljanica (Čerče & Turk 1995, 156). In the water beside one bank there were small items such as awls; by the other bank there were axes. In between them, within the main channel, was a group of spears. Here and in the north of Italy swords were sometimes driven into the edge or bed of a river.

The water finds of Southern Europe possess a distinctive feature. From the Neolithic period onwards they can be associated with mineral springs. A particularly striking example is recorded at St Moritz where a wooden building was associated with three wells, one of which has a dendro-date of 1456 BC (Seifert 2000). They provided a source of carbonated water that is still considered to have therapeutic properties. Inside one of these features were two bronze swords, part of another blade and no fewer than 300 pins. At about the same time another series of deposits were placed inside a massive wooden cistern at the Italian site of Nocete (Bernabo Brèa & Camaschi 2009). In this case pots, figurines, models of carts and four wooden ploughs were placed in the water. Although such collections coexisted with the finds from mountainous regions, it would be easy to make too much of the differences between them, for in the same part of Italy special deposits had long been associated with thermal springs and caves containing water.

In many parts of Southern Europe there was a particular emphasis on high ground (Schauer 1980; Wyss 1996; Guidi 2014). It is also illustrated by the *Brandopferplaze* in the Alps which generally contain different material from the metalwork hoards (Primas *et al.* 2001; Steiner 2010). Burnt offering sites are found close to settlements, but the other deposits occur in quite specific places. They are associated with high mountains – far higher peaks than the small selection of findspots in the North and West. They have been discovered on or close to summits up to 2500 m above sea level, on isolated rock pinnacles and amidst what have been described as 'wild plateaus'. They can be associated with prominent outcrops and blockfields where movement across the terrain would have been especially difficult. They are also found at the mouths of gorges and the foot of cliffs (Fig. 24; Čerče & Turk 1995; Soroceanu 2012).

Routes through the uplands were vitally important and their courses are sometimes indicated by finds of metalwork. A special feature of these regions is the significant number of artefacts from mountain passes, among them Iron Age helmets. These deposits do not have many equivalents in Western and Northern Europe (Wyss 1996). The same applies to discoveries of artefacts associated with burnt human and animal bones inside caves and rock fissures (Schauer 1980). It would be easy to mistake these places for seasonally occupied settlements, but such deposits were in positions that were

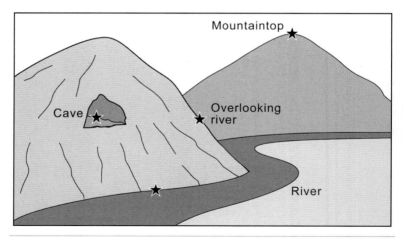

Figure 24. Typical locations for metalwork deposits in Rumania, including hilltops, caves and riverbanks. Information from Soroceanu (1995; 2012.)

virtually inaccessible. They were far removed from the domestic sites of the same date. That even applies to the by-products of Bronze Age metalworking which were dropped into cavities or crevasses that extended vertically into the bedrock. They might have been associated with the activities of smiths, but it is improbable that the metal was worked where these remains are found. Amber was deposited in the same locations. Most of the finds from caves date between about 1000 and 300 BC, but the sequence began in the Neolithic period and continued into Late Roman times when such places included burials and collections of coins.

A good example of one of these locations is the 'holy abyss' of Škocjan which contained a series of weapons and other items which had been damaged, broken and burnt (Čerče & Turk 1995). Among them were helmets, greaves, swords, spears and bronze vessels. Another is provided by two hoards from Kanalski Vrh in Slovenia (Žbona & Trkman-Bavdek 1995). One was found close to the summit of a 715 m high mountain in an area characterised by natural cavities and by blocks of stone up to 3 m high. In between two of the rocks was a collection of Late Bronze Age metalwork, containing a curious mixture of utilitarian and decorative items. They were inside a ceramic container with a group of ingots at its base. The collection included three axes, five phalerae, seven torcs, over 100 ornaments and 25 kg of bronze. Not far away there was a second hoard with a further 26 kg of unworked ingots. In another case a Roman helmet had been dropped into the same narrow cavity as pieces of metalwork that had been made 500 years before. Again distinctive locations attracted votive offerings during more than one period. It happened too often to be treated as a coincidence.

The wetland deposits of Southern Europe raise similar issues to those discussed in the previous section, and an obvious difference between them was a predilection for mineral springs (Guidi 2014). That was less common in the North and West. A more striking characteristic is the special importance of mountains and rock formations (Soroceanu 2012). It will be considered in greater detail in Chapter 10, but at this point one observation is very important.

Some of these deposits were on the very edge of the familiar world. They could be on exceptionally high peaks and rock formations where the earth touched the sky, or they might be in places that resemble Han-sur-Lesse which has been interpreted as an entrance to the Underworld. Caves, gorges, cavities and fissures all achieved a greater importance than they did in the West and North, and this is reflected by their distinctive contents and the ways in which they were treated. The archaeology of the South included openings leading into the earth, and peaks reaching into the sky. These features are so distinctive that they call for further research.

This account began with the remarkable site of Han-sur-Lesse for it epitomises many of the characteristics of the sacred places investigated in this chapter. It provides an excellent illustration of the problems and possibilities of studying a series of river finds. It also exploited its distinctive topography as one of the most impressive cave systems associated with later prehistoric artefacts in Europe. It is unusual for both these elements to be treated on equal terms. In the North deposits associated with water played a special role that in some cases extended as far back as the Mesolithic period and into the historical era as late as the Viking Age. The attention paid to upland landscapes was perhaps rather shorter-lived and may have focussed on a smaller variety of locations. The dramatic natural topography of Southern Europe must have had a decisive influence, but the fact that special deposits were made during the same periods from one end of the continent to the other is even more remarkable. There were many 'strange places' where specialised deposits have been identified. What is striking is not their diversity, but the extent to which they celebrated similar ideas – and dealt with similar concerns – over such enormous expanses of space and time.

A note of caution

Unfortunately, this cannot be (quite) the conclusion of this chapter, and it is right to say why such studies are – and always will be – incomplete.

The reason must be familiar from everyday experience. It is the contemporary practice of leaving flowers, messages and even small gifts in places where people have died, often suddenly and tragically. They are addressed to the dead, but the choice of location is entirely determined by the events that happened there. These informal memorials mark where accidents occurred and do not have any physical features in common. For that reason they would never be located by archaeological methods, nor would could their positions be explained by the kinds of argument put forward in this chapter. It is impossible to say whether, or how often, such collections might have formed in the past, but it would be wrong to exclude that possibility. Offerings could have been made because a particular place was where something dramatic had occurred. That could not be discovered by fieldwork. The implications are troubling and need to be kept in mind.

CHAPTER TEN

Thresholds and Transitions

Introduction

Both terms require a definition. For the purposes of this chapter *thresholds* are found where different elements were brought into contact with one another and where it was possible for people to move between them. They might be physical locations, like the edge of a lake, a riverbank, or the opening of a valley, but they could also be stages in a person's life, or even their death. The common feature is that rituals might have been required when those boundaries were crossed. This process of moving between one state or place and another is best described as a *transition* and in many cases it was accomplished by a rite of passage. Often this would have left no trace behind, but, where those thresholds achieved a physical form, offerings might be made as part of the process. In that case at least some of them can be identified.

Bridges, fords and causeways

Certain passages or thresholds might have an obvious manifestation, in which case it is quite easy to investigate their relationship with deposits of valuables. Those locations include fords, bridges, causeways or the entrances of settlements. In each case it is possible to identify a threshold in material terms, but it is more difficult to address its archaeology as the evidence is frequently ambiguous. Battles could take place at fords and bridges, and weapons might easily be lost there. The same applies to hillfort gateways where it is hard to distinguish between finds of human remains resulting from an attack, and sacrificial deposits containing similar material. Occasionally literary evidence can provide some assistance. In other cases it is useful to consider the character of the artefacts found there and the ways in which they were treated.

Examples of these relationships abound. Many of the Bronze Age weapons from Irish rivers were found in places where fords were documented in the Middle Ages. As Lorraine Bourke (2001, 120–27) has noted, they include the sites of battles described in early texts, but sometimes those encounters were by single combat. There are comparable finds from the English Fenland where Chris Evans (2002) has argued that each of the causeways leading to the Isle of Ely was associated with a concentration of metal finds. A comparable argument applies to the post alignment at Flag Fen, where most of the artefacts were deposited around the water's edge and could have been placed there before people ventured further into the wetland (Pryor 2001). During the Iron Age and Roman periods other bridges or causeways were associated with deposits of artefacts. Among the best known are the finds from La Tène and Mainz, but another is a large deposit of Roman coins recovered from the bed of the Thames beneath London Bridge where they were distributed over a limited area and associated with several statuettes (Rhodes 1991). They have been interpreted as intentional offerings (Fig. 25).

Some of these discoveries have been informative, but all too few were the result of careful excavation. It is the Viking Age that provides the clearest evidence for the significance of river crossings. Although bridges and fords are sometimes considered as the sites of battles, Julie Lund (2005) observes that few of the weapons from these places show any sign of damage; nor is there the defensive equipment which would be present if people were fighting. Some bridges might lead into important settlements, as happened at Tissø. In that case a hoard of tools was found not far away, and so were the graves of two men who had been beheaded. Similarly at the Danish site of Vaerbro a group of 19 weapons was associated with a wooden bridge communicating between a settlement and its cemetery on the opposite riverbank (Lund 2005). London Bridge remained important during this period, and here a group of Viking metalwork was deposited between AD 950 and 1050 (Wilson 1965, 50–51). Another example comes from Skerne

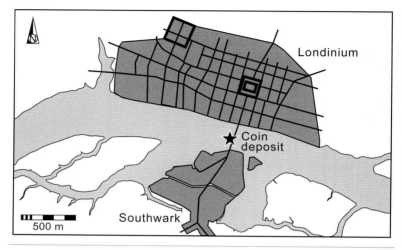

Figure 25. The location of a large deposit of Roman coins where a bridge communicated between Roman London and the settled area on the opposite bank of the Thames. Information from Rowsome 2008.

in north-east England where the remains of a bridge were identified together with a Viking sword, several knives and an adze (Dent 1984). This time they were associated with faunal remains. There was nothing to suggest that any of the animals had been eaten, and among them there was the skull of a horse which had been dispatched by a violent blow to the head. It could have been a sacrificial deposit.

Crossing such bridges may have entailed special obligations. Perhaps there were occasions when offerings had to be made. If so, such practices went through a lengthy history. Lund (2005) observes that by the time of the conversion of Northern Europe bridges were among the places where the souls of Christians would be judged. In England chapels were built there from the 12th century AD onwards (Harrison *et al.* 2010). Although they were meant to ensure divine protection for travellers, many were also chantries where prayers were said to shorten the time that the dead would spend in Purgatory. In such cases they were associated with the passage to an afterlife.

Other kinds of boundary

In other cases it is more difficult to identify thresholds in the landscape. Some boundaries were marked by fences, earthworks or lines of pits, but this did not happen widely. A good example is a recent find from Boest Mose in Jutland where two hoards dated between 1800 and 1600 BC were deposited by a wooden barrier consisting of four parallel lines of posts. On one side of that boundary there were bronze axes, and opposite it was a group of ornaments made of gold (I am grateful to Constanze Rassmann and Mette Løvschal for this information). Deposits of artefacts, human remains and animal bones can be found in other places, but they are not common compared with those at the entrances of settlements. Similarly, Caroline Von Nicolai (2014) has shown that burials and deposits of artefacts were associated with the defences of fortified sites throughout Central and Western Europe and were placed there throughout the period between the Early Bronze Age and the late pre-Roman Iron Age. She does not include the evidence from Britain and Ireland where similar deposits are recorded. On the Continent they were commonest in two very different periods – the Late Bronze Age and the Late Iron Age. Valuables also occur in seeming isolation, but in this case their positions may be related to topographical features. The most distinctive are associated with mountain passes where they are a widespread phenomenon (Wyss 1996). Others are connected with less dramatic landforms. Thus Martin Goldberg (2015) has argued that in upland areas of Scotland offerings of Iron Age metalwork were placed on local watersheds. In other cases deposits of valuables focussed on both natural and artificial boundaries. According to Torun Zachrisson (1998), the distribution of Viking hoards in part of middle Sweden followed the margins of different kinds of land as well as those of individual farms. At one time a comparable argument applied to bog bodies in Northern Europe which seemed to be located at, or even beyond, the limits of the occupied areas. That interpretation has been criticised (Hines 1989, 95–97). In Ireland, however, they do appear to be distributed close to boundaries which are known from documentary sources (Kelly 2006).

These are exceptional instances and in most regions the most obvious divisions were the streams and rivers. That is not surprising as they are where many valuables are found, but can they be investigated more effectively? One method is the study of place names of the kind described in Chapter 9. Do they identify rivers which were once considered significant? An alternative is to devote more attention to the character of the water itself.

River names and their associations

The theophoric names found in Northern Europe provide a useful starting point as they link certain rivers with Nordic gods and highlight their importance. At times the connection between them can be surprisingly direct – a river like the Gudenå ('God's river') includes a remarkable amount of metalwork (Frost 2013). The problem is that similar evidence is not found everywhere. It is true that some of the most important rivers must have been equated with divinities. Their names certainly imply this – the Seine was associated with Sequana; the Marne with the mother goddess Matrona; the Severn with Sabrina; and the Danube with Danu. The connection was by no means universal, but it is both striking and significant (Campbell 2012, chapter 4).

Rivers played an equally important role in Ireland. This is obvious from the first recorded myths. Like the Gudenå, the Shannon contains an unusual quantity of artefacts. It was associated with a goddess, Sinann (Waddell 2014, 126). There was a sacred well at Uisneach, which was thought to be the exact centre of the country. In this case the hilltop is described as the source of *all* the Irish rivers (Schot 2011). On the other hand, the goddess Bóand was linked with the origin of the Boyne. According to an early account, she visited another holy well in order to test its powers, but she was not sufficiently respectful and the water overflowed to form the river (Waddell 2014, 18–22). Its importance was enhanced by the monuments built beside it. In the early sources the Neolithic passage grave at Newgrange was the dwelling of the gods. During the Roman Iron Age the entrance to the tomb was associated with offerings of jewellery, coins and the remains of horses (Carson & O'Kelly 1977; Bendrey *et al.* 2013). The most recent version of the same idea comes from an unexpected source: James Joyce's *Finnegans Wake*, published in 1939. Its most famous section is *Anna Livia Plurabelle*, which was originally issued on its own. Its protagonist, Anna Livia, is identified with the River Liffey which enters the Irish Sea at Dublin, but Joyce's text incorporates hundreds of other river names. Like the Boyne, which was associated with a goddess, the Liffey was represented as a living being.

These may have been exceptional cases, for in England the majority of river names are purely descriptive (Ekwall 1928); the same applies to many of the earliest examples in Scotland (Nicolaisen 2001), although some of those with the prefix *aber* may refer to female deities (Nicolaisen 1997). For the most part they include terms that describe attributes of the water: they can be powerful, strong, swift, pure, friendly, dangerous or bad. Their appearance is equally important, so they may be clear, bright, grey, dark or even black. Gaelic names also refer to beasts, giants, spectres, ghosts and fairies (Murray 2014). A study by Margaret Gelling and Ann Cole (2014) considers the names of English rivers, marshes and bogs in greater detail. Many connected these features with the people who lived beside them, and very few referred to supernatural powers. Is there another way of assessing their significance in the past?

The character of water

The fact that English river names rarely refer to deities may be somewhat misleading. It is likely that some acquired their names from the Anglo-Saxon period onwards, long after any prehistoric and Roman artefacts had been placed in the water. That would explain the contrast with Ireland where traditional beliefs were more tenacious. Like the north of Scotland, the island received fewer settlers between the Atlantic Bronze Age and the Viking period, and for that reason traditional names could have remained largely unaltered. The British evidence could also be deceptive. Theophoric names may be uncommon, but there are many references to the character of the water itself. They suggest a distinctive perception of the world.

It is a cliché to say that water is both a source of human life and a potential cause of death, but, like other clichés, it is true. Water possesses an ambiguous character. Where it was considered as a boundary it separated different communities from one another, but where it could be crossed it also brought them together. That may be why bridges, causeways and fords were important places for conducting rituals. Rivers provided vital communication routes, but their volatile behaviour could make them threatening at the same time. They might protect settlements from hostile incursions, but when they flooded they could easily overwhelm them and their land. The important feature is that they could not be controlled. Springs would be impossible to explain, and the same applied to those Irish lakes – *turloughs* – which appeared unpredictably and then disappeared. The same argument could apply to underground rivers like the Lesse. In the British Isles systematic attempts to tame the major rivers did not start in earnest until the 12th and 13th centuries AD – a time when they no longer played such an important role in ritual (Blair 2007). There were some earlier initiatives, but not many.

One name which has not been mentioned so far is the Norse word *fors*, which means a waterfall. It was taken over in northern England where it changed to *force*, but its meaning remained the same. Quite by chance it suggests the power of cataracts, although these terms actually have different roots. In time both *fors* and *force* might have assumed similar connotations as rapidly flowing water could be treated as an active agent. It was as inexplicable as it was irresistible: a mysterious energy acting on a substance that might otherwise appear inert. In the same way a tidal surge could animate a lake of still water, or a sudden storm could transform a sluggish channel into a torrent. Powerful eddies might develop at confluences where tributaries joined the major rivers. In every case it must have seemed as if the water was alive or something was emerging from below.

Today water is considered as a natural resource. It can be measured, monitored, owned and portioned out, but in the past it may have been thought of as active, as possessing a vital force of its own. Sometimes rivers were described as living beings, but even where place names provide no indication of this connection, they had distinctive attributes. Many of their names suggest that they had an animate quality. Thus their waters can be friendly, dangerous or bad, just as they are described as powerful or strong. Much the same applies to lakes. Indeed, the character of votive offerings from at least the Bronze Age to the Migration period suggests that the contrast between still water and rapid currents was widely acknowledged. Christina Fredengren (2011) believes that these contexts were gendered. Weapons had male associations and were placed in active channels, but the ornaments, which she associates with women, are found in still water or bogs. John Waddell (2014, 126) has postulated a similar distinction in Late Bronze Age Ireland and David Fontijn (2003, chapter 12) observes something similar in the Netherlands.

One of the problems identified in Chapter 9 was that votive deposits might be made in the same places over enormous expanses of time, yet the intervals between those episodes were too great for the details of such events to be recalled with any accuracy. This would be explained if such locations shared similar attributes – they were places at which the same natural events occurred, and that is why they drew attention to themselves. They included springs, confluences, waterfalls and the tidal head. Not only were they used on quite different occasions, the same comparatively limited variety of locations was favoured in both Northern and Southern Europe. Of course, there were important contrasts – thermal springs and mineral springs were much more important in the South, and estuaries may have played a greater role in Scandinavia – but the common element was that the water itself behaved in inexplicable ways. In some parts of the North the shoreline retreated over time; and in the South the levels of lakes rose and threatened the security of the people living beside them. It has even been suggested that the skulls of children were placed around the edges of settlements in an attempt to arrest this process (Menotti *et al.* 2014). In south Scandinavia rock carvings may have been intended to achieve a similar result (Nimura 2016, 122–28).

Water and the dead

Still more abstract boundaries existed between different worlds, and here important thresholds are indicated by literary sources that describe the relationship between water, the dead and the supernatural. They even suggest that these processes were connected with particular locations. The evidence of place names is important here, and Chapter 9 suggested that certain physical features were thought to be especially significant. They were where people could communicate with otherworldly powers, and where their requests and offerings could be transmitted. Mircea Eliade (1954) describes such places as *hierophanies*; in literal terms they were the places *at which the sacred showed itself.* Not surprisingly, they include rivers, lakes and springs (Fig. 26).

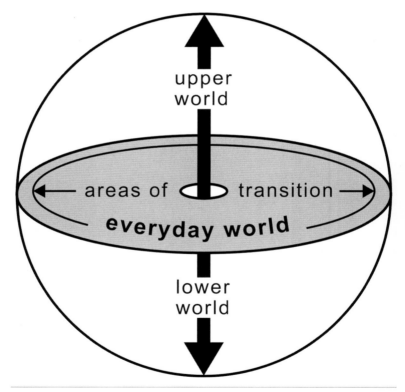

Figure 26. Interpretation of a three-tier cosmology postulated by Eliade (1954).

Eliade commented on the wide distribution of cosmologies in which the familiar world was positioned in between two others: an upper world or the heavens, and the underworld that Christians describe as Hell. Although this element was important in the medieval period, it figured much more widely. The Greeks knew it as Hades, and in Classical belief it is not by chance that a river separated the living from the dead who travelled there by boat (Wright 1995). The ship burials of Northern Europe show how a similar idea is reflected by archaeological evidence, but the same scheme was once associated with parts of the British Isles. Donn, who was known as 'the dark one', ruled over the dead and was associated with a conspicuous rock in the sea off the Irish coast (Ó hÓgàin 1999, 57–59). Here people who had died would enter the Underworld. In the same way, the 6th century author Procopius reported that Britain was an island of the dead (West 2007, 390). Souls were ferried there in the middle of the night. When the boatmen were summoned to undertake the task they found that the vessel was ready to depart and realised that it was carrying the weight of invisible passengers. Once the ghosts had reached land, the boat returned significantly lighter. The dead were no longer on board – they had made the crossing.

In his book on *Archaeology and Celtic Myth* John Waddell quotes a similar account, but this time it has a more direct reference to prehistoric archaeology. In the tale *Echtra Laegairi* (the Adventure of Laegiri), the hero travels across country to find the Otherworld. His journey takes him beneath 'the lake of the birds' and here he reaches a place where people are 'drinking mead from bright vessels' (Waddell 2014, 79). He never leaves again. Waddell (2014, 79–81) suggests that the lake can be identified with Loughnaneane in County Roscommon. It is relevant because it was the findspot of one of the finest and most unusual Late Bronze Age artefacts in Ireland.

The character of mountains

Again insular names can be revealing. Mountains and rock formations have attracted particular attention. In Scotland their names can refer to dreams, worship or sacrificial offerings. Some describe these places as if they were human or animals, and John Murray's study *Reading the Gaelic Landscape* lists no fewer than 27 terms which describe hills and mountains as if they were parts of the body (Murray 2014, 180–81). Others refer to otherworldly creatures. One of the most distinctive peaks is Schiehallion, 'the fairy mountain of the Caledonians'. It was especially significant because it was thought to be the precise centre of the country. It was also the findspot of an Iron Age metalwork hoard (Macgregor 1976, cat. nos 213 & 238).

Irish place names are equally intriguing (Flanagan & Flanagan 1994). Some may describe the appearance of areas of high ground – the beak of the eagle, for instance, or the horn of the cow – but others refer to supernatural beings. They include: the ravine of the monster, the cliff of the demons, the hollow of the hag, and, again, the hill of the fairies. Others refer to rather different elements: the hill of truth, or the mountain of the warriors. Whilst many names are purely descriptive, examples like these suggest that certain places had a particular significance.

It is obvious that, like rivers and lakes, high ground assumed a special importance in the ancient world. It included hills, mountains, plateaus, outcrops, and pinnacles of rock. Some were where Neolithic axes were made. Caves and rock fissures attracted particular attention as they extended into the earth. These places can be associated with cremated bone, but in Southern Europe they can also include quantities of artefacts – many of them burnt – together with the residues of bronze production. The transformation of the metal was like the treatment of the human body (Brück 2006). That is not surprising since the raw material had originally been obtained from mines. Similar deposits were associated with natural cavities and sinkholes.

In the South of Europe valuables were deposited in many parts of the uplands. In the North, however, there were fewer offerings of this kind, but cairns and mounds could still be constructed as far as possible above the habitable land. Mountains changed their character during the course of the year. They might be covered in snow during the winter and only accessible in the summer months. It was then that drawings of metalwork might have been created at Mont Bégo in the south of France and it is surely no accident that they should feature pictures of the sun (De Lumley 1995, 241–56). It seems possible that some of the carved surfaces were chosen because they commanded views of where it rose and set (Magail 2005). Mountainous regions like the Alps were subject to other natural processes and at times it must have seemed as if the rock itself was alive. They were affected by avalanches and the more gradual movement of screes. The area with the petroglyphs experiences violent thunderstorms even today – another natural event that would have been difficult to comprehend. All these features connected people to the sky.

The caves, mountains and gorges were among the principal sources of water that ran down to the lowlands. Deposits of valuable objects were made around their points of origin, far above any land that could be occupied all year. On the lower ground there were similar offerings, some of them closer to the settlements. In that way the movement of water linked three different domains: the high land which was associated with the sky; the familiar world of houses and fields; and an underworld that extended beneath the lakes and rivers. In good weather they were related for another reason, as the sky would be mirrored in the surface of the water. Mountaintops and riverbeds marked the limits of the familiar world and offerings of artefacts and living matter may have passed between them.

Eliade (1954) emphasises the importance of tripartite cosmologies, and his research draws together observations from many societies in the present and the past. The outcome is intriguing, but it lacks the specific detail that would make the argument more persuasive. It is a collage of observations made in different places with no obvious connection to one another. Fortunately, the basic notion of a tiered cosmology is supported by archaeological evidence from several different regions of Europe, but the plausibility of the argument depends on local evidence and not on cross-cultural generalisation. Such information is readily available from the Greek and Roman worlds (Wright 1995), but it has also been identified in the Nordic Bronze Age (Kaul 2005). A similar scheme is postulated in later prehistoric Ireland (Waddell 2014, chapters 3 & 4), and is clearly documented by early texts referring to Old Norse religion. In fact in the Late Iron Age of Scandinavia there seem to have been nine separate levels of the cosmos, linked to one another by the world tree, Yggdrasill, which may be represented by distinctive stone settings found in cemeteries (Andrén 2014, chapter 2). Votive deposits were made in every one of these regions, and it seems that they were located where it was possible to communicate between different worlds.

Mountains, waters and divinities

It is not possible to take the discussion further because the archaeological evidence shows too much variety. Certain places may have attracted attention over time, and they may have done so because they possessed qualities that were not found elsewhere. They may have been selected because of the unusual natural processes that happened there: processes that could have suggested that streams and rivers, rocks and mountains shared a certain animation, whether that was created by running water, avalanches, or storms. They might even be places where it was possible to imagine supernatural beings travelling between an overworld and an underworld, just as mountain streams cascaded from the high ground down to the sea. At certain points it could have been appropriate to offer gifts. They may have accompanied many different transactions, from crossing a significant boundary to celebrating the dead, and from propitiating the forces of nature to celebrating a successful harvest. It would be entirely wrong to reduce so much variation to a single scheme that somehow remained unchanged for five thousand years. If comparisons with other societies are helpful at all, it is useful to invoke analogies with the Classical world or with Old Norse religion, for in both cases sacred sites were found throughout the landscape and were used in many different ways. Notions of the Otherworld were equally diverse and supernatural forces were associated with an entire pantheon of gods and spirits. In that case modern Western monotheism would offer a poor analogy for beliefs in ancient Europe, and the sheer diversity of places, practices and offerings highlighted in this account must be allowed to speak for itself. There is no one answer. Instead this account concludes with an example that emphasises the sheer complexity of archaeological evidence.

The earth compels

The title of this section is taken from a poem by Louis MacNeice and describes the powerful impact exerted by the local landscape.

This book began with two hoards which dated from different periods and were discovered in different parts of Europe. It ends with a third example which was found in the Scottish Highlands. The Early Bronze Age metalwork from Dail na Caraidh dates from between 2100 and 1900 BC (Barrett & Gourlay 1999). The name means 'the field of the fish-trap' (Katherine Forsyth pers. comm.). It featured briefly in Chapters 4 and 9 as it belongs to a small group of sites in Scotland where collections of Early Bronze Age metalwork were associated with rock outcrops, boulders and natural hillocks (Cowie 2004). These artefacts might be decorated and some were deliberately broken before they were deposited. In this case the local topography was extremely distinctive. It consisted of an elongated mound of glacial debris on top of a conspicuous terrace overlooking the confluence of two rivers, the Lundy and the Lochy, 100 m away; the water can be heard from the findspot. It also commanded a view into the local mountains. Three different groups of artefacts were deposited in an almost level area by one end of the mound, but there is no obvious sign that they had been buried or concealed. One collection consisted entirely of axes, but in the other two they were combined with knives or daggers. At least one of the axeheads had been deliberately snapped before it was placed there, and at some stage another one was decorated. Some of these objects had also been coated with tin which made them shine. Brendan O'Connor, who reported on the finds for the excavators, suggested that the artefacts could have been placed there at intervals over a significant period of time (in Barrett & Gourlay 1999, 172–83). No other objects were associated with this assemblage.

Its position in a wider region was most important (Fig. 27). The land has risen since the Early Bronze Age but at that time Dail na Caraidh would have been at the head of a sea loch providing access to Ireland which provided most of the metal exploited in Britain. The site was also by the entrance to the Great Glen which was the most important land route across the northern part of Scotland. Prehistoric connections between Ireland and the eastern Scottish coast have attracted attention for a long time, but one of them is particularly significant here. Nearly all the deposits of Early Bronze Age metalwork are found in north-eastern Scotland or near to the North Sea coast (Needham 2004). The same applies to discoveries of moulds for making new objects; it is known that much of the imported metal was recycled in this region (Bray & Pollard 2012). Dail na Caraidh was exceptional because it was at the meeting between land and sea and equally close to the opening of a valley route that allowed people to travel through the mountains. It was in one of the main regions where metalwork first entered the country, yet similar hoards are unusual in western Scotland. In this respect the assemblage stands out.

The presence of high ground was even more significant, for the excavators of the site observed that it commanded a view of Ben Nevis – the highest summit anywhere in Britain. Pollen analysis showed that site had been in a largely open landscape, so the mountain was clearly visible in the past (Barrett & Gourlay 1999). That relationship takes on a new significance in the light of a more recent discovery, for it has become apparent that Dail na Caraidh was one of a small group of Early Bronze Age hoards from which the sunrise or sunset could be observed at the turning points of the year. In each case the sun passed behind a prominent mountain; it also happened at a natural mound on which a stone circle was built (Bradley & Nimura 2016, chapters 4 & 10). People visiting Dail na Caraidh could watch the midwinter sun emerging from behind Ben Nevis (Fig. 28). This was probably the most important point in the solar cycle, for it was when the hours of daylight started to increase and the natural world began to recover from the extremes of darkness and cold.

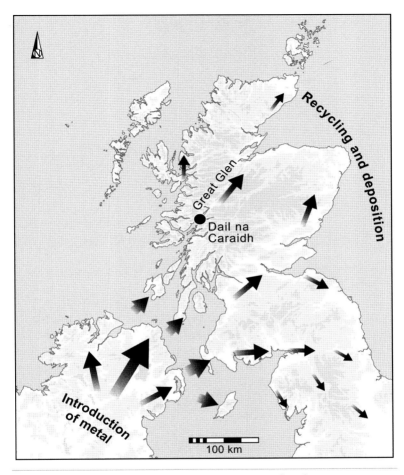

Figure 27. Map illustrating the movements of Irish copper into northern Britain and its recycling and deposition during the Early Bronze Age. It emphasises the pivotal location of Dail na Caraidh in relation to the Irish Sea and the Great Glen. Information from Needham (2004).

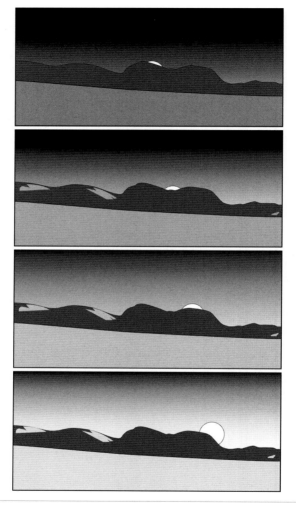

Figure 28. Reconstruction of the midwinter sunrise behind Ben Nevis as seen from Dail na Caraidh. The sun would have been in a slightly different position during the Early Bronze Age, but the difference would have been too small to affect the relationship between the site of the metalwork hoard and the view of the solstice. Analysis by Aaron Watson.

What is the right way of characterising such a distinctive place? Dail na Caraidh was at a pivotal point in the geography of ancient Scotland. It was where the sea met the land at the beginning of an important route leading across country. If people were bringing exotic objects with them, entering the Great Glen along the River Lochy might have involved a significant transition in physical and social terms. Perhaps this was acknowledged by offering bronze artefacts – one of them made in an Irish style – at such a significant threshold. The choice of this location for depositing valuables must have been influenced by an even more important consideration, for its position commanded a dramatic view of the midwinter sun as it emerged from behind the highest mountain in Britain. Thus it was associated with yet another important transition – the shortest day of the year. At Dail na Caraidh the metalwork was placed in, or on, the ground surface and coated with tin so that the individual objects would shine. All these were unusual features that it shared with few other places, but, like many of the deposits considered in this book, the site was where a watercourse joined a major river and possibly the sea. It encapsulated some of the most striking elements that influenced the placing of hoards.

A final reflection

To conclude an extended essay that threatens to become over-extended, there are really two ways of studying finds of this nature. Until recently the usual method has been to catalogue the artefacts, to determine their stylistic affinities, and to employ assemblages like this one to investigate the regional and chronological organisation of artefact production. That remains a perfectly legitimate exercise, and without that the detailed knowledge that specialists can bring to the task any other kind of analysis is liable to fail. The alternative route is more circuitous and involves some subjective judgements, but it is the one that has been followed here. It is to emphasise the distinctive places where specialised deposits are found and to investigate their settings in the ancient landscape, whether it was towards the beginning of the sequence during the Neolithic period or at its close during the late 1st millennium AD. This method involves a greater risk of failure, but at a site like Dail na Caraidh it may bring researchers a little closer to understanding the character of the events that left such distinctive traces behind. The midwinter sun still rises behind Ben Nevis as it did 4000 years ago. It takes the imagination to evoke a little of that drama. We must reanimate the objects we intercept in their passage between different worlds.

References

Primary Sources

Beowulf. 1999. Translated by S. Heaney. London: Faber & Faber.

Caesar: The Gallic War. 1996. Translated by C. Hammond. Oxford: Oxford University Press.

Egil's Saga. 2000. Translated by B. Scudder. London: Allen Lane.

The Nibelungenlied. 1965. Translated by A. T. Hatto. Harmondsworth: Penguin

The Ring of the Nibelung. 1993. Translated by S. Spencer. In S. Spencer and B. Millington (eds), *Wagner's Ring of the Nibelung: A companion*, 53–372. London: Thames & Hudson.

Secondary Sources

Abbate, C. and Parker, R. 2012. *A History of Opera*. London: Allen Lane.

Alberti, B. and Marshall, Y. 2009. Animating archaeology: Local theories and conceptually open-ended methodologies. *Cambridge Archaeological Journal* 19, 344–56.

Aldersey-Williams, H. 2011. *Periodic Tales*. London: Penguin.

Aldhouse-Green, M. 2015. *Bog Bodies Uncovered*. London: Thames & Hudson.

Allen, T., Hacking, P. and Boyle, A. 2000. Eton Rowing Course at Dorney Lake: The burial tradition. *Tarmac Papers* 4, 65–106.

Alves, L. B. and Commendador Rey, B. 2009. Rochas e metais na Pré-história para além da físico-quémica. In A. Bettancourt and L. Alves (eds), *Das montes, das piedras e das aguas. Formas de interpretaçção com o espaço natural da pré-história à actualidade*, 37–53. Braga: Centro de Investigação transdisciplina 'Cultura, Espaço e Memória'.

Anders, J. 2013. *Früh- und hochmittelalterliche Flussfunde in Nordost-deutschland: das Material aus Peene, Recknitz, Tollense und Trebel und seine siedlungsgeschichtliche Einbindung*. Bonn: Habelt.

Andersson, G. 2006. Among trees, bones and stones: The sacred grove at Lunda. In A. Andrèn, K. Jennbert and C. Raudvere (eds), *Old Norse Religion in Long-term Perspectives*, 195–99. Lund: Nordic Academic Press.

Andrén, A. 2014. *Tracing Old Norse Cosmology*. Lund: Nordic Academic Press.

Androschuk, F. 2010. The gifts to men and the gifts to the gods: Weapon sacrifices and the circulation of swords. In C. Theune, F. Biermann, R. Struwe and G. Jeute (eds), *Zwischen Fjorden und Steppe*, 263–75. Rahden: Leidorf.

Arrhenius, B. 2011. Helgö pagan sanctuary complex. In B. Arrhenius and U. O'Meachra (eds), *Excavations at Helgö XVIII*, 11–43. Stockholm: Royal Swedish Academy of Arts, Letters & Antiquities.

Arwidsson, G. and Berg, G. 1983. *The Mastermyr Find: A Viking Age tool chest from Gotland*. Stockholm: Almqvist & Wiksell.

Auden, W. H. 1948. *The Age of Anxiety*. London: Faber & Faber.

Barndon, R. 2004. A discussion of magic and medicine in East African ironworking: Actions and artefacts in technology. *Norwegian Archaeological Review* 37, 21–40.

Barnwell, E. 1873. The Broadward find – Supplementary note. *Archaeologia Cambrensis* 4, 80–83.

Barrett, J. and Gourlay, R. 1999. An early metalwork assemblage from Dail na Caraidh, Inverness-shire, and its context. *Proceedings of the Society of Antiquaries of Scotland* 129, 161–87.

Bazelmans, J. 1999. *By Weapons Made Worthy – Lords, retainers and their relationship to Beowulf*. Amsterdam: Amsterdam University Press.

Becker, C. J. 1971. 'Mosepotter' fra Danmarks jernalder. Problemer omkring mosefundne lerkar og deres tolkning. *Aabøger for Nordisk Oldkyndighed og Historie* 1971, 5–60.

Becker, K. 2013. Transforming identities – New approaches to Bronze Age deposition in Ireland. *Proceedings of the Prehistoric Society* 79, 225–63.

Behm-Blanke, G. 2003. *Heiligtümer der Germanen und ihre Vorgängern in Thüringen: die Kulstätte Oberdorla*. Stuttgart: Theiss.

Bendrey, R., Thorpe, N., Outram, A. and Van Wijngarden Bakker, L. 2013. The origins of domestic horses in northwest Europe: New direct dates on the horses of Newgrange, Ireland. *Proceedings of the Prehistoric Society* 79, 91–103.

Bennike, P. and Ebbesen, K. 1986. The bog find from Sigeradal: Human sacrifice of the Early Neolithic. *Journal of Danish Archaeology* 5, 85–115.

Berggren, Å. 2007. *Till och från ett kärr. Den arkeologiska undersökningen av Hindbygården*. Malmö: Malmö Kulturmiljö.

Bernabò Brea, M. and Camaschi, M. 2009. *Acqua e civilitatè nelle terremare. La vasca votive di Nocete*. Milian: Skira.

Berranger, M. 2006. Les dépôts de demi-produits de fer. Contexts and associations des mobiliers. In G. Bataille and J.-P. Guillaumet (eds), *Les dépôts metalliques au second âge du Fer en Europe tempérée*, 211–20. Bibracte: Collection Bibracte.

Bianco Peroni, V. 1979. Bronzene Gewässer- und Hohenfunde aus Italien. *Jahresbericht des Vorgeschichte der Universität Frankfurt A.M.* 1978–79, 321–35.

Bjork, R. and Niles, J. (eds). 1997. *A Beowulf Handbook*. Exeter: University of Exeter Press.

Blair, J. 2007. Introduction. In J. Blair (ed.), *Waterways and Canal-building in Medieval England*, 1–18. Oxford: Oxford University Press.

Blair, J. 2010. The prehistory of English fonts. In M. Henig and N. Ramsay (eds), *Intersections: The archaeology and history of Christianity in England, 400–1200*, 149–77. Oxford: British Archaeological Report 505.

Bloch, M. and Parry, J. (eds). 1989. *Money and the Morality of Exchange*. Cambridge: Cambridge University Press.

Boulestin, B., Lejars, T. and Testart, A. 2012. Annexe 1. Textes à l'appui. In A. Testart (ed.), *Les armes dans l'eau. Questions d'interprétation en archéologie*, 409–35. Paris: Errance.

Bourke, L. 2001. *Crossing the Rubicon: Bronze Age metalwork from Irish rivers*. Galway: Department of Archaeology, National University of Ireland Galway.

Bradley, R. 1985. Exchange and social distance: The structure of bronze artefact distributions. *Man* 20, 692–704.

Bradley, R. 1998[1990]. *The Passage of Arms: An archaeological analysis of prehistoric hoards and votive deposits*. Second edition. Cambridge: Cambridge University Press.

Bradley, R. 1997. *Rock Art and the Prehistory of Atlantic Europe*. London: Routledge.

Bradley, R. 1998. Daggers drawn: Depictions of Bronze Age weapons in Atlantic Europe. In C. Chippindale and P. Taçon (eds), *The Archaeology of Rock-Art,* 130–45. Cambridge: Cambridge University Press.

Bradley, R. 2000. *An Archaeology of Natural Places*. London: Routledge.

Bradley, R. 2002. *The Past in Prehistoric Societies*. London: Routledge.

Bradley, R. 2005. *Ritual and Domestic Life in Prehistoric Europe*. London: Routledge.

Bradley, R. 2009a. Beowulf and British prehistory. In D. Sayer and H. Williams (eds), *Mortuary Practice and Social Identities in the Middle Ages*, 38–45. Exeter: University of Exeter Press.

Bradley, R. 2009b. *Image and Audience: Rethinking prehistoric art*. Oxford: Oxford University Press.

Bradley, R. in press. The beach as source and destination. In R. Shaffrey (ed.), *Written in Stone*. Southampton: Highfield Press.

Bradley, R. and Edmonds, M. 1993. *Interpreting the Axe Trade*. Cambridge: Cambridge University Press.

Bradley, R., Haselgrove, C., Webley, L. and Vander Linden, M. 2016. *The Later Prehistory of North-west Europe: The evidence of development-led fieldwork*. Oxford: Oxford University Press.

Bradley, R., Lewis, J., Mullin, D. and Branch, N. 2015. Where water wells up from the earth: Excavations at the findspot of the Late Bronze Age hoard from Broadward, Shropshire. *Antiquaries Journal* 95, 21–64.

Bradley, R. and Nimura, C. 2013. The earth, the sky and the water's edge: Changing beliefs in the earlier prehistory of Northern Europe. *World Archaeology* 45, 12–26.

Bradley, R. and Nimura, C. (eds). 2016. *The Use and Reuse of Stone Circles: Fieldwork at five Scottish monuments and its implications*. Oxford: Oxbow Books.

Brandherm, D. 2007. Swords by numbers. In C. Burgess, P. Topping and F. Lynch (eds), *Beyond Stonehenge*, 288–300. Oxford: Oxbow Books.

Brandherm, D. 2011. Use-wear on Bronze Age halberds: The case of Iberia. In M. Uckelmann and M. Mödlinger (eds), *Bronze Age Warfare: Manufacture and use of weaponry*, 23–38. Oxford: British Archaeologocal Report S2255.

Bray, P. and Pollard, M. 2012. A new interpretative approach to the chemistry of copper-alloy objects: Source, recycling and technology. *Antiquity* 86, 853–67.

Brennand, M. and Taylor, M. 2003. The survey and excavation of a Bronze Age timber circle at Holme-next-the-sea, Norfolk, 1998–9. *Proceedings of the Prehistoric Society* 69, 1–84.

Briard, J. 1965. *Les dépôts de l'âge du bronze Atlantique*. Rennes: Becdelivère.

Bridgford, S. 1998. British Late Bronze Age swords: The metallographic evidence. In C. Mordant, M. Pernot and V. Richner (eds), *L'atelier du bronzier en Europe 2*, 205–19. Paris: Editions du comité des travaux historiques et scientifiques.

Brink, S. 2008. Naming the land. In S. Brink (ed.), *The Viking World*, 57–66. Abingdon: Routledge.

Brück, J. 2001. Body metaphors and technologies of transformation in the English Middle and Late Bronze Age. In J. Brück (ed.), *Bronze Age Landscapes: Tradition and transformations*, 149–60. Oxford: Oxbow Books.

Brück, J. 2006. Fragmentation, personhood and the social construction of technology in Middle and Late Bronze Age Britain. *Cambridge Archaeological Journal* 16, 297–315.

Bruen Olsen, A. and Alasker, S. 1984. Greenstone and diabase utilisation in the Stone Age of Western Norway. *Norwegian Archaeological Review* 17, 71–103.

Brunning, R. and McDermott, C. 2013. Trackways and roads across the wetlands. In F. Menotti and A. O'Sullivan (eds), *The Oxford Handbook of Wetland Archaeology*, 359–84. Oxford: Oxford University Press.

Burgess, C., Coombs, D. and Davies, G. 1972. The Broadward Complex and barbed spearheads. In C. Burgess and F. Lynch (eds), *Early Man in Wales and the West*, 211–83. Bath: Adams & Dart.

Burström, M. 1990. Järnframställning och gravritual: en strukturalistisk tolkning av järnslagg i vikingatida gravar i Gästrikland. *Fornvännen* 85, 261–71.

Burström, M. 2012. *Treasured Memories: Tales of buried belongings in wartime Estonia*. Lund: Nordic Academic Press.

Cahill, M. 2005. Roll your own lunula. In T. Condit and C. Corlett (eds), *Above and Beyond: Essays in memory of Leo Swan*, 53–62. Bray: Wordwell.

Campbell, B. 2012. *Rivers and the Power of Ancient Rome*. Chapel Hill: University of North Carolina Press.

Carlie, A. 2012. Forging for the household or specialised production? *Acta Archaeologica* 83, 55–81.

Carson, R. and O'Kelly, C. 1977. A catalogue of the Roman finds from Newgrange. *Proceedings of the Royal Irish Academy* 77C, 35–55.

Carver, M. 2005. *Sutton Hoo: A seventh-century princely burial ground and its context*. London: British Museum Press.

Carver, M. 2011. The best we can do? *Antiquity* 85, 230–34.

Cassen, S. 2009. *Exercise de stèle*. Paris: Errance.

Cassen, S., Grimaud, V., Lescof, L., Marcoux, N., Oberlin, C. and Querré, G. 2014. The first dates for the construction and use of the interior of the monument at Gavrinis (Lamor-Baden), France. *Past* 77, 1–4.

Čerče, P. and Turk, P. 1995. Hoards of the Late Bronze Age – The circumstances of their discovery and the structure of the finds. In B. Teržan (ed.), *Hoards and Industrial Metal Finds from the Neolithic and Bronze Age in Slovenia*, 7–30. Ljubljana: Narodni Muzej.

Childe, V. G. 1958. *The Prehistory of European Society*. Harmondsworth: Penguin.

Christensen, C. 2003. The sacrificial bogs of the Iron Age. In L. Jørgensen, B. Storgaard and L. Gebauer Thomsen (eds), *The Spoils of Victory: The North in the shadow of the Roman Empire*, 346–54. Copenhagen: National Museum.

Clarke, R. R. 1954. The Early Iron Age treasure from Snettisham, Norfolk. *Proceedings of the Prehistoric Society* 20, 27–86.

Close-Brooks, J. and Coles, J. 1980. Tinned bronzes. *Antiquity* 54, 228–29.

Coles, J. 1960. Scottish Late Bronze Age metalwork. *Proceedings of the Society of Antiquaries of Scotland* 93, 16–134.

Colquhoun, I. & Burgess, C. 1988. *The Swords of Britain*. Munich: Beck.

Cooney, G. and Mandal, S. 1988. *The Irish Stone Axe Project*. Bray: Wordwell.

Cowie, T. 2004. Special places for special axes? Early Bronze Age metalwork from Scotland in its landscape setting. In I. Shepherd and G. Barclay (eds), *Scotland in Ancient Europe*, 247–61. Edinburgh: Society of Antiquaries of Scotland.

Cunliffe, B. 1978. *Iron Age Communities in Britain*. Second edition. London: Routledge.

Cunliffe, B. 1988. *The Temple of Sulis Minerva at Bath, Volume 2: The finds from the Sacred Spring*. Oxford: Oxford University Committee for Archaeology.

Davidson, H. E. 1964. *Gods and Myths of Northern Europe*. Harmondsworth: Penguin.

De Jersey, P. 2014. *Coin Hoards in Iron Age Britain*. London: Spink.

De Lumley, H. 1995. *Le grandiose et le sacré*. Aix-en-Provence: Édisud.

De Navarro, J. M. 1972. *The Finds from the Site of La Tène, Volume 1: The scabbards and the swords found in them*. Oxford: Oxford University Press.

de Saulieu, G. 2004. *Art rupestre et statues-menhirs dans les Alpes*. Paris: Errance.

Dent, J. 1984. Skerne. *Current Archaeology* 91, 251–53.

Descola, P. 2003. *Beyond Nature and Culture*. Chicago: University of Chicago Press.

Detys, S. 1994. *Un people pélerins: Offrandes de pierre at de bronze des Sources de la Seine*. Dijon: Revue Archéologique de l'Est et du Centre-East, supplément 30.

Dietrich, O. 2014. Learning from 'scrap' about Late Bronze Age hoarding practices: A biographical approach to individual acts in large metal hoards of the Carpathian Basin. *European Journal of Archaeology* 17, 468–86.

Dobat, A. 2010. 'And hold therein feasts of sacrifice' – Archaeological perspectives on the sacral functions of sacrifice at Late Iron Age central places. *Neue Studien zur Sachsenforschung* 1, 362–75.

Ekwall, E. 1928. *English River-names*. Oxford: Clarendon Press.

Eliade, M. 1954. *The Myth of the Eternal Return*. London: Arkana.

Eogan, G. 1983. *The Hoards of the Irish Later Bronze Age*. Dublin: University College Dublin.

Evans, C. 2002. Metalwork and 'cold claylands': Pre-Iron Age occupation of the Isle of Ely. In T. Lane and J. Coles (eds), *Through Wet and Dry: Essays in honour of David Hall*, 33–53. Exeter: Wetland Archaeology Research Project.

Fabech, C. 1998. Kult og samfund i yngre jernalder: Ravlunda som eksempel. In L. Larsson and B. Hårdh (eds), *Centrala Platser, Centrala Frågor: Samhällsstrukturen under Järnåldern*, 147–64. Lund: Almqvist & Wiksell.

Fábregas Valcarce, R., Rodríguez Rellán, C. and Rodríguez Álvarez, E. 2009. Representacíons de armas no interior de Galicia. *Gallaecia* 28, 49–68.

Fallgren, J.-H. and Ljungkvist, J. 2016. The ritual use of brooches in early medieval forts on Öland, Sweden. *European Journal of Archaeology* 19, 681–703.

Field, D., Anderson-Whymark, H., Linford, N., Barber, M., Linford, P. and Topping, P. 2015. Analytical surveys of Stonehenge and environs, 2009–2013: Part 2 – the stones. *Proceedings of the Prehistoric Society* 81, 125–48.

Field, N. and Parker Pearson, M. 2003. *Fiskerton: An Iron Age timber causeway with Iron Age and Roman votive offerings.* Oxford: Oxbow Books.

Fischer, C. 1997. *Innovation und Tradition in der Mittel- und Spätbronzezeit.* Zurich: Monographien der Kantonsarchäologie Zurich 28.

Fischer, V. 2011. The deposition of bronzes at Swiss lakeshore settlements: An investigation. *Antiquity* 85, 1298–311.

Flanagan, D. and Flanagan, L. 1994. *Irish Place Names.* Dublin: Gill & Macmillan.

Fontijn, D. 2003. Sacrificial landscapes: Cultural biographies of persons, objects and 'natural places' in the Bronze Age of the southern Netherlands, *c.* 2500–600 BC. *Analecta Praehistorica Leidensia* 33–34, 1–392.

Fontijn, D. 2007. The significance of invisible places. *World Archaeology* 39, 70–83.

Forsgren, M. 2010. The divine appearance of Härn. *Current Swedish Archaeology* 18, 105–25.

Foucras, S. 2013. Inhumations de chevaux chez les Avernes. In G. Auxiette and P. Meniel (eds), *Les depots d'ossements animaux en France, de la fouille à l'interprétation,* 217–20. Montagnac: Editions Monique Mergoil.

Fox, C. 1946. *A Find of the Early Iron Age from Llyn Cerrig Bach, Anglesey.* Cardiff: National Museum of Wales.

Fredengren, C. 2002. *Crannogs.* Bray: Wordwell.

Fredengren, C. 2011. Where wandering water gushes – The depositional landscape of the Mälaren Valley in the Late Bronze Age and Early Iron Age of Scandinavia. *Journal of Wetland Archaeology* 10, 109–35.

Fredengren, C. 2015. Water politics: Wet deposition of human and animal remains in Uppland, Sweden. *Fornvännen* 110, 161–83.

Frost, L. 2013. River finds – Bronze Age depositions from the River Gudenå. *Germania* 91, 39–87.

Fugelsang, S. H. and Wilson, D. 2006. *The Hoen Hoard – A Viking gold treasure of the ninth century.* Rome: Bardi Editore.

Gansum, T. 2004. Roll the bones – From iron to steel. *Norwegian Archaeological Review* 37, 41–57.

Garrow, D. and Gosden, C. 2012. *Technologies of Enchantment? Exploring Celtic Art 400 BC to AD 100.* Oxford: Oxford University Press.

Gelling, M. and Cole, A. 2014. *The Landscape of Place-names.* Donnington: Shaun Tyas.

Gilchrist, R. 2012. *Medieval Life: Archaeology and the life course*. Woodbridge: The Boydell Press.

Giles, M. 2007. Making metals and forging relations: Ironworking in the British Iron Age. *Oxford Journal of Archaeology* 26, 395–413.

Glob, P. V. 1951. *Ard og plog i Nordens oldtid*. Aarhus: Aarhus University Press.

Goldberg, M. 2015. Belief and ritual(isation) in later prehistoric Scotland. In F. Hunter and I. Ralston (eds), *Scotland in Later Prehistoric Europe*, 211–23. Edinburgh: Society of Antiquaries of Scotland.

Goldhahn, J. 2007. *Dödens hand – en essä om brons- och hällsmed*. Gothenburg: Gothenburg University.

Gosden, C. 2005. What do objects want? *Journal of Archaeological Method and Theory* 12, 193–211.

Graham, W. S. 1977. *Implements in their Places*. London: Faber & Faber.

Graham-Campbell, J. and Williams, G. (eds). 2007. *Silver Economy in the Viking Age*. Walnut Creek: Left Coast Press.

Grane, T. 2003. Roman sources for the geography and ethnography of Germania. In L. Jørgensen, B. Storgaard and L. Gebauer Thomsen (eds), *The Spoils of Victory: The North in the shadow of the Roman Empire*, 128–45. Copenhagen: National Museum.

Grane, T. 2013. Roman relations with southern Scandinavia in Late Antiquity. In F. Hunter and K. Painter (eds), *Late Roman Silver: The Traprain Treasure in context*, 359–71. Edinburgh: Society of Antiquaries of Scotland.

Gräslund, B. 1987. *The Birth of Prehistoric Chronology*. Cambridge: Cambridge University Press.

Gregory, C. 2015. *Gifts and Commodities*. Second edition. Chicago, IL: Hau Books.

Guest, P. 2005. *The Late Roman Gold and Silver Coins from the Hoxne Treasure*. London: British Museum.

Guidi, A. 2014. Cult activities among Central and North Italian prehistoric communities. In A. B. Knapp and P. Van Domellen (eds), *The Cambridge Prehistory of the Bronze Age and Iron Age Mediterranean*, 635–49. Cambridge: Cambridge University Press.

Gullbekk, S. 2008. Coinage and monetary economies. In S. Brink (ed.), *The Viking World*, 159–69. Abingdon: Routledge.

Haaland, R. 2004. Technology, transformation and symbolism: Ethnographic perspectives on European ironworking. *Norwegian Archaeological Review* 37, 1–19.

Hagberg, U. E. 1967. *The Archaeology of Skedemosse, Volume 2.* Stockholm: Royal Swedish Academy of Letters, History & Antiquities.

Hallgren, F., Djerw, U., Geijerstam, M. and Steinicke, M. 1997. Skogsmossen: An Early Neolithic settlement and sacrificial fen on the northern borderland of the Funnel-beaker Culture. *Tor* 29, 49–111.

Hansen, S. 2016. A short history of fragments in hoards of the Bronze Age. In H. Baitinger (ed.), *Materielle Kultur und Identität im spannungsfeld zwischen Mediterraner Welt und Mittleeuropa,* 185–208. Mainz: Römisch-germanischen Zentralmuseums.

Hansen, S., Neumann, D. and Vachta, T. (eds). 2012. *Hort und Raum.* Berlin: De Gruyter.

Hårdh, B. 1996. *Silver in the Viking Age: A regional-economic study.* Stockholm: Almqvist & Wiksell.

Harding, A. 2007. *Warriors and Weapons in Bronze Age Europe.* Budapest: Archaeolingua.

Härke, H. 2000. The circulation of weapons in Anglo-Saxon society. In F. Theuws and J. Nelson (eds), *Rituals of Power from Late Antiquity to the Early Middle Ages,* 377–99. Leiden: Brill.

Harrison, D., McKeague, P. and Watson, B. 2010. England's fortified bridges and bridge chapels: A new survey. *Medieval Settlement Research* 25, 45–51.

Haselgrove, C. and Wigg-Wolf, D. (eds). 2005. *Iron Age Coinage and Ritual Practices.* Mainz: Von Zabern.

Hauptman Wahlgren, K. 2002. *Bilder av betydelse.* Lindome: Bricoleur Press.

Hedeager, L. 1992. *Iron Age Societies.* Oxford: Blackwell.

Hedeager, L. 2011. *Iron Age Myth and Materiality.* London: Routledge.

Helms, M. 1988. *Ulysees' Sail: An ethnographic odyssey of power, knowledge and geographical distance.* Princeton: Princeton University Press.

Helms, M. 2012. Nourishing a structured world with living metal in Bronze Age Europe. *World Art* 2, 105–18.

Herschend, F. 2001. *Journey of Civilisation: The Late Iron Age view of the human world.* Uppsala: University of Uppsala Occasional Papers in Archaeology.

Herschend, F. 2009. *The Early Iron Age in South Scandinavia: Social order in settlement and landscape.* Uppsala: University of Uppsala Occasional Papers in Archaeology.

Hines, J. 1989. Ritual hoarding in Migration-period Scandinavia: A review of recent interpretations. *Proceedings of the Prehistoric Society* 55, 193–205.

Hingley, R. 2005. Iron Age 'currency bars': Items of exchange in liminal contexts? In C. Haselgrove and D. Wigg-Wolf (eds), *Iron Age Coinage and Ritual Practices*, 183–205. Mainz: Von Zabern.

Hobbs, R. 2006. *Late Roman Precious Metal Deposits, AD 200–700*. Oxford: British Archaeological Report S1504.

Höck, A. and Sölder, W. 1999. *Culti nella preistoria delle Alpi: le offerte, i santuari, i riti*. Bolzano: Museo archeologico dell' Alto Adige.

Holmes, R. 1972. *Shelley: The pursuit*. London: Weidenfeld & Nicholson.

Hutcheson, A. 1996. Native or Roman? Ironwork hoards in Roman Britain. In K. Meadows, C. Lemke and J. Heron (eds), *TRAC 96*, 65–72. Oxford: Oxbow.

Hutcheson, N. 2004. *Later Iron Age Norfolk: Metalworking, landscape and society*. Oxford: British Archaeological Report 361.

Hutcheson, N. 2011. Excavations at Snettisham, Norfolk, 2004. In J. Davies (ed.), *The Iron Age in Northern East Anglia*, 41–48. Oxford: British Archaeological Report 549.

Innerhofer, F. 1997. Frühbronzezeitliche Barrenhortfunde. Die Schätze aus dem Boden kehren Zurück. In A. Hänsel and B. Hänsel (eds), *Gaben and die Götter*, 53–59. Berlin: Museum für Vor- und Frühgeschichlichte.

Insoll, T. 2012. Sacrifice. In T. Insoll (ed.), *The Oxford Handbook of the Archaeology of Ritual and Religion*, 152–65. Oxford: Oxford University Press.

Insoll, T. 2015. *Material Explorations in African Archaeology*. Oxford: Oxford University Press.

Jakobson, M. 1996. Burial layout, society and sacred geography. *Current Swedish Archaeology* 5, 79–98.

Jantzen, D. 2008. *Metallverabeitung im Nordischen Kreis der Bronzezeit*. Stuttgart: Steiner.

Jantzen, D., Brinker, U., Orscheid, J., Pick, J., Hauenstein, K., Kruger, J., Lidke, G., Lubke, H., Lampe, H., Lorenz, S., Schicht, G. and Terberger, T. 2011. A Bronze Age battlefield? Weapons and trauma in the Tollense Valley, north-eastern Germany. *Antiquity* 85, 417–33.

Ježek, M. 2015. The disappearance of European smiths' burials. *Cambridge Archaeological Journal* 25, 121–43.

Johns, C. 2010. *The Hoxne Treasure: Gold jewellery and silver plate.* London: British Museum Press.

Jones, A. M. 2015. Rock art and the alchemy of bronze: Metal and images in Early Bronze Age Scotland. In P. Skoglund, J. Ling and U. Bertilsson (eds), *Picturing the Bronze Age*, 79–88. Oxford: Oxbow Books.

Joy, J. 2009. Reinvigorating artefact biography: Reproducing the drama of object lives. *World Archaeology* 41, 540–56.

Joyce, J. 1939. *Finnegans Wake.* New York: Viking Press.

Jud, P. 2007. Les ossements humains dans les sanctuairies des Trois Lacs. In A. Daubigny, C. Dunning, G. Kaenel and M.-J. Roulière-Lambert (eds), *L' Age du Fer dans l'Arc Jurassien et ses marges – depots, lieux sacrés, et territorialité à l'Age due Fer*, 391–98. Besançon: Presses Universitaires de Franche-Comté.

Jud, P. and Alt, K. 2009. Les ossements humaines de La Tène et leur interpretation. In K. Honegger, D. Ramsmeyer, G. Kaenel, B. Arnold and M.-A. Kayser (eds), *Le site de La Tène: bilan de connaissances – etat de la question*, 57–63. Neuchâtel: Office et Musée Cantonal d'Archéologie.

Kaliff, A. 2007. *Fire, Water, Heaven and Earth.* Stockholm: Riksantikvarieämbetet.

Kappesser, I. 2012. *Römisch Flussfunde aus den Rhein gwischen Mannheim und Bingen.* Bonn: Habelt.

Karsten, P. 1994. *Att kasta yxan i sjön.* Stockholm: Almqvist & Wiksell.

Kaul, F. 2005. Bronze Age tripartite cosmologies. *Praehistorische Zeitschrift* 82, 135–48.

Kelly, E. 2006. *Kingship and Sacrifice: Iron Age bog bodies and boundaries.* Dublin: National Museum of Ireland.

Kerig, T., Edinborough, K., Downey, S. and Shennan, S. 2015. A radiocarbon chronology of European flint mines suggests a link to population patterns. In T. Kerig and S. Shennan (eds), *Connecting Networks: Characterising contact by measuring lithic exchange in the European Neolithic*, 116–64. Oxford: Archaeopress.

Kevenäs, A. and Hedenstierna-Jonson, C. (eds). 2015. *Own and be Owned: Archaeological approaches to the concept of possession.* Stockholm: Stockholm Studies in Archaeology.

Klassen, L. 2004. *Jade und Kupfer*. Aarhus: Jutland Archaeological Society.

Koch, E. 1998. *Neolithic Bog Pots from Zealand, Møn and Falster*. Copenhagen: Det Kongelige Nordiske Oldskriftselskab.

Kristiansen, K. 2002. The tale of the sword – swords and sword fighters in the Bronze Age. *Oxford Journal of Archaeology* 21, 319–32.

Krüger, J., Nagel, G., Jantzen, S., Lamper, R., Dräger, J., Lidke, G., Meckling, U., Schüler, T. and Terberger, T. 2012. Bronze Age tin rings from the Tollense valley in northeastern Germany. *Praehistorische Zeitschrift* 87, 29–41.

Kubach, W. 1979. Deponierung in Mooren der südhessischen Oberrheinebene. *Jahresbericht für Vorgeschichte der Universität Frankfurt a. M.*, 198–300.

Künzl, E. 1993. *Die Alemmannenbeute aus dem Rhein bei Neupotz: Plünderungsgut aus dem römisch Gallien*. Bonn: Habelt.

Lange, G. 1983. *Die menschlichen Skelettreste aus dem Oppidum von Manching*. Wiesbaden: Stein.

Larsson, T. B. 1986. *The Bronze Age Metalwork in Southern Sweden*. Umeå: University of Umeå.

Leahy, K. 2015. The Staffordshire hoard in context. In J. Naylor and R. Bland (eds), *Hoarding and the Deposition of Metalwork from the Bronze Age to the 20th Century: A British perspective*, 117–24. Oxford: British Archaeological Report 615.

Leahy, K. and Bland, R. 2014. *The Staffordshire Hoard*. London: British Museum Press.

Leahy, K., Bland, R., Hooke, D., Jones, A. and Okasha, E. 2011. The Staffordshire (Ogley Hay) hoard: Recovery of a treasure. *Antiquity* 85, 202–20.

Le Béchennec, Y. 2016. Thézy-Glimont (Somme), du site an territoire. In G. Blancquaert and F. Malrain (eds), *Evolution des sociétés gauloises du Second Age du Fer*, 303–16. Senlis: Revue Archéologique de Picardie N° Spécial 30.

Levy, J. 1982. *Social and Religious Organisation in Bronze Age Denmark: An analysis of ritual hoard finds*. Oxford: British Archaeological Report S124.

Ling, J., Hjärthner-Holdar, E., Grandin, L., Billström, K. and Perssen, P.-O. 2013. Moving metals or indigenous mining? Provenancing Scandinavian Bronze Age artefacts by lead isotope and trace elements. *Journal of Archaeological Science* 40, 291–304.

Lund, J. 2005. Thresholds and passages: The meanings of bridges and crossings in the Viking Age and Early Middle Ages. *Viking and Medieval Scandinavia* 1, 109–37.

Lund, J. 2006. Vikingetidens værktøjskister i landskab og mytologi. *Fornvännen* 101, 321–41.

Lund, J. 2008. Banks, borders and bodies of water in a Viking Age mentality. *Journal of Wetland Archaeology* 8, 53–72.

Lund, J. 2010. At the water's edge. In M. Carver (ed.), *Signals of Belief in Early England*, 49–66. Oxford: Oxbow Books.

Lynn, C. 1977. Trial excavations at the King's Stables, Tray townland, County Armagh. *Ulster Journal of Archaeology* 40, 42–62.

MacDonald, P. 2007. *Llyn Cerrig Bach: A study of the copper-alloy artefacts from the insular La Tène assemblage.* Cardiff: University of Wales Press.

Macfarlane, R. 2015. *Landmarks.* London: Hamish Hamilton.

Macgregor, M. 1976. *Early Celtic Art in North Britain.* Leicester: Leicester University Press.

Magail, J. 2005. Le calendrier agropastoral et religieux des graveurs. In J. Magail and J.-M. Giaume (eds), *Le site du Mont Bégo. De la protohistoire à nos jours*, 69–81. Nice: Serre Editeur.

Malim, T., Boreham, S., Knight, D., Nash, G., Preece, R. and Schwenninger, J.-L. 2010. The environmental and social context of the Isleham hoard. *Antiquaries Journal* 90, 73–130.

Malmer, M. 1981. *A Chorological Study of North European Rock Art.* Stockholm: Almqvist & Wiksell.

Malmer, M. 1992. Weight systems in the Scandinavian Bronze Age. *Antiquity* 66, 377–88.

Maraszec, R. 2006. *Spätbronzezeitliche Hortfund-landschaften in atlantischer und nordischer metaltradition.* Halle: Landesmuseum für Vorgeschichte.

Matthews, S. 2008. Other than bronze – substances and incorporation in Danish Bronze Age hoards. In C. Hamon and B. Qilliec (eds), *Hoards from the Neolithic to the Middle Ages*, 103–20. Oxford: British Archaeological Report S1758.

Mauss, M. 1925 [2007]. *Essai sur le don.* Paris: Presses Universitaires de France.

Melheim, L., Prescott, C. and Anfiset, N. 2016. Bronze casting and cultural connections: Bronze Age workshops at Hunn, Norway. *Praehistorische Zeitschrift* 91, 42–67.

Meniel, P. 2009. Les restes animaux de fouilles de 2003 sur le site de La Tène. In K. Honegger, D. Ramsmeyer, G. Kaenel, B. Arnold and M.-A. Kayser (eds), *Le site de La Tène: bilan de connaissances – etat de la question*, 65–73. Neuchâtel: Office et Musée Cantonal.

Menotti, F., Jennings, B. and Gollrisch-Moos, H. 2014. Gifts to the gods: Lake dwellers' macabre remedies against floods in the Central European Bronze Age. *Antiquity* 88, 456–69.

Milcent, P.-Y. 2012. *Le temps des élites en Gaule Atlantique*. Rennes: Presses Universitaires de Rennes.

Monikander, A. 2010. *Våld och vatten. Våtmarkskult vid Skedemosse under järnåldern*. Stockholm: University of Stockholm.

Möller-Wiering, S. 2011. *War and Worship: Textiles from the 3rd to 4th century AD weapon deposits in Denmark and Northern Germany*. Oxford: Oxbow Books.

Montari, F., Rengakos, A. and Tsagalis, C. (eds). 2009. *Brill's Companion to Hesiod*. Leiden: Brill.

Mörtz, T. 2010. Spätbronzezeitliche Waffendeponierungen Grossbritanniens. *Archäologische Informationen* 33(1), 153–57.

Moyler, S. 2008. Doing away with dichotomies? Comparative use-wear analysis of Early Bronze Age axes from Scotland. In C. Hamon and B. Quilliec (eds), *Hoards from the Neolithic to the Metal Ages*, 79–90. Oxford: British Archaeological Report S1758.

Murray, J. 2014. *Reading the Gaelic Landscape*. Dunbeath: Whittles Publishing.

Myrberg, N. 2009. The hoarded dead: Late Iron Age silver hoards as graves. In I.-M. Back-Danielsson, I. Gustin, A. Larsson, N. Myrberg and S. Thedéen (eds), *On the Threshold: Burial archaeology in the twenty-first century*, 131–54. Stockholm: University of Stockholm.

Myrberg Burström, N. 2015. Things of quality: Possessions and animated objects in the Scandinavian Viking Age. In A. Kevenäs and C. Hedenstierna-Jonson (eds), *Own and be Owned: Archaeological approaches to the concept of possession*, 23–48. Stockholm: Stockholm Studies in Archaeology.

Naylor, J. 2015. The deposition and hoarding of non-precious metals in Early Medieval England. In J. Naylor and R. Bland (eds), *Hoarding and the Deposition of Metalwork from the Bronze Age to the 20th Century: A British perspective*, 125–47. Oxford: British Archaeological Report 615.

Naylor, J. and Bland, R. (eds). 2015. *Hoarding and the Deposition of Metalwork from the Bronze Age to the 20th Century: A British perspective.* Oxford: British Archaeological Report 615.

Nebelsick, L. 2000. Rent asunder: Ritual violence in Late Bronze Age hoards. In C. Pare (ed.), *Metals Make the World Go Round*, 160–75. Oxford: Oxbow Books.

Needham, S. 1988. Selective deposition in the British Early Bronze Age. *World Archaeology* 20, 229–48.

Needham, S. 2004. Migdale-Marnoch: Sunburst of Scottish metallurgy. In I. Shepherd & G. Barclay (eds), *Scotland in Ancient Europe*, 217–45. Edinburgh: Society of Antiquaries of Scotland.

Needham, S. and Cowie, T. 2012. The halberd pillar at Ri Cruin cairn, Kilmartin, Argyll. In A. Cochrane and A. M. Jones (eds), *Visualising the Neolithic*, 89–110. Oxford: Oxbow Books.

Needham, S. and Bridgford, S. 2013. Deposits of clay refractories for casting bronze swords. In N. Brown and M. Medlycott (eds), *The Neolithic and Bronze Age Enclosures at Springfield Lyons, Essex: Excavations 1981–1991*, 47–74. Chelmsford: East Anglian Archaeology 149.

Nicolaisen, W. 1997. On Pictish rivers and their confluences. In D. Henry (ed.), *The Worm, the Germ and the Thorn: Pictish and related studies presented to Isobel Henderson*, 113–18. Balgavies: Pinkfoot Press.

Nicolaisen, W. 2001. *Scottish Place-names: Their study and significance.* Edinburgh: John Donald.

Nicolay, J. 2014. *The Splendour of Power: Early Medieval kingship and the use of gold and silver in the southern North Sea area (5th to 7th Century).* Groningen: Barkbuis Publishing.

Nielsen, P. O., Randsborg, K. and Thrane, H. (eds). 1994. *The Archaeology of Gudme and Lundeborg.* Copenhagen: Akademisk Forlag.

Nimura, C. 2016. *Prehistoric Rock Art in Scandinavia: Agency and environmental change.* Oxford: Oxbow.

Nørgård Jørgensen, A. 2009. Weapon-offering types in Denmark 350 BC to 1200 AD. In U. Von Freeden, H. Friesinge and E. Wamers (eds), *Glaube, Kult und Herrschaft*, 37–51. Bonn: Habelt.

O'Brien, W. 2014. *Prehistoric Copper Mining in Europe: 5500–500 BC.* Oxford: Oxford University Press.

Ó' hÓgàin, D. 1999. *The Sacred Isle: Belief and religion in pre-Christian Ireland*. Cork: The Collins Press.

Painter, K. 2013. Hacksilver – a means of exchange? In F. Hunter and K. Painter (eds), *Late Roman Silver: The Traprain Treasure in context*, 215–42. Edinburgh: Society of Antiquaries of Scotland.

Painter, K. 2015. Emergency or votive? Two groups of late-Roman gold and silver hoards. In J. Naylor and R. Bland (eds), *Hoarding and the Deposition of Metalwork from the Bronze Age to the 20th Century: A British perspective*, 67–91. Oxford: British Archaeological Report 615.

Pauli Jensen, X. 2009. From fertility sacrifices to weapon sacrifices: The case of the South Scandinavian bog finds. In U. Von Freeden, H. Friesinge and E. Wamers (eds), *Glaube, Kult und Herrschaft*, 53–64. Bonn: Habelt.

Pearce, M. 2013. The spirit of the sword and spear. *Cambridge Archaeological Journal* 23, 55–67.

Pétrequin, P., Jeunesse, C. and Jeudy, F. 1995. *La hache de pierre: carrières vosgiennes et échanges de lames polies pendant le Néolithique*. Paris: Errance.

Pétrequin, P., Cassen, S., Errera, E., Klassen, L., Sheridan, A. and Pétrequin, A.-M. 2012a. *Jade. Grands haches alpins du Néolithique européen*. Besançon: Presses Universitaires de France-Comté.

Pétrequin, P., Martin, A. and Vaquer, J. 2012b. Les haches en jades alpins pendant les Ve et IVe Millénaires: l'exemple de l'Espagne et du Portugal dans une perspective Européenne. *Revista de Gavà* 5, 213–22.

Planck, D., Biel, J., Süsskind, G. and Wais, A. (eds). 1985. *Der Keltenfürst von Hochdorf*. Stuttgart: Theiss.

Plisson, H., Mallet, N., Boucquet, A. and Ramsmeyer, D. 2002. Utilisation et role des outils en silex de Grand-Pressigny dans les villages de Charavines et de Portalban (Néolithique final). *Bulletin de la Société Préhistorique Française* 99(4), 793–811.

Pluskowski, A. (ed.) 2012. *The Ritual Killing and Burial of Animals: European perspectives*. Oxford: Oxbow Books.

Price, N. 2010. Passing into poetry – Viking-Age mortuary drama and the origins of Norse mythology. *Medieval Archaeology* 54, 123–56.

Primas, M., Schingler, M., Rott-Rubi, K., Diaz Tabernero, J. and Grüninger, S. 2001. *Wartau – Ur- und Frügeschichtliche Siedlungen und Brandopferplätz in Alpenrheintal*. Bonn: Habelt.

Pryor, F. 2001. *The Flag Fen Basin: Archaeology and environment of a fenland landscape.* London: English Heritage.

Pryor, F. and Bamforth, M. 2010. *Flag Fen, Peterborough: Excavation and research 1995–2007.* Oxford: Oxbow Books.

Quilliec, B. 2007. *L'épée atlantique: échanges et prestige au Bronze final.* Paris: Société Préhistorique Française.

Raffield, B. 2014. 'A river of knives and swords': Ritually deposited weapons in English watercourses and wetlands during the Viking Age. *European Journal of Archaeology* 17, 634–55.

Ramsmeyer, D. 2009. Le pont celtique de Cornaux-les-Sauges: accident ou lieu de sacrifice? In M. Honegger, D. Ramsmeyer, G. Kaenel, B. Arnold and M.-A. Kaeser (eds), *Le site de La Tène: bilan de connaissances – etât de la question*, 103–11. Neuchâtel: Office et Musée Cantonal d'Archéologie.

Randsborg, K. 1995. *Hjortspring: Warfare and sacrifice in early Europe.* Aarhus: Aarhus University Press.

Rassmann, K. 1996. Unterschungen du spätbronzzezeitlichen Hortfunde im nördlichen Schwartmeergebiet. In C. Huth (ed.), *Archäologische Forschungen zum Kultgeschehen in der jüngeren Bronzezeit und frühen Eisenzeit Alteuropas*, 535–55. Bonn: Habelt.

Ravn, M. 2010. Burials in bogs – Bronze and Early Iron Age bog bodies from Denmark. *Acta Archaeologica* 81, 112–23.

Rech, M. 1979. *Studien zu Depotfunde der Trichterbecher – un Einzelgrabkultur des Nordens.* Neumünster: Wachholtz.

Rhodes, M. 1991. The Roman coinage from London Bridge and the development of the City and Southwark. *Britannia* 22, 179–90.

Rivière, J.-C. 2012. Les raisons pour lesquelles on peut (ou pas) retrouver des armes dans les eaux au Moyen Age. In A. Testart (ed.), *Les Armes dans les Eaux. Questions d'interprétation en archéologie*, 237–49. Paris: Errance.

Roberts, B. 2007. Adorning the living but not the dead: Understanding ornaments in Britain c. 1400–1100 cal BC. *Proceedings of the Prehistoric Society* 73, 135–67.

Rock, T. and Barnwell, E. 1872. The Bronze Age relics from Broadward, Shropshire. *Archaeologia Cambrensis* 4, 338–55.

Rowlands, M. 1993. The role of memory in the transmission of culture. *World Archaeology* 25, 141–51.

Rowley-Conwy, P. 2007. *From Genesis to Prehistory: The archaeological Three Age System and its contested reception in Denmark, Britain and Ireland.* Oxford: Oxford University Press.

Rowsome, P. 2008. Mapping Roman London: Identifying its urban patterns and interpreting their meaning. In J. Clark, J. Cotton, J. Hall, R. Sherrris and H. Swain (eds), *Londinium and Beyond*, 25–32. York: Council for British Archaeology.

Roymans, N. 2004. *Ethnic Identity and Imperial Power: The Batavians in the Early Roman Empire.* Amsterdam: Amsterdam University Press.

Roymans, N. and Scheers, S. 2012. Eight gold hoards from the Low Countries. A synthesis. In N. Roymans, G. Creemers and S. Scheers (eds), *Late Iron Age Gold Hoards from the Low Countries and the Caesarian Conquest of Northern Gaul*, 1–46. Amsterdam: Amsterdam University Press.

Rundqvist, M. 2015. *In the Landscape and Between Worlds: Bronze Age deposition around Lakes Mälaren and Hjälmaren in Sweden.* Umeå: Archaeology & Environment 29.

Sallnow, M. J. 1989. Precious metals in the Andean moral economy. In M. Bloch and J. Parry (eds), *Money and the Morality of Exchange*, 209–31. Cambridge: Cambridge University Press.

Sanmark, A. 2004. *Power and Conversion: A comparative study in Christianization in Scandinavia.* Uppsala: Uppsala University.

Sauer, E. 2005. *Cult and Cultural Identity: Augustan coins, hot springs and early Roman baths at Bourbonne-les-Bains.* Leicester: Leicester University School of Archaeology & Ancient History.

Schauer, P. 1980. Unrnnenfelderzeitlicher Opferplatze in Höhlen und Fellspalten. In H. Lorenz (ed.), *Studien sur Bronzezeit*, 403–19. Mainz: Von Zabern.

Schot, R. 2011. From cult centre to royal centre: Monuments, myth and other revelations at Uisneach. In R. Schot, C. Newman and E. Bhreathnach (eds), *Landscapes of Cult and Kingship*, 87–113. Dublin: Four Courts Press.

Score, V. 2011. *Hoards, Hounds and Helmets: A Conquest-period ritual site at Hallaton, Leicestershire.* Leicester: University of Leicester Archaeological Services.

Schama, S. 1987. *The Embarrassment of Riches: An interpretation of Dutch culture in the Golden Age.* London: Collins.

Schulting, R. and Bradley, R. 2013. 'Of human remains and weapons in the neighbourhood of London'. New AMS C 14 dates on Thames 'river skulls' and their European context. *Archaeological Journal* 170, 30–77.

Seifert, M. 2000. Von 3466 Jahren erbaut! Die Quellen fassung von St Moritz. *Archäologie der Schweiz* 23(2), 63–75.

Skoglund, P. 2016. *Rock Art through Time: Scanian rock carvings in the Bronze Age and earliest Iron Age*. Oxford: Oxbow.

Snodgrass, A. 2006. Separate tables: A story of two traditions within one discipline. In A. Snodgrass (ed.), *Archaeology and the Emergence of Greece*, 105–13. Edinburgh: Edinburgh University Press.

Sofaer Derevenski, J. 2000. Rings of life: The role of early metalwork in mediating the gendered life course. *World Archaeology* 31, 389–406.

Sommerfeld, C. 1994. *Gerätegeld Sichel: Studien zur monetären Struktur bronzezeitlichen Horte in nördlichen Mitteleuropa*. Berlin: De Gruyter.

Sørensen, M. L. S. 1987. Material order and cultural classification: The role of bronze objects in the transition from Bronze Age to Iron Age in Scandinavia. In I. Hodder (ed.), *The Archaeology of Contextual Meaning*s, 90–101. Cambridge: Cambridge University Press.

Sørensen, M. L. S. 1997. Reading dress: The construction of social categories and identities in Bronze Age Europe. *Journal of European Archaeology* 5, 93–114.

Sørensen, M. L. S. 2004. Stating identities: The use of objects in rich Bronze Age graves. In J. Cherry, C. Scarre and S. Shennan (eds), *Explaining Social Change: Studies in Honour of Colin Renfrew*, 167–76. Cambridge: McDonald Institute for Archaeological Research.

Soroceanu, T. 1995. Die Fundumstände bronzezeitlicher Deponierungen. Ein Beitrag beiderseits der Karpaten. In T. Soroceanu (ed.), *Bronzefunde aus Rumainien*, 15–80. Berlin: Spiess.

Soroceanu, T. 2011. Le guerrrier des Carpathes à l'âge du Bronze. Particularités regionales et traits communs continentaux. In L. Baray, M. Honegger and M.-H. Dias-Meirinho (eds), *L'armament et l'image du guerrier dans les sociétés anciennes: de l'objet à la tombe*, 225–70. Dijon: Éditions universitaires de Dijon.

Soroceanu, T. 2012. Die Fundplätze der bronzezeitlichen Horte im Rumänien. In S. Hansen, D. Neumann and T. Vachta (eds), *Hort und Raum*, 225–54. Berlin: de Gruyter.

Sperber, L. 2006. Bronzezeitliche Flussdeponierungen aus dem Altrhein bei Roxheim. *Archäologisches Korrespondenzblatt* 36, 195–214.

Strathern, A. and Stewart, P. 2005. Ceremonial exchange. In J. Carrier (ed.), *A Handbook of Economic Anthropology*, 230–45. Cheltenham: Edward Elgar.

Stead, I. 1991. The Snettisham treasure: Excavations in 1990. *Antiquity* 65, 447–65.

Stead, I. 2006. *British Iron Age Swords and Scabbards*. London: British Museum Press.

Stead, I. 2014. Snettisham swansong. In C. Gosden, S. Crawford and K. Ulmschneider (eds), *Celtic Art In Europe: Making connections,* 297–303. Oxford: Oxbow Books.

Steiner, H. 2010. *Alpine Brandopferplätze – archäologische und naturwissenschäftliche Unterschungen*. Trento: Terri.

Stjernqvist, B. 1997. *The Röekillorna Spring: Spring-cults in Scandinavian prehistory*. Stockholm: Almqvist & Wiksell.

Taylor, R. 1993. *Hoards of the Bronze Age in Southern Britain: Analysis and interpretation*. Oxford: British Archaeological Report 228.

Teržan, B. (ed.) 1995. *Hoards and Industrial Metal Finds from the Neolithic and Bronze Age in Slovenia*. Ljubljana: Narodni Muzej.

Theuws, F. and Alkemade, M. 2000. A kind of mirror for men: Sword depositions in Late Antique Northern Gaul. In F. Theuws and J. Nelson (eds), *Rituals of Power from Late Antiquity to the Early Middle Ages*, 401–76. Leiden: Brill.

Timby, J., Brown, R., Biddulph, E., Hardy, A. and Powell, A. 2007. *A Slice of Rural Essex: Archaeological discoveries from the A120 between Stansted Airport and Braintree*. Oxford: Oxford Archaeology.

Torbrügge, W. 1971. Vor- und Frügeschlichtliche Flussfunde. *Bericht der Römisch-Germanische Kommission* 51–52, 1–146.

Toreld, A. and Andersson, T. 2015. Ny dokumentation av Kiviksgravens hällbilder. *Fornvännen* 110, 10–25.

Trump, B. 1968. Fenland rapiers. In J. Coles and D. Simpson (eds), *Studies in Ancient Europe*, 213–35. Edinburgh: Edinburgh University Press.

Turk, P., Istorič, J., Knific, T. and Nabergoj, T. 2009. *The Ljubjanica: A river and its past*. Ljubljana: Narodni Muzet.

Turner, L. 2010. *A Re-interpretation of the Later Bronze Age Metalwork Hoards of Essex and Kent*. Oxford: British Archaeological Report 507.

Vandkilde, H. 1996. *From Stone to Bronze: The metalwork of the Late Neolithic and earliest Bronze Age in Denmark*. Aarhus: Aarhus University Press.

Van Campen, J., Corrigan, K., Dierks, F., Gommians, J. and Gosselink, M. 2015. *Asia in Amsterdam: The cult of luxury in the Golden Age*. New Haven: Yale University Press.

Van Der Sanden, W. 1996. *Through Nature to Eternity*. Amsterdam: Batavian Lion International.

Van Gijn, A. 2010. *Flint in Focus: Lithic biographies in the Neolithic and Bronze Age*. Oxford: Oxbow Books.

Von Brunn, W. 1959. *Die Hortfunde der frühen Bronzezeit aus Sachsen-Anhalt, Sachsen und Thüringen*. Berlin: Akademie-Verlag.

Von Nicolai, C. 2014. *Sichtbare und unsichtbare Grenzen: Deponierungen an eisenzeitliche Befestigungen in Mittel- und Westeuropa*. Bonn: Habelt.

Vouga, P. 1923. *La Tène: Monographie de la station*. Leipzig: Hiersman.

Waddell, J. 2014. *Archaeology and Celtic Myth: An exploration*. Dublin: Four Courts Press.

Waller, M. 1994. *The Fenland Project, 9: Flandrian environmental changes in the Fenland*. Cambridge: East Anglian Archaeology 70.

Warmenbol, E. 1996. L'or, la mort et les Hyperboréena. La bouche des Enfers ou le Trou de Han à Han-sur-Lesse. In C. Huth (ed.), *Archäologische Forschungen zum Kultgeschehen in der jüngeren Bronzezeit und frühen Eisenzeit Alteuropas*, 203–34. Bonn: Habelt.

Warmenbol, E. 1999. Le solieil des morts. Les ors protohistoriques de Han-sur-Lesse (Namur, Belgique). *Germania* 77, 39–69.

Warmenbol, E. 2010. Drowning by numbers – nine lives, twelve deaths in the Bronze Age. In H. Meller and F. Bertemes (eds), *Der Griff nach den Sternen*, 563–76. Halle: Landesmuseum für Vorgeschichte.

Warmenbol, E. 2012. Une sequence radiométrique du Néolithique final à Le Tène final: le 'pilier stratigraphique' de Han-sur-Less. *Lunula* 22, 3–9.

Warmenbol, E. 2015. Nordic Bronze Age razors: 'Very like a whale'. *Archäologisches Korrespondenzblatt* 45, 487–97.

Webley, L. and Adams, S. 2016. Material genealogies: Bronze moulds and their castings in Later Bronze Age Britain. *Proceedings of the Prehistoric Society* 82, 323–40.

Webster, L., Sparey-Green, C., Périn, P. and Hill, C. 2011. The Staffordshire (Ogley Hay) hoard: Problems of interpretation. *Antiquity* 85, 221–29.

Weiner, A. 1992. *Inalienable Possessions: The paradox of keeping-while-giving*. Berkeley: University of California Press.

Wendling, H. and Winger, K. 2014. Aspects of Iron Age urbanity and urbanism at Manching. In M. Fernández-Götz, H. Wending and K. Winger (eds), *Paths to Complexity: Centralisation and urbanism in Iron Age Europe*, 132–39. Oxford: Oxbow Books.

Wentink, K. 2006. *Ceci n'est pas une hache: Neolithic depositions in the Northern Netherlands*. Leiden: Leiden University Faculty of Archaeology.

West, M. L. 2007. *Indo-European Poetry and Myth*. Oxford: Oxford University Press.

Wheeler, M. 1943. *Maiden Castle, Dorset*. London: Society of Antiquaries.

Williams, G. 2013. Hack-silver and precious-metal economies: A view from the Viking Age. In F. Hunter and K. Painter (eds), *Late Roman Silver: The Traprain Treasure in context,* 381–94. Edinburgh: Society of Antiquaries of Scotland.

Williams, M. 2003. Tales from the dead. In H. Williams (ed.), *Archaeologies of Remembrance*, 89–112. New York: Kluwer.

Wilson, D. 1965. Some neglected late Anglo-Saxon swords. *Medieval Archaeology* 9, 32–54.

Wirth, S. 2000. Die Funde aus der Donauschleife bei Schäftstill in Bayern. In L. Bonnamour (ed.), *Archéologie des fleuves et rivières*, 84–92. Paris: Errance.

Woodward, A. and Hunter, J. 2011. *An Examination of Prehistoric Stone Bracers from Britain*. Oxford: Oxbow Books.

Wright, M. 1995. *Cosmology in Antiquity*. London: Routledge.

Wyss, R. 1996. Funde von Pässen, Höhlen aus Quellen und Gewässenn der Zentral- und Westalpen. In C. Huth (ed.), *Archäologische Forschungen zum Kultgeschehen in der jüngeren Bronzezeit und frühen Eisenzeit Alteuropas*, 417–28. Bonn: Habelt.

Yates, D. and Bradley, R. 2010a. Still water, hidden depths: The deposition of Bronze Age metalwork in the English Fenland. *Antiquity* 84, 405–15.

Yates, D. and Bradley, R. 2010b. The siting of metalwork hoards in the Bronze Age of south-east England. *Antiquaries Journal* 90, 41–72.

York, J. 2002. The life cycle of Bronze Age metalwork from the Thames. *Oxford Journal of Archaeology* 21, 77–92.

Zachrisson, T. 1998. *Gård, gräns, gravfält*. Stockholm: Stockholm University.

Žbona-Trkman, B. and Bavdek, A. 1995. The hoards from Kanalski Vrh. In B. Teržan (ed.), *Hoards and Industrial Metal Finds from the Neolithic and Bronze Age in Slovenia*, 31–71. Ljubljana: Narodni Muzej.

Zemmer-Planck, L. (ed.) 2002. *Kult der Vorzeit in den Alpen*. Balzano: Casa Editrice Alteria.

Zvelebil, M. and Jordan, P. 1999. Hunter fisher gatherer ritual landscapes: Questions of time, space and representation. In J. Goldhahn (ed.), *Rock Art as Social Representation*, 1–26. Oxford: British Archaeological Report S794.